Brian L. Boley

What Do Evangelical Christians Believe?

Understanding Evangelical Christianity by Dispelling Common Myths

Oddparts Press

Lowell, Ohio, 45744 USA

www.oddparts.com

Copyright © 2007 by Brian L. Boley

All rights reserved. No part of this publication may be reproduced, stored in a retrieval system or transmitted in any form by any means – electronic, mechanical, photocopying, recording, or any other – except for brief quotations in printed reviews, without the prior written permission of the publisher.

Unless otherwise specified, Scripture taken from the New King James Version. Copyright © 1979, 1980, 1982 by Thomas Nelson, Inc. Used by permission. All rights reserved.

ISBN 978-0-6151-4461-0

First Edition Copyright © 2007 by Brian L. Boley

Additional Copies of this book may be purchased at our website: oddparts.com

Mr. Boley is available for speaking and consulting. He may be contacted through oddparts.com

To all those people who honestly search for Truth.

Table of Contents

Table of Contents ___ *4*
What Do Evangelical Christians Believe? ___ *6*
A Word to the Knowledgeable Reader ___ *15*
Who are Evangelical Christians, Anyway? ___ *18*
Myth #1 - Understanding the People in the Churches. ___ *33*
FAQ #1 – Where Can I Find Evangelicals? ___ *58*
Myth #2 - I Am a Good Person, so I Will Go to Heaven When I Die. ___ *63*
Myth #3 - I Believe in God, so I Am a Christian. *84*
Myth #4 - I Think Jesus Was a Great Teacher, so I Am a Christian. ___ *113*
FAQ #2 – Why do Evangelicals Constantly Talk About God? ___ *143*
Myth #6 - Christians Who Die Become Angels. *183*
Myth #7 - Christian Denominations Believe Radically Different Things. ___ *199*
FAQ #3 What Are the Major Evangelical Denominations? ___ *257*
Myth #8 - The Existence of God is a Matter of Opinion and Personal Faith. ___ *264*
Myth #9 - Christianity is All a Bunch of Rules. *286*
FAQ #4 – What Do Evangelical Christians Think About Current Social Issues? ___ *318*

Table of Contents

Myth #10 - Scientific Evolution and Christianity Are Contradictory Ideas. *328*

Myth #11 - All Groups That Claim to be Christian Are Christian. *364*

Myth #12 - Christians Are Dull, Unhappy, Weak people Who Never Have Fun. *376*

Appendix - How Do Mormons Fit into Evangelical Christianity? *387*

Index *393*

Contact Information *399*

What Do Evangelical Christians Believe?

Understanding Evangelical Christianity by Dispelling Common Myths.

Introduction

> *For who is like Me?*
> *Who will arraign Me?*
> *And who is that shepherd*
> *Who will withstand Me?*
> Jeremiah 50:44

Evangelical Christians are all over the news today. According to some, Evangelicals are responsible for all the hate in society. According to others, Evangelicals are also responsible for the electoral victories of George W. Bush. In Russia and France, evangelicals are called cults, while in most of Africa and Latin America the Evangelical Movement is the fastest growing religion. In the United States, Evangelicals may be the largest group, surpassing Catholics, "mainstream" denominations, and fundamentalists in church-going attendance.

Introduction

If you are in business, journalism, entertainment, or politics, you have certain questions about Evangelicals: Who are these people? What do they believe that is different – and the same – as other Christian groups? Additionally, how do their doctrinal differences affect their lives, their daily decisions about what television to watch, which products to buy, what stores to shop at, which news channel to view, which politician to vote for, and which movies to watch?

If you are new to an Evangelical church, you have other questions: Just what do your new friends believe? Are their beliefs grounded in sound ideas, or are they flaky? What will be expected of you?

Additionally, there are other questions of an even more personal nature: Are you an Evangelical Christian – or should you be one? Why are so many people becoming Evangelical Christians? Do Evangelical Christians truly understand God or are they just another cult, deluded by charismatic leaders?

How should you relate to an Evangelical Christian you know at work? Why does he keep talking to you about God and Christ? For that matter, how do God and Christ relate to each other?

If any of these questions are important to you, then you will want to read this book. For that is our subject matter.
- Who are Evangelical Christians?
- What do they believe?
- What do they culturally value – and hate?

Introduction

- How mainstream are they in religious belief?
- How can you understand an Evangelical Christian?

Several incidents and friends led me to write this book. Perhaps you have had a similar experience or belief.

- The distinguished National Public Radio commentator Daniel Schorr remarked one Saturday morning that he didn't know any Evangelical Christians. Yet, they were becoming a key part of the political scene.
- When I studied astrophysics back in college, I had some Evangelical Christian friends. I had serious questions about the nature of God and how to know about Him. Yet they used odd terminology that made little sense to me. One of my Christian friends said, "God is like a father." Another said that I had to "have faith" and believe. Another told me "God is Holy". (I certainly had no idea what *that* meant!). Frustrated with not getting my questions answered, I gave up on Christianity for many years.
- My wife has a friend who sadly lost a couple of children as infants. She firmly believes that those children have been turned into angels who are watching over her and her other children, based upon the Hollywood idea that people become angels when they die.
- Another friend believes that Hell is "party city", while Heaven must be the dullest place conceivable. He thinks that

Introduction

- Evangelical Christianity is about giving up his freedom.
- Another Christian friend says that you can't possibly be a Christian if you believe in modern science. I have other friends who *aren't* Christians because they agree.
- Another friend won't go to church because of "all the hypocrites" he knows that actually attend. He also "hates all those Christians."
- We have a Chinese friend who is an Evangelical Christian. When she met a guy, they began to talk religions. He was shocked to find she was Christian and said, "Since you are Chinese, you are supposed to be Buddhist! Why are you Christian?"
- I have a Moslem friend who thought the Christian Trinity was God, Mary, and Jesus. We have another friend who believes that all Catholic Christians are going to go to Hell. And a homosexual friend once said that his hand "would fry" when he touched the doorknob of a church.
- An acquaintance has decided to "find God in herself" and says that she is a Christian. Another woman we know refuses to condemn or discipline some out-of-control teenagers who visit her household, because she says that Christians "should not judge".
- I know others who spend their time reading conspiracy theory books. They believe that the entire world is controlled by a handful of families who have run the world for the last several thousand years. They think that Christianity is a temporary mechanism by which these families control people.

Introduction

- And finally, I have many, many friends who think that all preachers are either the scary old man from "Poltergeist", the anti-fun fellow from "Footloose", political people like Jerry Falwell, or money hustling fakes.

The Evangelical Christian Myths

All of the people I've listed above (and myself) fell prey to one or more Myths about Evangelical Christianity. The Evangelical Christianity that they "know" is as much like real Evangelical Christianity as cheap hot dogs are like filet mignon. And each of us has been poorer for believing those myths. As the saying goes, "A *little* knowledge is dangerous."

Throughout history, many of the greatest thinkers and leaders of our world have been Christians – Christians in the tradition that led to modern Evangelical Christianity.

- Presidents: Washington, Adams, Lincoln, F. Roosevelt, Eisenhower, Reagan, G.W. Bush
- Leaders: Churchill, Patton, McClelland, Macarthur, Martin Luther King, Jr.
- Entertainers: Jimmy Stewart, Maria Von Trapp, Bing Crosby, Charlton Heston, Mel Gibson,
- Scientists: Newton, Boyle, Franklin,
- Authors: C.S. Lewis, James Dobson, John Bunyan, Patrick O'Brien, Robert Heinlein, Tom Clancy, John Grisham
- Explorers: Christopher Columbus, The Pilgrims, Buzz Aldrin, Rick Husband

Introduction

- Philosophers: Augustine, St. Francis, Blaise Pascal and many others.

These intelligent, capable, and talented people would not have been attracted to a fringe concept without a solid, logical basis for their belief. Yet, the "Christianity" of today's popular culture is filled with myths. Many people think that real Christianity is what Hollywood teaches. But "Hollywood Christianity" is not the True Faith that is held by mature Evangelical Christians.

Why Read This Book?

The purpose of this book is to explode those myths and explain what Evangelical Christianity is.

- *If you are a journalist, politician, or businessman* and need to understand Evangelical Christianity, you'll get a solid background on the beliefs of this large group of "red-state" people.
- ***If you are searching for Truth***, after you have read this book you'll understand what Evangelical Christianity really is about. You will have been intellectually honest with yourself. You'll better understand where the Evangelicals are coming from and you'll be better equipped to discuss with them philosophical and moral issues.
- *If you are a Believer*, you'll be better equipped to explain Evangelical Christianity to your friends. You might want to use this book in a group study for new Christians.

Introduction

- *If you are truly searching for Truth*, this book should help you by stripping away the Hollywood myths and bringing out the True Faith that two hundred million Americans claim as their own.

About the Author

Now a bit about me, your humble author: I am a semi-pastor. Although I have apprenticed under an ordained minister, I haven't been to seminary, or to Christian college. I spend a considerable amount of my time explaining Evangelical Christianity to international college students and friends in my local community, and to people who visit my website, oddparts.com, and I teach at a local church.

My college background was astrophysics, and thus, a few years ago I was a devout atheist who argued strongly with my Christian friends over their "stupid religion". I found that many of my friends who claimed to be Christians couldn't explain Christianity to me. They didn't really understand the subject - they had "just believed" since childhood and couldn't bridge the gap to my questions. They had no answers, and thus I felt that *Christianity* had no answers either. I needed a logical track; I needed logical answers. For I understood that the questions posed by religion are the most important questions to be answered. So I continued to search and tormented my poor Christian wife with questions.

When we moved to Atlanta, I took the opportunity of a neighbor's invitation (thanks, Mike!) to attend a local Evangelical church service -- where I listened

Introduction

to Dr Douglas Macintosh, who has since authored several excellent books on Christian beliefs with Moody Press. Dr. Macintosh is a mature Evangelical Christian who understands Christian beliefs and expresses them in an exceptionally clear manner every Sunday morning and evening. In his sermons, he didn't rant and rave -- he taught. And thus I finally had my questions answered by one who understood the subject. I understood that Christianity attracted all those greats of philosophy because it is so very rational. When you dig into it, Evangelical Christianity really *does* make sense.

Since then, I have read and studied and read some more. Plus, I have the benefit of years of Dr. Macintosh's and many other teachers' sermons. People tell me that I have a gift of explaining things on paper -- perhaps I do. You can be the judge.

In any event, this book is an attempt to clearly distinguish between what is truly Evangelical Christian belief -- and what is mere myth and Hollywood fantasy about Christianity and Evangelical Christians. For if you are going to report on Evangelical Christians, sell to Evangelical Christians, represent Evangelical Christians, or become an Evangelical Christian, you ought to understand what we really believe.

Introduction

How to get the most out of this book.

As you read this book, you will find references to the Bible. Some are quoted fully. Others are not. You will learn much more about the Evangelical Christian mind if you keep a Bible handy to look up the references and read them, especially the Suggested Scripture Readings at the end of each chapter.

In addition, there are a series of Discussion Questions that are designed to focus your thoughts upon a particular area. Keep a pencil with you and fill in your answers to the questions. The act of writing the answer will stimulate a burst of understanding in most cases. (Sometimes the lecture just can't take the place of a few minutes of quiet thought.) If you are reading this book in a small group, the group should discuss most of these questions.

Finally, at the end of most chapters are a series of suggested Actions. Some of the actions are to watch a movie – others are to do something that is normally outside your comfort zone. This is the laboratory section of the course. Get out and do! It's the only way to really grow.

    Brian L. Boley

    Lowell, Ohio

A Word to the Knowledgeable Reader

> Receive one who is weak in the faith, but not to disputes over doubtful things. Romans 14:1

Gentle Reader, if I were to take you and all the other readers of this book into a nearby paint store and ask you and the others to mix the color of paint that represents the color of sunshine, I expect that several things would happen.

- First, some people would choose not to do this.
- Second, of those that did this, almost all would mix a shade of yellow to represent sunshine.
- Third, very few people would mix exactly the same shade of yellow.
- Fourth, some people would mix their shade quickly and almost haphazardly, finishing in a few minutes, while others would mix their paint meticulously and take hours, indeed even days to get the shade "just right".
- Five, several people would then argue over how their shade better represented sunlight than the next person's shade of yellow did.

And the same is true of the subject of this book. I fully expect that some Christians will disagree with the exact words I use to describe our joint beliefs,

A Word to Knowledgeable Readers

and will insist that they do not believe what I say that they do. That is fine – I agree with you – you probably do not believe everything I have written, although some of your fellow Evangelicals will agree with me on just the very points where you disagree. Meanwhile, they will disagree with me where you agree. But, in the main, Evangelicals believe and act according to how I've stated.

When you disagree with me, you are quite welcome to write letters to *Christianity Today* explaining why I am a heretic and heathen. (Please be sure to send me a copy as well, for I enjoy learning about the lines in the sand that people draw.) Any movement as vital and growing as Evangelical Christianity is bound to have members with strong opinions of what is right and wrong – especially when a key purpose of the movement is to help people understand right and wrong.

This book is a beginner's book on Evangelical Christianity. It is not intended as a theological treatise – I'll write that some other time. In other words, I am not attempting to mix the precise shade of yellow that is sunlight at 4 pm on the afternoon of June the fifth after a light rainstorm. No, I've walked into the paint store and simply grabbed a bright "sunny" yellow that most people would agree is a reasonable representation of sunshine for an amateur artist. I'll let the perfectionists and the theologians argue over the precise shade for that rainy afternoon.

In the same way, I've tried to lay out for the beginner some of the debates that occur within Evangelical Christianity and between Evangelicals

A Word to Knowledgeable Readers

and other groups, for that is a good way to understand us. If you are new to Evangelical Christianity, please keep in mind that we all agree that "yellow" is the color of sunshine – just not exactly which yellow. We all affirm Jesus Christ as our Lord and Savior – we often emphasize different aspects of Him in our worship and ministry.

Perhaps the one weakest point of our movement is our failure to follow the point that Paul makes in Chapter 14 of Romans, that disputes over minor theological points confuse and cause despair in the new Christian. For the chapter is not just about the holding or not holding of feast days, and it is not limited to clean or unclean food discussion, but applies the principles of Grace and brotherly love to all of life and reminds us that these principles trump the law of Moses. In particular, verses 12 and 13 are very, very important.

- Brian Boley
  February 14, 2007

Who are Evangelical Christians, Anyway?

> You are the salt of the earth; but if the salt loses its flavor, how shall it be seasoned? Matthew 5:13

Generalizations

One rainy day, a man got off the train in a small town on the Plains. He went into the local diner and sat down to eat. While he was eating, the guy beside him asked what he did for a living. "I'm an engineer," the stranger replied.

"Great," the local said. "Come with me. We need you here."

The two of them walked to the edge of town where a crowd was gathered. People were looking at a road bridge that spanned a gorge. The bridge was obviously in trouble due to the high water. Since it was still raining, the townsfolk were trying to figure out a way to strengthen the bridge.

"Hey, everybody! I've brought us an engineer!" the local man yelled. The crowd quieted down and waited for the stranger to speak. An engineer! What a miracle for one to arrive right at this moment!

"Eh, although I am an engineer, I don't think I'll be of much use to you here", the stranger began. "You

Who are Evangelical Christians, Anyway?

see, I'm a software engineer. I write computer programs for a living. This is clearly a hardware problem."

At that moment the bridge collapsed.

Defining Christians

Like the townsfolk who forgot that there are many different types of engineers, we often forget to define whom we are talking about when we say the word "Christian". This word must be understood well before we can truly understand Christianity. We'll start with Christianity in general and then narrow our focus to Evangelicals.

Perhaps the most common Christian myth in our society revolves around the definition of who Christians are. Are Christians

- White, northern European-descended Americans?
- People who attend church?
- People who believe in God?
- Catholics?
- Mormons?
- Intolerant white Southerners?

Many people are very confused about what makes a Christian a Christian. And many people are also confused about the relationship of various other group-defining words (such as Evangelical, Catholic, Mormon, Baptist, Jehovah's Witness, and such) to the definition of Christian. So the first thing we're going to do is define a few things about Christians.

A Few Basic Points about Christian History

Christianity began in approximately 30 A.D. at Jerusalem, in the land that was then the Roman province of Judea and is now the focal point of the Palestine/Israel conflict. Christianity takes its name from Jesus Christ, who was a historical figure who claimed to be the Son of God. Other comments and actions which He and others made establish that "Son of God" means that Jesus is actually part of God, the Creator of the Universe in a rather complicated manner that we will deal with in later chapters. After arrest by the Jewish authorities, He was tried for blasphemy and executed by the Roman authorities by crucifixion -- death through slow suffocation by being hung on a cross. As a proof that Christ was truly the Son of God, He was resurrected three days later and appeared in bodily form to several of his followers, or *disciples*, and then to over 500 people. Christ then ascended into Heaven.

His followers began to preach the message of the good news, or *Gospel,* to anyone who would listen. This Gospel was that God had removed all barriers between Himself and humans by the atoning sacrifice of His Son Jesus Christ, and had demonstrated the Truth of this through miracles such as the Resurrection of Jesus and many other events documented in a series of three eyewitness and one journalistic account known collectively as *The Gospels*. Jesus promised eternal life and a substantial healing in this life if we would accept this and follow Him as Lord.

The new religion grew rapidly, and became the state religion of the Roman Empire in the early 300's. The Bible is the compilation of the writings of these disciples (the *New Testament*), combined with much older writings sacred to Jews and Christians alike (the *Old Testament*). Gradually, the leader of the church in Rome -- the *Pope* -- became acknowledged as the leader of the religion. In 1054, the Eastern Mediterranean churches broke from Rome in what is known as the Eastern Schism. The Eastern churches today are known as Orthodox churches, while the Roman church is known as the Roman Catholic Church.

In the 1530's, another great break came. Martin Luther, a German priest, became upset at the differences he noticed between the New Testament teachings and current practices in the Roman Catholic Church. His protests started the Protestant Reformation, which created a second large break in Christianity. In this case, Northern Europeans split from the Roman Catholic Church and formed other groups, or *denominations*. Luther's term for his followers, translated from the German, is Evangelical -- those who proclaim the "good news". Today this term is applied in a narrow sense to the specific groups known also as Lutherans, in a more general sense to a wide range of denominations which emphasize the doctrine of salvation through grace (as opposed to works), and in the widest sense to most Catholic and Protestant groups which argue that salvation can come to almost any man who believes in Christ (as opposed to legalistic groups that require specific behaviors and liberal groups which argue that salvation has already come to all). We'll have more details on this in a later chapter.

Who are Christians?

- Although increasingly used to define an ethnic group, Christians are not a coherent racial group. Christians are found throughout the world in almost every country. Christianity is the dominant religion of Europe, North America, South America, Australia, The Philippines, South Korea, Russia, and Sub-Saharan Africa. Millions of minority Christians are found in China, Japan, India, Vietnam, and Indonesia. Christians are sprinkled throughout North Africa, the Middle East, and Central Asia -- areas dominated by Islam.

    In the USA, Christianity is the dominant religion in most racial groups, including whites, blacks, Hispanics, American Indians, Eskimos, Pacific Islanders, Vietnamese, and Filipinos. Over 1 billion people claim to be Christians worldwide.

- Christians divide themselves into "Denominations" or sects. (For details on Denominations, see Chapter 7.) Most people

Who are Evangelical Christians, Anyway?

who study Christianity divide Christians at the highest level into four main groups:
- Catholic - The largest group, the Roman Catholic Church looks to the Pope as its leader. Catholics are the dominant group in Belgium, France, southern Germany, Austria, Poland, Italy, Spain, Portugal, Croatia, Hungary, Ireland, South and Central America, the Philippines, southern India and the northern USA.
- Protestant - The Reformation led to the creation of the groups commonly known as Protestant, Reformed, or Evangelical. These include the subgroups of Evangelical, Lutheran, Anglican, Methodist, Baptist, Presbyterian, Pentecostal, Congregational, Church of Christ, Disciples of Christ, and many, many smaller subgroups. Protestants are the dominant group in the United Kingdom, Holland, northern Germany, Scandinavia, Australia, Canada, southern Africa, and the USA outside of the Northeast and Chicago.
- Orthodox - The Orthodox church split from Rome around the year 1054. It is strongest in Russia, Ukraine, Greece, Bulgaria, Rumania, Serbia, and Macedonia.
- Coptic - The Coptic church dates from the 1st Century, and has survived in Egypt.

We will cover Denominations in greater depth in a later chapter.

Who are "Evangelical Christians"?

"Evangelical" is an important word to Christians. The root of the word comes from the Greek word that means "good news" or "Gospel". Thus, an Evangelical is one who shares the Good News of Jesus Christ. But when we look closer, we find that Christians use the word in three specific ways.

1. The oldest and narrowest use of the word comes to us from Germany. The German priest Martin Luther applied the word to describe his followers and to distinguish them from the Catholic Church, the Reformed Churches founded by John Calvin, and the Protestant Church of England, as well as the Eastern Orthodox Church. Thus, in Germany, the denomination we call "Lutheran" is known as "Evangelische", or "Evangelical".

   When these Germans came to America, many chose to call their churches "Evangelical". In many cases, this means that the church has a specific connection to Luther's doctrines, or is "Lutheran". These groups are extremely strong in a belt extending from Ohio west through Montana and south to Missouri, all areas that were settled by Lutheran Germans, Swedes, Danes, and Norwegians.

Who are Evangelical Christians, Anyway?

2. In the broadest usage of the word, "Evangelical" refers to an outgoing style of church, where a core teaching is that each Christian should demonstrate love for others by helping outsiders come to an understanding of the Gospel. This outward focus can occur in any church. So, there can be "Evangelical Baptists", "Evangelical Methodists", "Evangelical Catholics", "Evangelical Anglicans", and "Evangelical Lutherans". There is even an article in the December 2006 issue of *Christianity Today* that was written by an "Evangelical Orthodox".

   (In some sense, I have even seen usage pointing towards "Evangelical Jews", or "Evangelical Islam", but this usage of the word leaves out the essential Christian Gospel meaning of the word.)

3. The most common and least technical meaning of the word "Evangelical" is closely associated with Billy Graham. At the end of World War II, American Christianity was divided into four major groupings. The first group was the Roman Catholic Church, which gradually became more open to talking to other Christians, particularly with the significant reforms pushed by the Vatican II Council in 1960.

   In the second group were the liberal denominations, known in the press as "mainline denominations", such as the Episcopal Church, the United Methodists, liberal Presbyterians, Congregationalists, the United Churches of Christ, and Unitarians (the Christianity of Unitarians is in dispute, particularly by Unitarians). This group generally tended to uphold tradition in ceremony. Members were encouraged to attend church once per week. Bible reading was not encouraged (it wasn't necessarily discouraged, but it was not a key part of an individual church member's life.) Social welfare programs – both in the church and in government – were a key focus of the congregation's energy.

Politically, the leadership of many of these groups began to move toward the very liberal, indeed socialist, viewpoint. It became difficult to tell which was more important – Christ or political power. By the 1990's these groups were researching convoluted "Biblical" support for abortion, as the political position began to come before the historical clear message of the Bible and Christianity against child murder.

At the other end were the Fundamentalists, a collection of many small denominations that found a focus around a literal reading of the Bible, particularly around the first chapter of Genesis. Fundamentalism also emphasized a separation from the secular world, with various groups opposing television, movies, government social welfare programs, and most modern science teaching, particularly in the biological and geological sciences.

Many of these groups founded schools to teach their worldview to their children.

Fundamentalist groups moved politically toward the right, increasingly equating liberal politics with the work of the Devil. Just as their liberal opponents had lost their focus on spreading the Gospel, the fundamentalists began to look towards conservative politics first and Christ secondly. Despite clear support by Christ for rulers showing justice to the poor, these groups frowned upon anything that looked like such an idea as the approach of Communism.

Billy Graham organized the fourth group. Reverend Graham began preaching a series of mass meetings in football stadiums and major arenas around the country. These "Crusades" were different from previous revival meetings because the Graham organization took much care to involve as many churches as possible in the meetings. A wide range of churches were involved in following up with the people who became Christian at these events. Graham simply wanted Christian groups to keep in contact with the new Christians. Unlike his predecessors, Graham believed that the details of denominational doctrinal differences were not nearly as important as getting the new Christians connected with SOME Christian church. And this became the core of a new movement, known today as "Evangelicals".

(It is notable that many Fundamentalists opposed Graham and would not participate in his events.)

Graham's Evangelicals required two other items to help them coalesce.

The first item was a Presbyterian preacher from Missouri by the name of Francis Schaeffer, who became a missionary to Europe and settled in Switzerland in the early 1950's. Schaeffer's retreat "L'Abri" attracted a host of young intellectuals from all over Europe and America for philosophical conversations about the nature of God. Schaeffer's key points were that God exists, Jesus is historically real, science and Christianity will eventually reach the same Truth, a life which follows Biblical principles work, and following Christ is something that involves our entire life, not merely Sunday mornings. These young men and women returned from their time at L'Abri and radically transformed the concepts of ministry. Schaeffer's book *"The God Who is There"* became the philosophical core of the movement. "What would Jesus Do?" became a key slogan of the Evangelical Movement.

The second item was a magazine founded by Graham, *Christianity Today*. If Graham recruited churches and individuals, and Schaeffer trained them, then Christianity Today became the magazine which kept them communicating. With over a dozen

Who are Evangelical Christians, Anyway?

magazines in the family today, Christianity Today International is the key way to reach Evangelical Christianity and to understand current evangelical thinking.

The major denominations and types of churches that are found in the Evangelical camp today include the Southern Baptist Convention (the nation's largest non-Catholic group), Conservative Baptists, most non-denominational churches, "Christian" churches, Restorationist Churches of Christ, many Presbyterians, conservative Methodists and Wesleyans, Reformed, Charismatics, Pentecostals, Mennonites, and yes, Evangelical Lutherans.

These churches are unified not by doctrine – there are many disagreements here – but by one common theme:

> *Jesus Christ has helped me – I am to love you – So I must tell you about Jesus since that can help you more than anything else I can do.*

Sharing the Gospel is the key value shared by these churches and their members. These churches also have the following values:

- A focus upon Bible study and upon understanding the Biblical message.
- An understanding that everyone individually must make up his or her mind about Christ.

Who are Evangelical Christians, Anyway?

- Belief in the reality of God and His ability to change the world.
- Belief in the reality of Jesus Christ and His ability to make us whole people.
- Belief in the Holy Spirit and His very real guidance in our life today.

The Barna Group Definition

The Barna Group is a marketing and research organization founded by George Barna, which focuses upon religion in America. On the Barna Group website, www.barna.org, Evangelicals are described as follows:

"Born again Christians" are defined as people who said they have made a personal commitment to Jesus Christ that is still important in their life today and who also indicated they believe that when they die they will go to Heaven because they had confessed their sins and had accepted Jesus Christ as their savior. Respondents are not asked to describe themselves as "born again."

"Evangelicals" meet the born again criteria (described above) *plus* seven other conditions. Those include saying their faith is very important in their life today; believing they have a personal responsibility to share their religious beliefs about Christ with non-Christians; believing that Satan exists; believing that eternal salvation is possible only through grace, not works; believing that Jesus Christ lived a sinless life on earth; asserting that the Bible is accurate in all that it teaches; and describing God as the all-knowing, all-powerful, perfect deity who created the universe and still rules it today. Being classified as an evangelical is not dependent upon church attendance or the denominational affiliation of the church attended.

Who are Evangelical Christians, Anyway?

Also, according to the Barna Group, 38 percent of Americans describe themselves as Evangelical, yet only 8 percent meet the criteria given above.

Understanding the Evangelical Worldview

Evangelicals often talk about "worldview". That word describes our way of looking at the world. It includes our most basic ideas about how the world functions, how we know things, how we learn things, what is important – and what is not. It covers our understanding of what is good and what is bad, what is beautiful and what is ugly. In summary, it is how our philosophy and religion affect our entire outlook.

If you want to understand Evangelicals, you must understand our worldview. Or world*views*, for there is not a single coherent view. Yet, there are certain ways we look at the world that are unique to us. If you can understand these ideas, you will be much closer to understanding us and will be able to communicate better with us.

The next few chapters will cover the Evangelical Worldview. We will cover some basic misunderstandings about Evangelical Christianity, or *Christian Myths*, that most non-Evangelical people have in *their* worldview.

Who are Evangelical Christians, Anyway?

Discussion Questions

1. Why do you think South Korea is mostly Christian?

2. If you attend a church, which major group does it fall into?

3. Why do you think that many non-Christian academics think of Christianity as a white, European religion?

Myth #1 - Understanding the People in the Churches.

> I know your works, that you are neither cold nor hot. ...Because you are lukewarm...I will vomit you out of My mouth. Revelation 3:16

Have you ever wondered why "Christians" don't behave like Christians are supposed to? The Myth is that Christians are supposed to act in a particularly moral way. The reality is that few uphold that high standard.

The reason is that Christians mature over time – there is not a sudden change in most people the day that they call themselves a Christian.

People who call themselves Christians fall into four categories:

- **Ethnic Christians** - People whose parents or grandparents were believing Christians, yet who never attend church except during an occasional Easter or Christmas service. About two-thirds of self-described "Christians" fall into this category.

- **Attending Christians** - People who attend church on a regular basis, but appear to do so out of habit rather than for religious reasons. "Attendees" are seen in Sunday morning services or Saturday evening Mass, but almost never visit the church at any other time. Although they may have become believers, they do not do anything with that belief. To them, church attendance is a duty, a social club, or a habit - not a religion. About 80 percent of church-attending Christians fall into this category.

- **Believing and Growing Christians** - These people are true believers. I'll explain in a later chapter what that means. They are involved in their church. Many of them serve the church as teachers, deacons, committee chairs, youth group leaders, choir members, etc. (Note that it is possible to do these things and still not be a believer!) About 15 percent of a typical church's attendees fall into this category.

- **Mature Christians** - These people are not new to the faith. They have learned many things about God, Jesus, and the Holy Spirit. They have a reputation for wisdom within their church. They teach the deepest classes on Sunday mornings and on Wednesday evenings. They often become missionaries or found new churches. Only a handful of these people are found at any normal church. (Many churches don't have any!) People talk about them in reverent tones and use words like "godly", "Christ-like", and "wise" to describe them. They only represent about 5 percent of church attendees. Less than 1 in

Understanding the People in the Churches.

50 people who call themselves "Christian" fall into this category.

Discussion Questions

1. Why do you think people move from one maturity category to another category?

2. Are you an Ethnic Christian, an Attending Christian, a Believing Christian, a Mature Christian, or a non-Christian?

3. Think about other people you know. Do you know a Mature Christian?

A Bit More About Ethnic Christians

To understand the concept of the Ethnic Christian, let's first discuss Ethnic Jews. Many Jews are familiar with the difference between observant and non-observant Jews. "Jewishness" refers not only to the religion of a Jew, but also his ethnic traditions and ancestry. Jews have traditionally not intermarried with *gentiles* (non-Jews), and thus form a semi-racial group with generally common physical features.

Understanding the People in the Churches.

Since World War II, many American Jews do not attend synagogue services. However, they still identify themselves as "Jewish". In essence, the Jewish religion has been tied so strongly to the Hebrew ethnic group that it is possible to be "Jewish" and never attend synagogue or have any understanding of the Jewish religion. These people are ethnic, non-observant Jews. Observant Jews attend synagogue regularly and observe the festivals and laws of Judaism. Observant Jews have the Jewish religion -- ethnic, non-observant Jews are commonly atheists or agnostics. An "in-between" group also exists: Jews who are circumcised, have a Bar-Mitzvah, are married under a canopy, and occasionally have a Passover meal, yet do not attend synagogue regularly.

In the same way, many descendents of Christian believers now identify themselves as "Christian", "Catholic", "Methodist", or "Baptist", even though they never attend church and have never read significantly in the Bible. These people are ethnic non-observant Christians in the same way as the ethnic, non-observant Jews. Ethnic Christians do not have an understanding of the Christian religion - merely a vague feeling of identity. *Are you an ethnic Christian?*

Ethnic Christians do a lot of harm to the image of Christianity. Ethnic Christian children picked on a Jewish friend of mine when at an early age. A mature Christian believer would detest the actions of these children because their actions go against every core teaching of Christianity.

Let's review our definition of an "Ethnic" Christian:

Understanding the People in the Churches.

> An Ethnic Christian is someone who rarely attends Christian services, yet calls himself or herself Christian because their parents or grandparents went to church regularly.

In reality, Ethnic Christians (EC's - pronounced "ee-sees") are unbelievers. Many profess a vague belief in God - but that isn't really what Christianity is all about. Some may have been baptized at an early age -- but that isn't really what Christianity is all about, either. Some feel "spiritual" -- but that isn't Christian belief either.

Since EC's don't attend regular Christian services, they are violating one of the key Christian teachings: *Christians should assemble together regularly to strengthen one another*. A Christian who lives as a hermit is a contradiction; Christians are supposed to gather together in groups. Even medieval monks joined together in monasteries. Christianity is a social religion. A man who claims otherwise may be spiritual, and he may be trying to reach God, but he is not a practicing Christian.

Why EC's don't attend church

One EC I know (we'll call him "Sam") told me that he doesn't go to church because of the "hypocrites" in the church. When Sam was a teenager, he saw that many of his church-going teenage friends went to the same parties he did and behaved just as badly as Sam. In a spirit of self-justification, Sam adopted the high moral ground by maintaining that since

    A) both him and his friends misbehaved at these parties, and

B) his friends went to church and Sam didn't, then
C) Sam was a better person – his friends were "hypocrites".

(The word "hypocrite" is actually of Greek origin and refers to the theatric masks that were worn by ancient Greek actors. Thus, when you say that someone is a "hypocrite", you are saying that they are "putting on the mask".)

Many people I know who are EC's justify their non-church-going position on this basis. "There are people at that church who behave as badly as me or worse, so I will not associate with them". Let's see what these EC's are really saying.

1. "Christians are supposed to be morally perfect".
2. "The Christians which I know are not morally perfect".
3. "I will only go to a church where there are morally perfect people".
4. "Therefore, I will not go to church."

Sometimes I've been tempted to say, "Why don't you go to that church so that you can teach those people moral perfection!" But I've managed to restrain myself. (One of the nice things about writing a book to you, whom I don't know, is that I don't have to restrain myself quite as much....) Notice that EC's understand one thing about Christianity - you are supposed to improve your morals when you become a Christian. But they mistake the classes (church) for the result (a Mature Christian's behavior).

Understanding the People in the Churches.

Clearly, EC's are missing something. And the concept that they are missing is that they think the day a person begins to attend church, that person will become a Mature Christian. Yet, Evangelical Christians share a concept with Mature Christians of almost all denominations when they agree that attending church does not make you a Christian any more than walking in the woods makes you a deer.

The Journey

Christianity is a journey. Like any journey, it has its rivers to cross and landmarks to attain. But still, a Christian's spiritual development is a journey and takes time. An EC may someday begin to attend church more regularly. He may do this for decades before he decides to attend a Sunday school class to learn more about a particular book of the Bible. Or he may dive right in. Some Christians mature by the time they're twenty-five. Others never mature. But when you are learning about Christianity, don't confuse the man or woman who just started lap 2 with the Mature Christian who's run 497 laps.

Imagine someone who has never heard Mozart attending a 4th grade orchestra concert. Ouch! Then imagine that same person later refusing to attend a London Symphony concert because she **knows** that Mozart sounds terrible. That's just what my friend Sam was doing when he confused all of those teenage Christians-in-Training with the end result and condemned all Christians.

No, just like anything else, the people at any church have to improve themselves to behave like Christians are supposed to behave. And some will

Understanding the People in the Churches.

become good at Christian behavior and others will not. But at least the ones going to church are taking lessons. After all, that's one of the key reasons Evangelical Christians attend church.

Discussion Questions

1. Do you know any EC's? Are you an EC?

2. Why do EC's call themselves Christian even if they never attend church?

3. Have you ever had a "4th grade orchestra" experience?

Choose your Teachers

Evangelical Christians are concerned with good teaching. And the best way to get good teaching is to choose your teachers well.

Imagine that you are sixteen years old and want to learn how to play golf. You have a choice of three teachers -- your best friend Fred who's been playing for a year, your Dad who's been playing for 25 years at local courses and shot par once, or a friend of your neighbor -- a guy named Tiger Woods that's supposed to be really good.

If you choose golf teachers like most people choose religion teachers, you'll choose Fred. If you are a bit wiser, you'll choose your Dad. But if you are really

Understanding the People in the Churches.

wise, you'll find the best teacher you can find -- and pick Tiger Woods.

Fred and the EC's

Let's say that you choose Fred. Fred will probably teach you how to point the club the right way, give you a terrible swing, and you'll be lucky to ever get a chance to use a putter since you'll take so many strokes to get the ball on the green. After playing a few times, you'll decide that golf's a stupid game, you don't have the knack for it, and spend your weekends watching baseball.

When you ask Fred for religion advice, you'll get the same sort of overview. The lesson on Christianity won't make much sense and you'll probably end up spending Sunday mornings watching "Meet the Press" on TV.

This is how many EC's get their religious training. They talk to a Christian friend who knows little more than they do about Christianity. They watch a TV show such as "Touched by an Angel" or a movie such as "It's a Wonderful Life" and think that they now understand Christianity. (Incidentally, Christians don't believe that you become an angel when you die...but more about that in a later chapter). Naturally, Christianity from Hollywood doesn't make much sense or have much depth. (What did you expect from people who specialize in having people fall in love in 90 minutes?)

Most people who learn about "Christianity" this way don't see any particular relevance to their life. And thus, EC's take the easy way out -- they don't

Understanding the People in the Churches.

go to church and they don't think much about religion. After all, they believe in God, don't they? But a belief in God is only a small part of Christianity.

The fact is EC's, many atheists, and New Age types have their religion - the religion of "me". Down deep, they believe that they are the ultimate judges of what Truth should be -- they would put God on trial and decide whether He is good enough for them. They want a God that will approve of their behavior, regardless of what it is. They want a forgiving God who will accept them as they are. (In this they are close to the Reality). But in essence, EC's want to create their Universe and put a god in it who will behave himself and treat them like a kindly old grandfather would. But that's not Christian belief, either.

So learning about Christianity from your newly baptized friend Fred is not such a good idea. Maybe we can get a bit wiser.

Discussion Questions

1. What is it like to develop a golf swing without lessons?

2. Can you imagine learning how to cook without lessons?

Understanding the People in the Churches.

3. Right now, list your characteristics of a perfect God.

Dad and the Attendees

Let's say that you choose good ole' Dad. Dad knows that the swing is important, but he's not sure how to put it all together. He helps you a bit by telling you to use a wood for long strokes and irons for shorter strokes, but can't really tell you the difference between when to use a 7 iron and a 9 iron. Dad also has a problem with a nasty slice when he swings in the rough and he teaches you that slice, too. You'll enjoy playing with Dad and may actually play regularly. Golf will be a nice social sport for you, but you'll be lucky to win your foursome.

When you ask Dad about religion, he knows a bit. You'll get a few of the major pieces and understand the seriousness of the subject. You'll probably come away with a few rules to follow: "Go to church every Sunday and tithe". You may even get some additional details such as "Jesus is the Son of God" and "Don't commit adultery". But you won't understand how it all hangs together - you won't understand the "why" of it all. And there will be a couple things that Dad will get wrong -- and you'll learn those, too!

There are many people who learn about Christianity from their parents, or by going to church as young children. This is not bad in itself -- the danger occurs when the "what" of religion dominates and the "why" is ignored.

Understanding the People in the Churches.

Children are very focused on black-and-white rules. A child is most comfortable when he is given hard and fast rules for living:

- "Don't chew gum."
- "Clean your plate before you have dessert."
- "Do your homework before watching television."
- "Don't ever drive the car."
- "Don't hit anyone."

Children run into difficulties when they are faced with "sometimes" rules. For example, you know that you can't explain to an average 8-year-old how to determine if a new blouse on a store rack should be bought or not -- there are too many things to consider, such as the weight of the fabric, the chance that the blouse will go on sale next week, the amount of other bills due, the money in the purse, the time of the year, the cut of the blouse, the rest of your wardrobe. But it is easy to tell that same 8-year old: "Never buy a sleeveless blouse."

We call the simple rules "black-and-white" reasoning. We call the more complicated adult decision making "gray" reasoning. "Gray" reasoning involves understanding the "why" of something in depth and takes time and effort to teach. "Black-and-white" reasoning is easy to teach, but the results aren't satisfactory for most adult situations.

Many times people who are taught only "black-and-white" reasoning end up as adults who are either fanatically devoted to a few principles, or are incapable of making sound judgments because they

Understanding the People in the Churches.

can always see both sides of an issue. They have resorted to avoiding decisions because most adult situations present the adults with conflicting principles. It is not an easy thing to teach "gray" reasoning, but it is necessary to make proper adult decisions.

Teaching religion to children is an excellent idea and I recommend it strongly. We do it every day in our household. But the danger occurs when you teach *a little* religion to children. Then, they will remember only the hard and fast rules and forget the more subtle issues. They remember who David and Goliath were -- but not why they were fighting. (Do you?)

They remember that they shouldn't have pre-marital or extra-marital sex -- but don't remember *why* they shouldn't. Oh yes, they know that "it's wrong", or "the Bible says not to", but if faced with a debating opponent who denies the validity of the Bible, they aren't able to go to the next step and defend their religion and its teachings. And this means that they are just like my Christian friends of 20 years ago who couldn't answer my questions about God and Jesus.

In many places, the Bible talks to us about the differences between new Christians and Mature Christians. Mature Christians eat spiritual meat where new Christians need spiritual milk, just as infants need real milk. A sound knowledge of the "why" concepts behind the black and white "what" rules gives you the ability to understand the faith fully and eat that spiritual meat. And this only comes with sound teaching and a commitment of

Understanding the People in the Churches.

time – not by a casual visit to church once or twice a year.

Once again let me say I support teaching Christianity to young children. But be sure to follow up as the children get older and teach the "why" as much as the "what". If you aren't sure how to teach it -- then find the person in the church who **can** teach the course.

Discussion Questions

1. Have you ever tried to teach a child "gray" rules?

2. West Point requires a cadet to take classes in moral reasoning. Do you think that this class involves "black and white" reasoning or "gray" reasoning? Why?

3. Have you ever had your decision-making paralyzed by conflicting principles? How did you settle the conflict?

4. Do you know anyone who can't make decisions about right and wrong?

Understanding the People in the Churches.

5. Read 1 Corinthians 8 to see how Paul suggested that Christians handle the Law.

Legalism

Some (but not all) Christians who learn about Christianity in this "black and white" way develop a way of thinking that Mature Christians refer to as "legalism". This is the exact same problem that had developed in first century Palestine, for Jesus spent a considerable part of His ministry reminding the legalistic sect of Pharisee Jews that religion was not about the "what" of do's and don'ts, but rather about the "why" of the heart.

> **Evangelical Christian Teaching**
>
> Christianity is about your heart -- not your actions.

Legalism is an excessive focus on the "what". Legalistic Christians exercise an influence upon society's view of Christianity completely out of proportion to their numbers. This is perhaps because legalistic Christians are often outspoken and often act distinctively.

For example, a particular group may decide that card playing is contrary to Christian teaching. In most cases, this concept developed during a time that card playing meant gambling. Gambling was what was bad. This was clearly understood by the first generation of group members. However, later generations simply repeated the words "don't ever play cards", even after the rise and popularity of recreational games of skill such as contract bridge and Hearts. The original prohibition didn't apply, but because of poor teaching, the entire group avoids a behavior enjoyed by millions of Christians worldwide. This is legalism: Following the rule even when the "why" of the rule no longer applies.

I've seen the same issue develop regarding alcohol. Some groups argue that no Christian should ever drink alcohol because it is likely to lead to abuse. While other groups may disagree with this prohibition -- many Christians regularly drink alcohol in moderation and have biblical support for this position -- it is a reasonable concept given the availability of safe, non-alcoholic drinks in our society. However, I know of some people who have gone so far as to avoid excellent meals because the chef put wine in the sauce before cooking. Any alcohol would have evaporated during the cooking. Even the tablespoon or so the chef began with would not cause anyone problems. This is legalism in extreme. These people would have a much lower stress life if they understood the "why" of their beliefs.

It should be noted that groups such as the Amish and Holiness Pentecostals may appear to be legalistic due to their distinctive dress and behaviors, but this misses the point. The Amish dress as they do for the precise purpose of being distinctive and calling attention to the influence of God in their lives. Many Holiness women wear their hair long expressly to demonstrate that they are more obedient to God than to fashion. A

Understanding the People in the Churches.

legalistic Christian is overly concerned with dress or a particular behavior as an end -- the belief that a particular behavior is irreconcilable with God. This is a myth that we will deal with in a later chapter.

Discussion Questions

1. Do you know any legalistic Christians?

2. Do you have any examples of legalism in your own life?

3. Read Matthew 15:1-9 to see how Jesus dealt with legalistic Jews.

College

Another problem with children who missed the "why" of Christianity occurs when they reach college. At this point, all people question their basic beliefs. When pressed by a clever philosophy professor, or a sharp fellow student, a Christian student can loose his or her faith and fall into one of the cults that prey upon lonely college students. However, well-educated students will quickly spot the fallacies in cults and will find their faith to be a source of tremendous strength during a difficult period of life.

Understanding the People in the Churches.

Mistakes Happen

Every Christian at one time or another finds his mind wandering during Sunday school, or during the sermon. "Is this really necessary?", he thinks. Here's a quick story about why you need to understand the details.

Mohammed was the founder of Islam. When he was a traveling merchant he apparently encountered some Christians. After his encounter with the Christians he returned to Arabia and founded Islam.

There is a curious problem with Islamic belief. This problem is about core Christian belief. Most Moslems believe that the Christian Trinity is God, Mary, and Jesus on the basis of the Koran Sura 5.116 The Dinner Table. (The actual Trinity is God, Jesus, and Holy Spirit.) The Koran records Mohammed's words, and can roughly be considered the Moslem "Bible". What makes this so interesting is that the false trinity was very repugnant to Mohammed and is a key part of most Moslem's rejection of Christianity.

Did Mohammed make this mistake in translation? Or did he get a garbled view of Christianity from a supposed Christian? Was Mohammed trying to bring Christianity to Arabia? Whichever it was we will not know in this life, but it led to the development of a new religion - one which dominates North Africa, the Middle East, Central Asia, Iran, Pakistan, Bangladesh, and Indonesia. All of this was because of a mistake in Mohammed's understanding of Christian doctrine. Understanding doctrine correctly really can make a difference. You

Understanding the People in the Churches.

never know what that passing acquaintance of yours will do in later life. And parents - you really need to understand that doctrine to teach your children properly.

Tiger Woods and the Growing Christians

Now, let's go back to our golf lessons. If you get your golf lessons from Tiger Woods, you'll probably find that you practice that swing over and over again, since Tiger won't let you get a bad swing. He knows that a minor mistake in your swing can mean a difference worth millions of dollars on the pro tour. And he'll make you understand why you should choose each particular club and why you should have a particular set of clubs. He'll help you get the big picture *and* the details straight. After your lessons, you might go on the pro tour yourself!

Now Tiger Woods isn't an expert on religion. But there *are* professionals in the field of religion. For example, C. S. Lewis wrote many excellent and witty books on the Christian religion in the mid-twentieth century. Charles Stanley has a superb radio and TV teaching ministry today. Likewise David Jeremiah. Paul E. Little, Rick Warren, and Doug Macintosh have in-depth books on details of Christianity. Chuck Colson, Bruce Wilkerson, and Chuck Swindoll in our time. St. Augustine, Martin Luther, and Charles Spurgeon from the past. These gentlemen are the leaders on the Christian "pro tour".

But you have local pros, too. Just as every major golf course has a local pro, most major churches

Understanding the People in the Churches.

have local pros, too. Although the pastor is often one of the pros, all pastors aren't pros and all pros aren't pastors. Instead, start looking for in-depth teaching at a local church. Look for churches where the sermons are explanations of biblical passages conducted by learned men rather than mere exhortations to "follow Jesus". Look for teachers who answer the question "what did Jesus do?" and back up their teachings with detailed and clear answers.

A man who cannot teach something clearly really doesn't understand it himself.

These teachers aren't always men. Although it is less common, many churches have well-educated women who teach women's Bible studies. These women focus upon what the Bible says -- they don't hold social gatherings masquerading as Bible studies.

BSF International

If you are serious about the study of Christianity or can't find a teacher who can answer your questions, then you should contact BSF. An interdenominational organization, Bible Study Fellowship operates men and women's bible course studies around the nation and around the world. Their website lists class locations. (www.bsfinternational.org)

These classes are open to all people who want to learn about Christianity in detail. And one of the rules of BSF is that attendees may not attempt to recruit people to come to their churches. In almost

Understanding the People in the Churches.

every case, the classes are free, but are taught as if you were at an extremely expensive private college.

In these courses you will find the Growing Christians. These courses are taught by Mature Christians who undergo a difficult "train-the-trainer" class themselves. Here is where you can get real biblical training. I highly recommend it.

The Ultimate Pro

The nicest thing about Christianity is that the inventor of the game wrote the Book. The Bible is full of detailed God-inspired instructions to Christians. (More on that later...) If you read the New Testament and take time to reflect on everything you read, you will get many insights even without finding one of the local pros - but you will learn quicker and better if you have a "Pro".

The Pro Tour and the Mature Christians

The men I listed above as the "Pro Tour" of Christianity have one thing in common -- they all were quick to talk about what they had *yet* to learn about Christianity. In many ways, Mature Christians believe that this life is simply Boot Camp for eternity. Here we learn how to behave. There are a few experienced drill instructors - and most of us are raw recruits. Paul of Tarsus, the man who brought Christianity to Europe and the heart of the Roman Empire, wrote that the more he learned, the more things he found wrong with himself and his attitudes. So the Pros are the quickest to tell you that they have flaws. And they all spend hours every week reading and re-reading their Bibles.

Understanding the People in the Churches.

Discussion Questions and Actions

1. Who are your local Pros?

2. Read 2 Timothy 3:13-15. This short passage contains many truths about learning Christian teachings.

3. Read the next verse. Don't despair if you can't find a Pro! Studying the Bible will answer many questions.

Finding Mature Christians

By now, you probably see the point of this chapter. Just because a person calls himself a Christian doesn't make him a Christian who can teach you anything about Christianity. There are many people who call themselves Christians who don't even attend church and really don't understand much about Christianity; there are also many who are just learning to behave as Christians. Judging all Christianity by the behavior of young Christians or EC's is like judging an army by the marching of recruits their first week in boot camp.

Look for the Mature Christians. Just as in other walks of life, flashy doesn't mean best. If you see a TV preacher who is flashy -- he probably will disappoint you later. Billy Graham drives old cars and lives in a modest home -- humility is the mark of a Mature Christian. Yet, even Billy Graham has his flaws. The Bible and church history talk about preachers and teachers as different people. It has been rare to find someone who has the outgoing nature needed to preach to large crowds of unbelievers and make them believers. We call these people "evangelists". It has also been rare to find someone who could teach Christianity to serious students and teach it correctly. It is almost unheard of to find both abilities in one person.

The Mythical Christian

So the First Myth is the Mythical Christian -- the man who says he is a Christian but doesn't know what that means well enough to explain it to another. If you are not a Christian, I ask you to look for a Mature Christian who can explain things to you. If you *are* a Christian -- an EC or an Attendee -- I suggest that you should look for a deeper meaning to Christianity than that which you already know. The next few chapters will move deeper into Evangelical Christian belief.

Actions

1. Make a list of Mature Christians you know.

2. If you don't know any, find one. Visit a nearby church, talk to a few Christian friends, or contact a BSF group.

Understanding the People in the Churches.

3. Decide which Mature Christian will be your "Pro".

4. Talk with your Pro and explain that you want to learn more about Christianity. Ask your Pro where you can find a good class.

Understanding the People in the Churches.

Suggested Scripture Readings

- Acts 11:25-26 The First Christians

- Matthew 28:18-19 The Great Commission - Why Christians Spread the Word.

- 1 Corinthians 3:1-3 New Christians are Spiritual Infants

- 1 Corinthians 1:10-13 Fighting over Sects is not Proper

- John 1:1-5 Jesus as the Word.

FAQ #1 – Where Can I Find Evangelicals?

> However, many of those who heard the word believed and the number of the men came to be about five thousand. Acts 4:4

Evangelical Christians are an increasingly common part of our society, but there are many people who don't know any Evangelicals. In this short chapter, I'll give some basic information which should help you find some Evangelicals, whether you are trying to find a couple to talk with, or millions to sell to.

Geography

Evangelical Christianity has four strong geographic bases.

First, there is Chicago. Chicago is the home of the key Evangelical universities of Moody Bible Institute, Wheaton College, and Trinity Evangelical Divinity School, as well as *Christianity Today* magazine, the flagship publication of Evangelical Christianity. In addition, the huge megachurch, Willow Creek Community Church, influences churches around the world by leading the Willow Creek Association, an organization that connects like-minded churches.

The second base of Evangelical Christianity is Orange County, California. This wealthy suburb,

Where can I find Evangelicals?

nestled between Los Angeles and San Diego, is the home to a series of powerful ministries and Evangelical colleges, including Saddleback Church, the home of Rick Warren. Only the Bible itself surpasses Pastor Warren's recent book in worldwide sales. Interestingly enough, *The Purpose-Driven Life* is the follow-on book to an earlier best seller, *The Purpose Driven Church*, which has helped many churches duplicate the growth and success of Saddleback Church.

The third center of Evangelical Christianity is Texas. Dallas Theological Seminary, Wycliffe Bible Translators (a huge missionary organization – wycliffe.org), Baylor University, several other significant colleges, Trinity Broadcasting Network, and a host of megachurches with wide exposure are found here.

Atlanta represents the fourth center of Evangelical Christianity. Ravi Zacharias International Ministries directly engages academics that would dismiss Christianity, while megachurches are scattered all around the area, many with significant television and radio ministries.

In a more general sense, Evangelical Christianity is strongest in middle-class and wealthy suburbs. Almost every city has an Evangelical megachurch (defined as having over 2000 regular Sunday attendees.) These churches are found throughout the United States, from the heart of Brooklyn to rural Amish country in Sugarcreek, Ohio.

Where can I find Evangelicals?

Although strongest in the suburbs, inner-city neighborhoods are not left out. Huge ethnic churches can be found who follow Evangelical principles in every major city. The largest church in the world is a charismatic Evangelical church in Seoul, Korea, where over 250,000 people worship each week.

Demographics

Evangelicals are spread over a wide demographic range. Although politicians refer to "white Evangelicals" as though this is the defining label, it only represents a portion of the Evangelicals. Most black churches are very Evangelical. Evangelicals are becoming the majority in many central American countries, and this has led to a large number of Hispanic Evangelical churches in the United States, as well as Spanish language services being conducted in many Evangelical churches. Particularly in the West and South, each large city has a growing number of Chinese and Korean Evangelical congregations.

Evangelicals are not limited to one particular salary or job type. In major cities, Evangelical churches will be found that cater to various groups, from the poorest of the poor to the wealthiest entrepreneurs.

Media

The flagship Evangelical publication for pastors and those heavily involved in ministry is *Christianity Today*. Conceived and founded by Billy Graham about fifty years ago, this publication covers worldwide developments in Evangelical

Where can I find Evangelicals?

Christianity, and to a large extent, defines the field. Regular articles cover foreign missions, new American church concepts, church leaders, authors, new books, movies, developments in denominations and colleges, and theological concepts. Although the circulation is roughly 300,000, the organization also has another dozen publications covering in detail the field, from foreign missions to the business of running a church.

More political in its outlook is *World* magazine, based in Asheville, North Carolina. World is a weekly newsmagazine similar to Time or Newsweek, but with an explicitly Christian perspective. *World* also has a circulation of roughly 300,000.

On television, there are a plethora of channels that aim toward the Evangelical viewer. Trinity Broadcasting Network provides a 24-hour diet primarily of charismatic preachers. Sky Angel is a satellite television service that delivers over 30 channels of Christian programming.

On the radio, there are many, many locally owned Christian radio stations, mostly supported by a single church or group of churches. Three common formats are found. First, there are the traditional sermons alternated with traditional hymns stations. Bible Broadcasting Network and Moody Broadcasting Network are key suppliers for these stations. Christian rock stations are found in major cities, some of which are even for-profit. And there are the stations that offer more contemporary easy listening Christian music interspersed with sermons.

Where can I find Evangelicals?

In the general field of Christian bookstores, Family Christian Bookstores (formerly Zondervan) is the largest national chain.

On the web, Crosswalk.com provides a series of resources that are aimed at Christian readers.

Walden Media and Fox Faith are two film distributors that are interested in the Evangelical Christian market.

Suggested Actions

- Find an Evangelical Christian church in your area. (One way to do this is to go onto the web and look up an Evangelical seminary, such as Dallas Theological Seminary, where you can find churches that are led by a graduate.) Visit it on Sunday morning.

- Investigate some of the Evangelical media described above.

I am a good person, so I will go to Heaven.

Myth #2 - I Am a Good Person, so I Will Go to Heaven When I Die.

> By the deeds of the law no flesh will be justified in His sight. Romans 3:20

Despite the common belief of many Americans, mature Evangelical Christians do not believe that good people will go to Heaven when they die. Here's why:

Christians believe that God is perfect and good. (In another chapter we'll explain why we believe these things of God.) He created the Universe and mankind, and put us on the Earth. He was present before there was an Earth.

The Nature of Cats

Imagine a bachelor who built a house for himself. Everything in the house has been created to perfection. The house is kept clean and neat, and everything has its place. This bachelor also hates cats. (Is this like anyone you know?). Now, he doesn't really hate cats - he likes stroking their fur and playing with them. But he will never, ever have a cat in the house, because cats by their very nature will cause problems with his home. They make messes in the corner and shred the furniture legs. They require stinky food and have stinky litter

I am a good person, so I will go to Heaven.

boxes. They occasionally leave fur balls on the floor and hair on the couch. And so he will never let a cat into the house.

Now imagine that the bachelor marries. The man and his wife have a daughter who is the joy of his life. He loves this little girl more than anything he has ever loved before. And one day -- she shows up with a stray kitten in her arms and says, "Daddy, can we keep it? P-U-L-E-E-Z-E?"

What did this kitten do? It simply trusted the daughter enough to come into her arms and believed that the daughter would be good to it and would take care of it. It isn't any different from any other cat. It isn't any "better" than any other cat -- it isn't even housebroken!

Now you know exactly what will happen. The man will let the kitten into the house. And, true to form, there will be stinky food, stinky litter boxes, shredded furniture, messed carpet, fur balls and hair. The cat behaves according to its nature and hasn't changed a bit. It isn't a particularly good cat, after all. It's just a stray kitten the daughter found who was smart enough not to run from the daughter.

So why'd the guy let the cat into the house?

The reason is clear -- the daughter has told the father "That cat is mine!". And because of his love for the daughter, he lets the cat into the house -- not because the cat is particularly good. And he'll take good care of the cat even when the daughter isn't around.

I am a good person, so I will go to Heaven.

Now, we are just like cats: We do some pretty awful things, shred the furniture, and make messes in the corner. We have some lovable qualities, but our basic nature is to cause problems.

In this story, God is the Father; Jesus is the daughter. And we are the cats. We get into the house of God not on our own goodness, but solely because we are Jesus' "cats".

Evangelical Christians believe that what Jesus and His disciples said is true. By our nature, we cannot be good enough to associate with God. But because of the love of God for Jesus, God can tolerate us. We have one thing do in return: Jump into the arms of Jesus and trust that He will take care of our needs.

Goodness isn't enough

Now why can't a "good" person get into heaven?

Christians and Jews believe that a long time ago, a man called Moses (Moshe) led the Jewish people from slavery in Egypt into the Sinai Desert, where they paused. During this pause, God gave Moses a set of laws of which the Ten Commandments are the core. God explained through these laws what behavior He expected from the Jewish people. These are found in the second book of the Old Testament, Exodus, in Chapter 20.

I am a good person, so I will go to Heaven.

The Ten Commandments

1. You will have no other gods before Me.
2. You will not worship carved images.
3. You will not take the name of the LORD lightly. ("In vain")
4. Keep the Sabbath day holy.
5. Honor your father and your mother.
6. You will not murder.
7. You will not commit adultery.
8. You will not steal.
9. You will not bear false witness against your neighbor.
10. You will not covet your neighbor's possessions.

Their Meaning

Notice the first four commandments. Collectively, they say "Treat God as unique and very, very special". Have you ever used the name of the LORD in an unholy way? If so, you've broken Commandment Three. Have you ever worked on the Sabbath? Then you've broken Commandment Four. Have you treated a sports event, a job-related goal, or a special present as more important than prayer or attending church? Then you've broken Commandment One. Have you ever worshipped a sculpture? This one is not so common in Western countries today, but it is the core of Commandment Two.

Commandment Five - Have you ever been disrespectful to your father or your mother?

I am a good person, so I will go to Heaven.

Jump to Commandment Ten - Notice that coveting (wanting very badly) your neighbor's possessions is breaking this Commandment. You don't have to actually *take* anything. God's standard of goodness includes your *thought processes* as well as your overt actions. In the Book of Matthew (5:27), Jesus further explains this by pointing out that whoever *looks* at a woman with lust has already committed adultery (Commandment Seven) in his heart. *This is how high God's standards are!*

So now look at the other Commandments:

Commandment Six: Ever *hated* someone enough to wish they were dead? You've broken this commandment.

Commandment Eight - Have you ever taken home a pencil from work? Ever drank your college roommate's soda without asking? "Borrowed" some cosmetics?

Commandment Nine - Ever exaggerated your little sister's actions when the two of you did something wrong? Ever slanted a story to make you look better and another look worse? Have you ever lied? Any of these will break the Commandment.

Measuring Up

So, how did you measure up to God's Standards? Are you like most people and broke most of the Commandments?

If we break even **one** of the Commandments a **single** time, then God considers us to be guilty. And

I am a good person, so I will go to Heaven.

He will not want to associate with us. Our bachelor would not bring in a cat who behaved perfectly (except for the occasional fur ball) - simply because of the occasional fur ball. And so, God, who demands perfect behavior from us, will not tolerate the least bit of Commandment breaking.

Discussion Questions

1. Which commandments did you break?

2. Have you ever met a cat-hater? Why does he/she hate cats?

3. The cat-hating story is an example of substitute love. The love the man has for the daughter is substituted for the actual feeling the man has for the cats. Have you ever seen substitute love in action?

4. Have you ever gained entrance to an event based upon a friend or relative's standing rather than your own?

5. Have you ever been in a situation where you needed to know the "right person" to accomplish something?

I am a good person, so I will go to Heaven.

6. Read Romans 3:10-20. This is the classic statement of our imperfection.

All are guilty

So we've all broken most of the Commandments and we are guilty.

But what about our good deeds? With a Just God, wouldn't our good deeds be strong enough to get us into Heaven?

No. There are a couple points to be made here about the way Evangelical Christians believe.

First, let's look at ourselves the way God looks at us.

Jolly Old Men and Crabby Old Ladies

Have you ever met a really jolly old man or woman? Someone who always treats the children nice, who smiles at your very presence, and laughs when your dog runs over their feet? I'll tell you a secret: He or she didn't get to be that nice overnight. They didn't just turn 70 one day and suddenly decide to become nice. No, they began a long time ago and *practiced* being nice.

In contrast, you've also probably met a crabby old man or woman who hates the world. She complains about the presents you just gave her and can't stand

I am a good person, so I will go to Heaven.

the hot/cold/mild/wet/dry weather. You know, she didn't get to be crabby overnight, either. She began a long time ago and practiced being mean and nasty.

Now from God's perspective: He knows better than anyone what happens over time to people. Imagine your jolly old man after 10,000 years of practice. Imagine your crabby old lady after 10,000 years of practice. (Now you understand Hell much better!)

God knows that if we are left to ourselves we will become meaner and nastier. Left to ourselves, our hidden evils will take us over. Our envy, lust, violence, pride, boasting, backbiting, hatred, and other evil tendencies will grow and grow over time. Just like the cat, it is in our nature to hiss and spit and make messes on the carpet! God understands that one bad habit in a person who isn't willing to take instruction from Him will become a terribly bad problem in a thousand years or so. It's like a cancerous mole that starts out as a minor blemish on your skin but will spread throughout your body to affect every organ unless you remove it quickly.

Everyone has these cancers. Everyone started out with a problem or two. It's built into our very nature. Evangelical Christians have a name for this disease – it is called our "sin nature". We believe that the Adam and Eve and the serpent story explains how this happened. (There is conflict within the church about whether this story is literally true or merely figuratively true, but most Evangelical Christians believe it is literally true.)

Evangelical Christians believe that God initially created man and woman perfectly. However, He

I am a good person, so I will go to Heaven.

intentionally left us with free will so that we would be more than robots. He gave us everything – the Garden of Eden – and had only one rule: Do not eat from one particular tree.

Eventually, Adam and Eve both ate from that tree and disobeyed God. Through that act, they defined being human as being in rebellion to God. Once we tasted that concept, we were by nature creatures that would look for our own way, which leads us into conflict within a Universe created by Another.

God isn't willing to have you in His Universe – His house - unless you are willing to take instructions from Him about how to cure your problem – the disease of "being human".

When you agree to accept Christ as your Lord, you implicitly sign up for His personality improvement program. And that means that you will be a much more pleasant and happy person in a few thousand years or so. Most people begin to see the effects very quickly, sometimes within hours, but others take years to see the effects

Self-Examination

Now let's look at yourself today in a totally honest way. Look deep.

- How many good things have you done today?
- How many unkind words have you said today?
- How many times have you broken a Commandment in your heart today?

I am a good person, so I will go to Heaven.

- How about when you mentally cussed out your wife/husband/friend/child/mother/father?
- What about the secret, horrible things that you've done in your life, when you did something awful which hurt someone (or would if it became public knowledge)?

Would you *really* like to have God judge you fairly and justly?

Look at it this way: Assume that God, the Perfect Policeman, were to bring all the proper evidence to court and were to apply the proper punishments to you that you deserve according to *human* laws. What would your punishments be?

Start with traffic tickets that you deserved, but weren't ticketed for because a policeman didn't see you. The Perfect Policeman caught all of those. Would you be bankrupt from the fines?

What about the other crimes you've committed? How many years in prison would you serve if all those crimes were public knowledge? (Oh, you say that you've never committed any crimes? Did you ever hit your brother? Isn't that assault and battery? Did you ever steal a pencil or piece of paper, or a paper clip? Added a couple of dollars to a meal on an expense account? That's theft!)

Now what about the crimes that you *thought* about committing? How many men have you killed in your mind? How many friends have you punched out in your daydreams? How many times have you

I am a good person, so I will go to Heaven.

committed adultery or worse in your mind as you watched TV?

No, there are very few of us that would like to take our chances with God's judgment. We would be in big trouble -- even by man's laws -- if we actually got what we deserve. And this ignores the worst crime of all.

Discussion Questions

1. Have you known the crabby old woman or man? How about the jolly one?

2. Have you ever broken a human law and avoided being caught?

3. What is your proper sentencing by human laws if you were caught with proper evidence?

4. What if you added those crimes you only thought about committing?

The Greatest Commandment

"Love the LORD your God with all your heart, with all your soul, and with all your mind". Jesus calls

I am a good person, so I will go to Heaven.

this the first and greatest Commandment. Breaking it would be the worst crime. If so, then we all have a problem. None of us can live up to Christ's reading of the Commandment. Do you actually love Him totally? It is impossible, but this is what Christians believe we are to attempt. For we know that if you don't make the *attempt*, you are actually saying, "I love *ME* with all my heart, with all my soul, and with all my mind". And so most people break this Commandment.

What does it mean to love myself more than God? Most people want to set the rules, decide what is fair, decide what is just, and get upset when the Universe doesn't operate according to their ideas. In reality, everyone naturally wants to be *the god*. It's more fun that way -- or so we think. (Go watch the movie *Bruce Almighty* for a sobering view of this).

Christians believe that God has a tremendously just punishment for those who break this Commandment. God simply says, "If you are not going to follow this Commandment, then you can live by yourself. Love Me or love yourself without Me. It's your choice." He does not kill us, or send us straight to Hell. He simply says, "If you can live by yourself, go ahead." And here is the center of Christianity.

The Center of Christianity

God does not demand that we love Him. But He is very just, and very polite. If we don't love Him, we are politely left to our own devices. We can figure out how to live in a Universe that He made and designed to *His* specifications – not *our*

I am a good person, so I will go to Heaven.

specifications. We can follow our desires and end up with broken lives, with broken hearts, and with broken spirits. Some of the systems that we develop will work better than others. But ultimately, our best efforts will fall short, because we didn't design the Universe – He did. And because of that, our best efforts and plans will always have a fatal flaw that will eventually fail us.

We can continue to muddle through in our own way. We are afraid of death, so we exercise, eat fruits and vegetables, avoid smoking, and work to look young. Yet, in the end, because He made the Universe and we didn't, we lose. And finally when our hearts stop and our breathing stops, it is then up to us to figure out what to do next.

If we don't obey God, then we can just save ourselves. He doesn't kill us – He just lets us live or die by ourselves. Do *you* know how to live forever without divine help? *I* don't.

But God gave us a way out of the problem. Christ said, "Whoever believes in Me will have eternal life." Therefore, God gave us a simple choice: Accept His gift of eternal life by believing that His Son Jesus has the ability to save your life, by which act you are acknowledging Him as greater than you -- or show everyone just how much a god you are.

"Save yourself", He says, "or let My Son save you." This is Just and Fair.

It's something worth thinking about for a while...

I am a good person, so I will go to Heaven.

Discussion Questions

1. Can you save your own life? Permanently?

2. Does this line of thought disturb you? Why?

3. Do you want to be the god? Can you?

4. What would you do if you were the god?

5. Why do you suppose God hasn't done that?

Beings and Creatures

Words have inherent meanings. God is a Being. He exists by His Will. We are creatures. We were created. Create-ures. God is a Creator. We acknowledge that a boy who creates a Lego® block man owns him and can dispose of him in any way he wishes. What is the difference between a boy and God? More than the difference between a Lego block man and the boy who builds him. And how much more should we acknowledge that God the Creator owns us - His creatures?

I am a good person, so I will go to Heaven.

Can a creature save himself? No. And that is why we need to be saved.

Sins versus Sin

When you break one of God's laws, you commit a "sin". A sin is an offense against God, in the same way that a crime is an offense against the government. However, there is another, slightly different usage of the word "sin" that Christians also use.

The Condition of Sin

Christians also understand that that there is something broken about this world. It was not made in a broken condition, but very early on it became broken. The story of Adam and Eve and the Serpent tells about the breaking of Mankind and the world. It really doesn't matter whether or not you take the story literally or as an allegory, the message is clear. Things were once perfect on this earth and mankind was right with God. Mankind disobeyed God through the urging of an evil creature, and ever after the world and mankind were broken. This condition of brokenness is what we call the Condition of Sin.

Today, if we look around at the world, we see many problems. Clearly, the world is broken. You may be trying to "fix" part of the world. Blood is shed, pain is caused, and ugliness spreads. At one time, people dreamed of fixing all the problems of the world. Now we know better. We know that Jesus was right when He said, "there will always be the poor". Yet we keep trying.

I am a good person, so I will go to Heaven.

Ugliness. As the movie *The Preacher's Wife* says, "God don't like ugly!" And that is why we cannot be perfect. This world is broken by our disobedience -- and God is too perfect to tolerate the ugliness that stains our hands. And we can't help but be part of that ugliness. We are broken, also. Our relationships are often ugly, we offend people unnecessarily, we hurt others, and we hurt ourselves even with our very best efforts. Things go wrong. We cannot be perfect even when we try. We are "in Sin".

The Purpose of Christ

Because men could not live up to the laws of Moses, God sent Jesus to establish a new agreement with mankind.

Under the Mosaic Law, if a man committed a particular sin, he had to pay by a sacrifice. For example, he might have to sacrifice a bull. The man would put his hand on the bull and kill the bull, thus signifying that the innocent and very valuable bull was dying in the place of the man. This is similar to our paying a fine for breaking a human crime. We often have criminals sacrifice part of their lives in jail if they commit a crime.

Under the old laws, every year a special sacrifice was made to apologize for all of the sins of the people of Israel for that year. The blood of the sacrifice was brought into the Temple of God and placed by the high priest upon a special spot in the center of the Temple - the spot where God looked upon Israel. God could then look at Israel through the filter of the special sacrifice for the next year. Man had apologized to God and acknowledged God

I am a good person, so I will go to Heaven.

the Creator's ownership of the man's life and property.

When Jesus was crucified, His blood became the perfect sacrifice that could pay for all of the sins of the entire world forever. Jesus was God. He was of infinite value. His life was of infinite value. An infinitely valuable sacrifice could pay for all of the sins of the world. It was the only sacrifice that was valuable enough.

One thing wasn't mentioned in the stray cat story. The daughter had work to do. Because she loved the stray kitten, she had to clean up all of the messes that were made -- if she wanted to keep the kitten. So she vacuumed fur shed on furniture, and changed the litter box. She fed the kitten and brushed it. She cleaned up fur balls and other messes. She tried to teach the kitten not to make the messes. She sacrificed a tremendous amount of her life for the kitten to allow it to enjoy life in the house and avoid the cold of winter. It was a cost she was willing to pay.

In the real story, Jesus wanted us in His Father's House so much that He was willing to sacrifice his entire life for us. It was the cost He was willing to pay. But no matter how much He sacrificed, there was one action that His Love left for you. You have to jump into His arms.

If you agree that this sacrifice happened, and you understand that your particular sins were also paid for in this act, then you are ready to become a believing Christian. You agree that you have done

> I am a good person, so I will go to Heaven.

wrong, need to apologize to God, and acknowledge God the Creator's ownership of your life.

The next step is simply to state the obvious in prayer.

> Father, I have sinned many times and I'm sorry for this. Please forgive me. Although I don't understand fully how it happened, I do understand that Jesus was your Son and He died as payment for my sins. I want to try to understand Your ways better and live life the way You want me to. Please guide me. Amen.

When you pray this prayer, it is the same as the kitten jumping into the arms of Jesus. You become a Christian through this belief and action.

Once you pray this prayer, tell someone else about it. Most Christians believe that you should now be baptized to announce this fact to the Christian community. The next step is to find a mature Christian to guide you in this and your next steps. Call a mature Christian friend, the pastor at a local church, or call us (1-888-728-2465) for advice. *Do it now!*

Can you get to Heaven by yourself because you are good? No. And now you know why believing Evangelical Christians don't believe this, either.

I am a good person, so I will go to Heaven.

Discussion Questions

1. Discuss the difference in meaning between Beings and Creatures.

2. Describe a sacrifice you once made for an animal or another person you loved.

3. What questions do you have about the sacrifice issue?

4. Discuss becoming a Christian and what it has meant or might mean to you.

I am a good person, so I will go to Heaven.

Actions

1. List your sins on a separate sheet of paper.
2. Keep going - you've forgotten some minor ones.
3. Now write down your really big sin.
4. Now pray this prayer or something similar:

>   Father, I've listed many of
>   my sins. I'm sorry for them.
>   Please forgive me for them.
>   I'll try to do better. Guide me,
>   Father, so that I may not sin.
>   Amen.

5. Go to the sink, light a match, and burn the paper. Water down the ashes and throw them away.
6. God now forgives you for those sins. Permanently.

I am a good person, so I will go to Heaven.

Suggested Scripture Readings

- Hebrews 9:16-28 This explains the need for a blood sacrifice.

- Hebrews 10:1-14 This is why Christ was needed.

Movies/DVD's to Watch

The Preacher's Wife (Copyright 1996; DVD 2003 Buena Vista Home Entertainment **ASIN:** B000065V3J)

Bruce Almighty (Copyright 2003; DVD 2004 Universal Studios Home **ASIN**: B0000AKCKI)

Myth #3 - I Believe in God, so I Am a Christian.

> There will be one flock and one shepherd. John 10:16

This is one of the most common Myths about Christianity. It isn't true, but it is widely believed. However, it is a major milestone on the way to becoming a Christian. In fact, you can't be a Christian without a belief in God. But it isn't enough. There are other things that you must understand and believe, too. And it's time we had a serious discussion of those things.

The following story illustrates how far some people will go to avoid a serious discussion of God and Christianity.

Figments

A friend of mine was having a discussion with a couple of sharp college students. One was an Evangelical Christian; the other was an argumentative atheist. The atheist was enjoying the discussion immensely, for every time my friend made a point the atheist would not concede the point but would counter with another point -- simply to debate. If my friend had said, "The sky is

I believe in God, so I am a Christian.

blue," the atheist would have said: "no, it is often white or gray."

Finally, the atheist said, "...but I can't even grant that you exist. You may be a figment of my imagination." My friend was at a loss. But at that point the Christian student stepped in and said, "Since I am a figment of your imagination, you won't mind if I take my imaginary fist and shove it into your nose at high speed, will you?"

The atheist stopped, thought, and laughed. He said, "I guess maybe you do exist." The discussion continued from there in a friendly way.

Approaching God and Christ

Let's talk a bit about the steps by which most people approach Christian belief.

Step One - Belief in Existence

It has been said that sanity begins when you believe in Existence. This seems natural to most people, but certain philosophers -- known as Solipsists -- believe in a different form of Existence - or perhaps they don't really believe in Existence. Solipsists believe that the Universe exists totally in your mind -- everything that you see and sense is actually part of your own mind. In essence, you have created your own Universe.

But this is not quite true. You see, the Solipsist doesn't believe he created the Universe. Only that the Universe exists in his own mind. The people,

I believe in God, so I am a Christian.

dogs, cats, and homes exist only in his mind. The world isn't really real -- only the illusion is real.

Solipsism is a neat philosophy, since it allows the Solipsist to be all-powerful. Solipsists do not need to acknowledge the presence of God in their lives. To the Solipsist, he is his own God. This philosophy is quite popular with young college-age philosophy students (who often wish that they *were* God!). However, the philosophy has some basic problems:

- Solipsism rejects the real presence of other people. After all, to a Solipsist, you and I do not *really* exist. We are simply figments of his imagination. This means that a Solipsist cannot ever have an equal relationship with another person, since all people are part of his imagination.
- Solipsists have a difficult time managing their Universes. For example, why would a Solipsist ever have an automobile wreck, a cold, or be unemployed? After all, can't he adjust his Universe to provide for a pleasant life? (The heyday of Solipsism was in the 1960's. Many Solipsists claimed that LSD would let them get closer to their reality. After several of them tried to fly out of second story windows, LSD and Solipsism both gained bad reputations.)
- A Solipsist must take the blame for all the problems of the world. If the world only exists in his own mind, then the Solipsist clearly is responsible for all the poverty, hatred, crime, and evils of the world. And when he notices this, he should be able to

I believe in God, so I am a Christian.

> affect the Universe. But he can't. At least, not in any major way.
> - The biggest problem with Solipsism is when the Solipsist tries to tell us that his reality is different from what us mere "figments" perceive. That is why many of the most ardent practicing Solipsists are know by their more common name: "psychotics".

In other words, Solipsism fails because it does not describe reality. It is a fantasy escape from reality.

The Ultimate Reality Check

The Evangelical Christian philosopher Francis Schaeffer made a profound conclusion in his book *"The God Who is There"*. Schaeffer pointed out that we all have opinions about what is correct in religious thought. In fact, many of us like to sit back and say, "I don't think that God would allow such and such to happen" and then we go on with our opinions. But isn't there a method that can shake out all the opinions and help us determine who is right?

When we look around at the Universe and attempt to answer spiritual questions, the one test that most people can agree upon is the Reality Check. ***Does this religion or philosophy describe the world in a way that agrees with Reality?*** Is this what we see and smell and taste and hear and touch?

This was one of Schaeffer's key points. *We can know about God through the clues He gives us in His Creation.* (And furthermore, if we accept the Bible as the Word of God, we can learn more

I believe in God, so I am a Christian.

detailed information about Him). Let's just check to see if our ideas check with Reality.

Solipsism fails because it doesn't describe reality. Solipsism doesn't account for certain observed facts about reality. Solipsism, like any religion or philosophy, must account for these and other observed facts:

1. There is pain and suffering in the world. Evil exists.
2. Beauty exists in the world. Good exists.
3. "*I*" am separate and distinct from "*you*".
4. The world appears to operate according to basic principles which we call laws of nature.
5. People are born and die.
6. People constantly refer to behaviors as "good" or "bad".

Solipsists have considerable trouble with the third fact, for they believe that you are part of them. This logically leads to all sorts of questions, the most important of which is "Why do Solipsists need friends?"

Each of these points causes trouble for Solipsists.

- They must take responsibility for all of the pain and suffering and evil. Yet, they must explain the presence of Beauty.
- We are expected to believe that the mind that designs the Universe creates all the laws of nature yet has problems with ordinary daily interactions with co-workers.

I believe in God, so I am a Christian.

- Furthermore, the Solipsist causes people to be born and people whom he loves to die.

Interesting set of contradictions, isn't it?

Solipsism is an interesting idea to toy with in college philosophy classrooms, but falls quickly on its face. Taken to its logical conclusions, Solipsism becomes insanity. The first step toward a sane philosophy and religion is recognizing that an objective reality exists.

Discussion Questions

1. Have you ever talked with or read writings by a Solipsist?

2. Are there any other key facts that that a true religion should explain?

3. Should a religion be tied to reality? Why?

4. Why do you think Beauty exists?

5. What does it mean to be a distinct person?

I believe in God, so I am a Christian.

6. Should a religion explain what the Purpose of Life is? What do you think the Purpose is?

Step Two - Belief in a Higher Power

Belief in a Higher Power does not mean that you are a Christian. Which specific Higher Power you believe in is very important. There are many people who believe in a Higher Power -- Hindus, Buddhists, and Jedi Knights (from *Star Wars*). Many Pagans believe in the higher power of an Earth goddess. Zoroastrians, adherents of a religion found mainly in Iran, believe in two equal higher powers -- a good power and an evil power. Many UFO cults believe in benevolent aliens as their higher powers. Many people today still believe in the power of Fate or Luck, similar to many ancient Greeks. And some people believe that natural laws operate by themselves to develop the Universe.

Once again, we go back to the basic Reality Test.

- God-like aliens don't really explain the existence of stars - or of rainbows. If they exist, aliens began in a Universe that already existed.
- The Zoroastrian Dualism approach has a simple weakness -- if one power is "good" and the other is "evil", then what do we use as the reference for determining good and evil? For example, we know that mercy is morally better than cruelty, but why? In the end, the Dualism is resolved only by

I believe in God, so I am a Christian.

> postulating a third Higher Power as a Referee or Standard who has determined the definitions of good and evil. Thus, we find that Dualism is not logically self-consistent. A single Higher Power is necessary.

Impersonal Forces

Many people put forth that the Higher Power in the Universe is actually one or more Impersonal Forces. What about those ideas?

The Force was admittedly a creation of a man, George Lucas, the creator of Star Wars. Lucas never intended anything deep for the Force. He simply wanted to entertain you for a couple of hours and separate you from a few dollars.

Fate and Luck are two sides of the same coin. One says, "things had to happen in this way", and the other says, "Things just happened to happen in this way." Neither answers the questions about Beauty and suffering. Neither answers the question about why you and I are separate. Fate and Luck (and their modern scientific cousins, Natural Law and Evolution) only explain how or why events occur -- they don't answer the questions about why the Universe exists, and why it exists with the operating rules which it has. Any honest scientist will agree with this. Although the laws of physics can tell you when a rainbow will appear and how people die, they don't answer the questions about why rainbows are beautiful, and why the Universe has Death in it.

I believe in God, so I am a Christian.

Natural laws don't explain the ultimate beginning of the Universe, nor of documented miracles. Even string theory and "brane" theory don't explain the creation -- they explain what happened after the creation.

This is also the problem with the "anthropic principle". This principle put forth by cosmologist Steven Hawking and other skeptics, states that the rules of physics are the way that they are because if they were significantly different, we would not be able to live. A simple reduction of this principle is that the laws are the way they are because they had to be the way they are. Fate and Luck. The answer is inadequate. The "why" is not answered. To this type of philosophy, the Purpose of Life is a meaningless quest.

If Fate or Luck ruled the world – or their more philosophical names, *Determinism* or *Randomness*, there would be no need or advantage to working hard. This may be why inveterate gamblers -- who believe in Fate and Luck -- often are unemployed. They have seen the lack of control and purpose that is the logical result of their philosophy.

The belief in an impersonal force that runs the Universe ultimately leads to meaningless. If the power behind the Universe is impersonal, then we are all simply created and swept to-and-fro by the laws of chance, quantum mechanics, and physics. We only exist as *creatures-that-somehow-think* in a totally purposeless Universe. We are like images on a screen saver, moving around the Universe at random. There is no purpose.

I believe in God, so I am a Christian.

But why do *we* think yet maintain that *everyone else's* apparent thinking is merely the action of the laws of chance, quantum mechanics, and physics? This is not logical, is it?

There are only three options:

a. Perhaps we don't actually think. We are caught up in the grand machine that is the Universe. We are therefore hopelessly without meaning. But yet we are self-aware and *believe* that we have a purpose. After all, everything else in the Universe appears to have a purpose when we think about it, if only to make us feel happy or uncomfortable. So how is it that we *think* we think? How is it that we are the only things in Universe without purpose?
b. Perhaps I am the only thinking creature in the Universe (the Solipsist approach). We've already dealt with the conclusions of Solipsism, haven't we?
c. Without any other options, we are led to the conclusion that the force must be a God with personality – a Personal God.

Step Three: Belief in a Personal God

There are impersonal Forces and there is a Personal God. (A Personal God is the term we use to mean that God is a Person with a personality.) Scientologists and many Buddhists believe in a Force. But Hindus, Moslems, Jews, many Buddhists, pagans, and Christians believe in a

I believe in God, so I am a Christian.

Personal God. What are the justifications in Reality for the belief in a Personal God?

One key justification for a Personal God is the presence of Beauty. A Force has no need of Beauty -- only personalities can appreciate Beauty. Thus, a Personal God exists.

Another justification is the presence of Self-Awareness in people. There doesn't appear to be any logical manner in which personalities develop. We can't give you a formula for the development of self-awareness. In self-awareness, you have something that we realize a computer program, no matter how complex, does not have. You know that you exist. You have your own desires. A Force doesn't.

The 2nd Law of Thermodynamics shows that in a closed system, disorder must increase. This is mathematically equivalent to the information theory concept that information degrades with time. Clearly, self-awareness contains more information than non-awareness – it is more complex and more ordered. Only personality has the ability to consistently increase the information content of something. (Non-living self-ordering units are limited to specific routines. Personality allows new routines to be developed.) It seems logical to conclude that that which creates the Universe must ultimately be greater than the Universe. We know that an impersonal Force contradicts the evidence of our own existence and self-awareness. Thus, our self-awareness is evidence for the existence of a Personal God.

I believe in God, so I am a Christian.

To these arguments are added the arguments directly in support of the Christian God that we will develop in a later chapter.

Belief in God

Belief in a Personal God does not mean that you are a Christian. If so, then all Hindus, Moslems, Jews, and pagans would be Christians. Belief in God means that you are a *Theist*. Theists simply believe in the existence of a higher Being.

The word "Theist", like many words, has two meanings. It can be applied to all people who believe in a personal God, which would include such people as the Pope, Billy Graham, the Ayatollahs, various Rabbi's, Noam Chomsky, and various Hindu leaders. It also would include the vast majority of Americans.

In the second meaning, which we are going to use, the word Theist actually means "a person who vaguely believes in the existence of a personal God, but does not explicitly believe in the attributes of the Traditional Triune God of Christianity."

Some people prefer the term "Vague Theist" to describe these people, but we'll stick to "Theist" simply because the longer term is cumbersome to use.

Now, an awful lot of people who claim to be Christian are actually (Vague) Theists. This is because a (Vague) Theist can believe anything he or she wants to believe about the nature of God -- and

I believe in God, so I am a Christian.

still "believe in God". In effect, the Theist decides what attributes he or she wants in God and runs with it.

This is very nice but Schaeffer pointed out one obvious flaw -- Since God created the Universe, **He probably should be consulted about what His Attributes are** -- even if those attributes are somewhat unpleasant from time to time. If you are a Theist, you are not divorced from the Reality Check. You can't simply stop by stating that "God exists", and then creating Him with *your* list of attributes.

Doesn't it make sense that if God exists, then He has certain definite attributes that exist regardless of what you or I prefer. Aren't we fools when we say, "I can't believe in a God that would..."?

Either He is God, or He is not. You cannot decide what God is like. He is the way He is. In the Old Testament Book of Exodus, He says that His Name is "I AM THAT I AM". He proclaims self-existence -- his "style" and attributes do not depend upon our opinions.

Let's understand one basic point:

> A Personal God exists and has a very definite personality.

Whenever you walk into the house or office of someone, it is obvious that the person has put his or her personality on the place. If the person is warm and friendly, the home probably is, too. If the person is a golfer, you'll expect to see some golf-

I believe in God, so I am a Christian.

related items in his office. In fact, good salesmen love to take time to understand their customers by looking at the office walls for a few minutes at the beginning of a sales call.

God has been decorating this Universe for millennia. Don't you think that His personality can be found in the decorations and design of the place?

When you hear someone talking about God like He is a warm, fuzzy teddy bear, you are probably dealing with a Theist -- not a Christian. The Christian writer C.S. Lewis, in his *Narnia* series of books, compares God to a lion -- warm, furry, and attractive, yet there is a terrible awesome nature which surfaces from time to time. In one of the books, a girl approaches Aslan, the God-lion and says, "You won't eat me, will you?" Aslan replies, "I make no promises." God does not answer to us - we answer to Him. He has the warm and fuzzy, and He also has the frightening aspects that control the storms.

Vague Theists are the most popular denizens of the "create your own religion" camp. They pride themselves in being "spiritual" and "communing with God" and "approaching God our own way", but never want to do the study of the books where God talked to men about Himself -- that collection of books we call the Bible.

It is so easy to dismiss the Bible as irrelevant when what you really want to do is create your own religion. Wouldn't you rather see what may actually be True? Have you actually read the entire Bible?

I believe in God, so I am a Christian.

Or do you just like to talk about what you heard is in the Book?

Discussion Questions

1. How much of the Bible have you personally read?

2. If you haven't read the entire Bible, why not?

Truth, Tolerance, and the Theist

Vague Theists are also the people who love to talk about being tolerant of the beliefs of others. According to Theists, you must accept all the beliefs of your friends, no matter how weird. In particular, you must accept the beliefs of the Theist himself.

This is because the Theist's greatest good is not Truth, but Tolerance -- something he accepts as the most important value in his life.

At the root of all philosophies and religions are certain assumptions about Existence, how we come to know Truth, and what constitutes Reality. The great debate of the late twentieth century and early 21st century is the philosophical debate between Truth and Tolerance.

The society of the three hundred years preceding 1970 was commonly referred to as "Modern". Modern society and the Modern worldview was

I believe in God, so I am a Christian.

defined by an absolute search for Truth, driven by a belief that man could ultimately understand and control the Universe if he simply researched and studied long enough. Modern society was profoundly optimistic, since eventually man could solve any problem. Newton and Jefferson represent the roots of modern philosophical belief. Today, most Westerners still hold this philosophical worldview.

As the number of PhD candidates expanded dramatically in the 1960's and 1970's, a problem arose in many disciplines. In the past, a key test for a PhD thesis was that the thesis be tested and correct. With so many more papers being written, it was necessary to relax the requirements. So in many fields, particularly in history and the other social disciplines, the concept arose that a thesis would be adequate if it "brought forth new insights". This effectively meant that it was not necessary that a thesis be correct -- only that it have a different point-of-view. Getting the "correct" knowledge was seen to be too difficult or impossible. Now, it was only necessary to re-interpret existing knowledge to get published. Gradually this concept of knowledge began to filter into the overall society.

Today's society is "post-modern". Post-modern society believes that certain problems cannot be solved by any combination of technology and knowledge. Justified somewhat by the quantum mechanical uncertainty principle, post-moderns believe that certain knowledge cannot be found. The most direct implications of this philosophy apply to religious and moral beliefs, as well as the political expressions of those beliefs.

I believe in God, so I am a Christian.

"Clearly", says the post-modern, "religious and moral beliefs differ. Therefore it follows that we must not be able to come to any definite statements in this field. 'Judge not...' after all! We will therefore limit our advances to attacking any definite statements, since they will obviously be wrong."

Opinions and Words

The post-modern Vague Theist really doesn't believe that a personal God exists. Instead, he believes that thoughts about God are an intellectual exercise, an arguing of opinions, a testing of our minds. He soundly believes that religious and philosophical questions cannot be answered – only debated. To the Vague Theist, God does not *actually* exist – it is all a matter of opinion and words.

Avoiding Conflict

A post-modern society is defined by certain attributes, but the key defining statement is "Whatever". If I make a statement you disagree with, you say "whatever". If I make a statement that makes you uncomfortable, you say "whatever". If I do something strange and weird, you say "whatever".

"Whatever" is our shorthand for a much longer statement: "Whatever you say is ok to say. I may not agree with it or follow your suggestion, but I will let you say it without explicitly disagreeing with it. I will tolerate the statement and not challenge it, because to directly challenge it would

I believe in God, so I am a Christian. create a conflict that might make me uncomfortable."

"Whatever" is the statement of Tolerance. Above all, a post-modern must avoid making definite statements that may lead to conflict. And this leads to the Tolerance idea.

Tolerance

In our post-modern society, Tolerance is more important than Truth. This is because accepting that there is a single Truth about anything starts a line of thought that leads to moral restrictions upon our behaviors. Let me explain this.

If I accept anything as True, I must accept certain behaviors as more correct than other behaviors. For example, if I say that the proper color for bricks is red, then this leads to the concept that there are proper colors for homes. This might lead me into conflict with a neighbor who has a chartreuse-and-violet-striped home. This also means that a second neighbor might tell him that his chartreuse-and-violet-striped home is a disgrace to our neighborhood. Any statement of Truth ultimately and logically leads to a standard for behavior.

If I state that rivers flood, a logical conclusion of that is that it is stupid to build your home beside a river. In a post-modern world, this statement is seen as harsh because some people have chosen to live beside rivers. This simple statement leads to a standard for behavior -- It is wrong to build beside a river.

I believe in God, so I am a Christian.

Accepting *anything* as Truth ultimately means that I should not do certain things because they are *not true*. Those actions are *wrong*. I must accept a moral law and moral values.

If I do this, then I will begin to think some very uncomfortable thoughts. Thoughts about where moral laws and moral values come from -- what makes certain things right and other things wrong?

It is clear that there must be an ultimate Standard that is used to determine what is right and what is wrong. Some will say that it is Survival. Others will say that it is Pleasure.

Unfortunately, this only detours our thoughts. For there must be someone or something which determined the physical and sociological laws that lead certain behaviors to be pro-survival or pro-pleasure and others to be anti-survival or anti-pleasure. If there are rules to the game, then Someone must have developed the rules.

If I follow this line of thinking, I will eventually conclude that there must be a Law-Giver and Value-Giver and Judge. God must exist and I must give to Him the authority to judge my behavior -- and I know that there are many, many wrong things that I have done. What will be His Judgment upon me?

Furthermore, He will have certain attributes and preferences – some of which may make me very uncomfortable. I no longer can define Him – I am led to the idea that He should define me, and which of my behaviors are proper. And that is very frightening to most people.

I believe in God, so I am a Christian.

For many people, Tolerance is the value that keeps us from walking down that very scary path.

A Judgmental God?

In our emerging post-modern society, Vague Theists prefer that their gods be Tolerant rather than "Judgmental". ("Judgmental" means that the god decides what is Good and what isn't Good.) A Tolerant god doesn't put demands on our behavior. A Judgmental God suggests that some behaviors are better than other behaviors. And – at first glance – this feels very restrictive.

Theists are good at using this dodge. A Theist will say, "*I can't believe* that God really doesn't want me to be happy" when his "happiness" means that the Theist has the freedom to sleep with a different woman (or man) other than the Theist's spouse. (God *does* want him to be happy. God understands that traditional monogamous marriage leads to the most happiness for all.)

This is similar to the teenager who prefers a parent that tolerates all her bad behavior rather than one that points out where she's done stupid things -- "Don't you know that driving 80 miles per hour on that road will get you killed?" -- "Don't wear those clothes unless you want to end up pregnant at age 17!" In the end, the tolerant parent harms the teenager, and the intolerant loving parent teaches the teenager how to live a long, happy life.

The loved teenager faces a tongue-lashing, grounding, or some similar punishment from a loving parent. We face a much more definite

I believe in God, so I am a Christian.

punishment from our Loving God. The parent can *point out* that you will be killed "or paralyzed like the Smith kid" when you drive too fast: God will *actually* paralyze you. Your Mother will *tell* you that only sluts wear those clothes: God will make sure that you get pregnant the one time you take a chance. Your grandmother *told* you to never gamble for you'd lose your wife: God will take your home and car and family. Dad told you that your attitude was rotten: God takes away your job when you cuss out the boss. Grandfather told you not to borrow money: God sends you collectors who call you every hour of the day and night.

The real God *is* very judgmental -- He does not take kindly when we break His rules. He loves us too much to let us do stupid things repeatedly.

The Changing Meanings of Tolerance

Let's go back to that word "Tolerance". Tolerance is a word that has changed meaning over the years. In 1950, if I was tolerant, that meant that I would let my Jewish/Hindu/Moslem/Buddhist neighbors live in peace and worship as they chose. If I talked with them, I might politely point out what I thought were problems with their systems, but since I was tolerant, I would stay on friendly terms with them. People had a friendly give-and-take.

Today (2006) Tolerance has a different meaning. If I am to be tolerant, I must not only allow my neighbors to live in peace -- I must accept the "goodness" of the Al-Qaida terrorists who killed many innocent men and women in the Twin Towers, the Pentagon, and the airplanes. I must

I believe in God, so I am a Christian.

accept that "one man's terrorist is another man's freedom fighter". I must proclaim the equal moral validity of their religion with my religion. My religion that says, "turn the other cheek" and "do unto others as you would have them do unto you" must be equated with a religion that instructs believers to destroy Jews and Christians.

In 2006 Tolerance means that I must not only "tolerate (1950)" your beliefs, but I must now accept them as equal to my own in Truth and Goodness. I must ignore the Reality Check and *any* moral standard to accept all conduct and beliefs as equally good or bad if the topic under discussion is remotely connected to moral behavior or religion.

Coming Back to our Senses

In any rational logic, Truth must be more important than Tolerance. Let us assume that you have a belief that killing others is the best and most sure way to go to heaven. Surely this is in stark contrast to a belief that says you should be kind to others.

In our world, thankfully, most people still understand that serial murderers are morally inferior. We all understand – no matter where we live – that murder is somehow "less good" than kindness.

We live in the same Universe with those serial murderers. A single God created the Universe. If this is so, then He could not make both kindness and cruelty equally good. One is superior to the other. This is a statement of an absolute Truth every

I believe in God, so I am a Christian.

bit as much as when a physicist states that objects fall toward the center of the earth due to gravity.

Another example of the contradiction inherent in the Tolerance cult: If you maintain that "there are many paths to God and all are True and should be Tolerated", then logic has this response: "Christianity claims that there is only one Path. So does Islam. So does Orthodox Judaism. Thus, how can all be True? In addition, how can your "many paths" concept and our "one Path" concept both be True?" Are you *really* saying that all paths are true except the Christian path?

No, Christians and God follow the 1950 definition of tolerance. We tolerate people - not untrue beliefs. Theists want all of us to be Tolerant (2006) -- for this is the only way that they can keep their beliefs from being ridiculed. Yet God will continue to be Intolerant of untrue beliefs and sin, despite anything Vague Theists do or say.

Discussion Questions

1. Have you encountered this difference in meanings?

2. Why do you think this difference in meanings developed?

3. What do you think? Is Truth or Tolerance more basic?

I believe in God, so I am a Christian.

The Vague Theist's Dilemma

A Vague Theist thinks that he avoids the problem of God's Intolerance by defining God as he chooses. But the Theist only fools himself - God is still there and is still judging everyone -- even the Theist.

Each Theist ultimately must come to a certain dilemma. He must both develop his theology logically to its conclusion and face the fact that he is creating his god rather than describing God as He is - or the Theist must choose to not think.

Follow me on this. If God created the Universe, then He will choose either to be found or He will choose not to be found. He has the power to accomplish either of those possibilities. If He does not want to be found, our task is hopeless. God can simply hang out around the bald spot on the back of your head until you die, and you will never see Him.

On the other hand, if God wants to be found, He can let us know about Himself. Christians believe that He did this in several ways. First of all, He left a Creation that has the footprints of the Creator. It has flowers and rainbows, as well as many other beautiful natural things that have no purpose other than to glorify God. In this way, all people can understand some things about God.

A very few people He appeared to directly. According to the Bible this was extremely frightening to the people involved. He also sent

I believe in God, so I am a Christian.

messengers - Angels and Prophets - to tell people about Him. God even sent His Son, Jesus, to explain things in detail to us. (You may not believe this yet. That's ok. Go back a couple pages and explain to yourself again why Beauty exists.)

Many Vague Theists are very arrogant. They do not want to accept the evidence recorded in the Bible - simply because so many people believe it. Theists say, "God must be more subtle." And this particular type of Theist believes that only smart people like him will be able to get the picture about God. Thus, the obvious messages from God are rejected, because of the arrogance of the Theist. The arrogant Theist prefers to believe that God intentionally tries to make Himself difficult -- yet not impossible -- to be found. Only someone as smart as the Theist can find Him. But once again, the Theist is actually creating his own god.

Christians believe that anyone truly seeking God can find Him. In fact, Christians believe that we all start out knowing God but most then become arrogant and blinded by that arrogance. We turn our backs on God and have to rediscover Him.

The arrogance of the Theist is the same as the arrogance of the Solipsist. The Solipsist claims to have created his Universe: The Theist creates the Creator. Both types of men at their cores are simply refusing to accept that a Creator exists and that all men are simply creat(e)-ures. (It's more fun to be God than creature, isn't it?)

C. S. Lewis wrote an essay entitled *God in the Dock* (Copyright 1970 Wm. B. Eerdmans Publishing

I believe in God, so I am a Christian.

ISBN: 0802808689) where he points out that most people want to put God on trial and see if He is good enough. But this completely ignores the fact of God's existence. If God exists, then he has certain definite attributes that do not depend upon our opinion of Him. Ultimately, we will understand God, Christianity, and the entire Universe better when we finally accept this point. It is the key issue -- accepting the Creator on His terms -- not yours. God is God -- and we're not!

Belief in God?

The non-Christian Vague Theist, because he is defining his own god, is not a Christian. In the same way, Jews and Moslem Theists are not Christians, but we are getting closer to the Truth. Jews have a substantial portion of God's Truth -- Christianity completes that Truth. Moslems have a distorted picture of God's Truth, but at least have decided to let another define God for them.

Thus, we come full circle. You must let God define Himself. This is Christian belief. Despite the fact that many, many people are willing to give you their opinion of what God is like, the fact remains that God is a real Person, who has a personality and abilities which are His, no matter what people say.

The next effort is to discover God and His attributes and personality. The best way to do this is by reading the books that Christians claim are the inspired Word of God. In particular, the best place to start is in the *Gospel of Mark*, which is the life of

I believe in God, so I am a Christian.

the Man who claimed to be the Son of God and who spoke for God: Jesus Christ.

It really matters which god you believe in. Simply believing in a god is not enough to be considered a Christian. In the next chapter we will consider what the particular belief in Christ means to Christianity.

Discussion Questions

1. What attributes do you wish for God?

2. How do these attributes differ from Reality?

3. Have you fallen into the create-your-own-God trap?

Actions

1. Ask a non-Christian friend to describe God to you.

2. Ask a Christian friend to describe God to you.

I believe in God, so I am a Christian.

3. Make a list of Reality Check items.

4. Read the Gospel of Mark. You will find it about 2/3rds of the way into a Christian Bible.

Suggested Scripture Readings

- Romans 1:20-21 explains how we can see the presence of God in this world.

- Daniel 4:1-3 Nebuchadnezzar points out the presence of God.

- Psalm 147 tells us of the attributes of God.

- 2 John verses 9-11 points out the centrality of Christ to understanding God.

I believe in God, so I am a Christian.

Sidebar - A Brief Word about Polytheism

Polytheism is the belief in multiple gods. Pagans, Wicca, Hindu, many American Indian religions, and many other groups believe in multiple gods, usually arranged in a hierarchy.

In these religions there is almost always a stronger god who rules. For example, in ancient Greek mythology, there was Zeus who was stronger than all the other gods combined. Yet, Zeus allowed Poseidon and Hades to rule their domains without interference. In other polytheistic religions, a particular mountain may be sacred to a particular god or goddess.

Despite these issues, it is always fairly clear in any polytheistic religion that there is only one boss god -- often the creator god. So despite protestations to the contrary, polytheistic religions still point to a single god as the ultimate authority. For example, the Greeks understood that Zeus could have fought all of the other Olympian gods and won, while the Norse religion understood the power of Odin/Wodan. In the end, the arguments against these multiple god religions are essentially the same as the arguments against Theism.

Jesus was a great Teacher.

Myth #4 - I Think Jesus Was a Great Teacher, so I Am a Christian.

> I and my Father are one. John 10:30

A key part of what it means to be an Evangelical Christian revolves around the nature, character, and historical reality of the man we know as Jesus Christ of Nazareth. More than anything else, this detailed understanding of Jesus is what distinguishes the culture and behavior of Evangelical Christians from most other people. Understanding Jesus, as we know him, is critical to understanding Evangelical Christians.

In the 1959 movie classic *Some Like it Hot (DVD 2005* MGM/UA Video **ASIN:** B00003CXCR), Jack Lemmon and Tony Curtis play a couple of musicians who witness a gangland slaying and are forced to disguise themselves as women to escape. Because of events, the disguise must be maintained for many days. A man even begins to date Lemmon's character, which becomes more and more female as he is forced to remain in disguise. Eventually, the disguises come off -- yet the man continues to think of Lemmon as a woman. Lemmon's character had become to himself and the man a hybrid man-and-woman.

Jesus was a great Teacher.

Evangelical Christians believe that the God Jesus Christ adopted the disguise of being a man while He was on earth. However, we also believe a bit more happened. He actually *was* human as well as God -- and still is. Unfortunately, two thousand years after the episode, many men still have the story confused.

The greatest argument for Christianity is the fact that Christianity is True. You can conduct the research and evaluate the evidence. The claims of Christianity are special and unique. Their validity completely depends upon their Truth. And – contrary to what you may have been told –there is no need to make a "leap of faith" to determine the Truth of Christianity. Investigating the historical, archeological, literary, sociological, psychological, and personal evidence available can determine the Truth. In this chapter, we will cover some common fallacies about the nature of Christ and then cover some of the evidence for the claims of Christians.

In the last chapter we saw where belief in a generalized God is not the same as being a Christian. A belief in one particular God is necessary. In addition, in this chapter, we will explain that Evangelical Christians do not believe in anything less than the full deityhood of Christ. A Christian is not a follower of the human man, Jesus. Instead, a Christian believes that Christ was the Spirit Being God who lived as a human man during His time on Earth - and is still in this fully hybrid God-man state today.

Jesus was a great Teacher.

Common Fallacies

In the early years of the Christian church, there were several commonly held beliefs about Christ:

1. Christ was a spirit being who existed on earth for some thirty years. This was called Eutychianism.
2. Christ was a man who had been captured by the Spirit of God for a few years. This was known as Monarchism.
3. Christ was created by God and was part Deity and part man. This was called Arianism.
4. Christ was a mysterious person about whom special knowledge could be gained through special studies. This was called Gnosticism.
5. Christ was a great fully human teacher with no divine nature. This belief was held by skeptics and is still common today.
6. Christ was both completely God and completely man, and co-existed with God before the birth of Jesus. This was the standard view of Christianity. Today, this view is still held by Orthodox, Catholic, and Protestant Christians around the world.

These beliefs were not held by equal numbers of believers. On the contrary, the final standard view was held by over 80 percent of Christians at all times, and was by far the dominant belief among the earliest Christians -- those who were alive during the time of Christ Himself.

However, as Christianity grew, philosophers from other religions moved into the new religion and

Jesus was a great Teacher.

brought certain pre-conceptions. Since most Christians, then as now, believe largely what they have been taught, these various beliefs acquired groups of adherents centered on a charismatic teacher.

Each of these beliefs was debated in theological circles for many years. Finally, the Emperors of Rome and Constantinople called great councils to decide the questions. And the standard view won out. The others were declared to be "heresies" or "false teachings".

These councils were not political discussions. They were groups of very learned men who were debating and searching for the Truth, since they all recognized that many souls were relying upon their conclusions. And so they came to the standard view of Christ -- the view that is still held today by groups as different in other ways as the Roman Catholic Church, the Greek Orthodox Church, Lutherans, Southern Baptists, Presbyterians, Methodists, Assemblies of God, and all the other "mainline" denominations.

A key part of this is expressed in the first chapter of the *Gospel of John*.

Scripture Reading/Action

- Read John Chapter 1 now and discuss it with a Christian "pro".

Jesus was a great Teacher.

Eutychianism – the Spirit-Being Christ

This heresy came from a somewhat skeptical reading of the scriptures by men coming from a Greek pagan and Platonic philosophical background where many gods were expected to exist. The argument went this way:

"Christ clearly did miracles, died, and miraculously arose from the dead. Only a god could do these things. Gods are perfect beings -- men are not. Since it is clearly impossible for the perfect nature of a god to mix with the imperfect nature of man, Christ must have been a god and the men around him just thought He was human."

This was refuted by the obvious fact that Christ had everyone fooled during His Life on earth. No one stood up and said "Jesus, You are God and not a man". Peter said that Jesus was "the Son of the living God". Only after His Resurrection did most men get idea that Jesus was divine. Christ also died -- something that a pure God does not do.

Thus, Christ must have had some human nature to Him, as is pointed out in Romans Chapter 5, Verse 15 and Hebrews Chapter 10 Verse 12.

In addition, Christ often referred to Himself as the "Son of Man", a reference from Daniel 7, which continually points to His human Messianic nature.

Jesus was a great Teacher.

Monarchism – Possessed by the Spirit

Monarchists believed that Christ was a normal man until the moment of His baptism, when the Spirit of God came upon Him and worked through Him for the next few years. This is a more persistent heresy, with adherents present today. However, it is refuted by the supernatural events surrounding His birth, the terribly intelligent and wise 12-year-old child who taught at the Temple (See Luke 2:41-52), and His own statements. For example, He says, "I came from the Father...." He never said, "I was chosen by God..." as was the style more commonly used by prophets who were spoken to by God. He was clearly abnormal throughout His life.

Arianism – Created by God

This was the strongest heresy of the early days of the Church. The Arian heresy is still a common belief among newer Christians today. (Note that Arian has nothing to do with Hitler's Aryans).

The Arians believed that Christ was created at the time of His conception and was part God and part man. But Christ Himself refuted this by clearly using verb tenses that state that He was present from the Beginning. Christians believe that Christ was always present -- indeed many of the appearances of Angels on the earth in the Old Testament are appearances of Christ on earth before his birth - "the pre-incarnate Christ". Perhaps the most concise refutation of Arianism is John 1:1. Christians also believe that Christ is still alive in Heaven -- not in spirit form, but alive in the flesh.

Jesus was a great Teacher.

Gnosticism – the Hidden Knowledge

Gnosticism returns time and time again throughout history. Gnostics believe that the key to understanding Christ and God comes about through special knowledge that is revealed in mysterious, secret books. Gnosticism underlies belief in magical spells, in the desire for and fears of a secret society conspiracy, and in the popularity of such utterly (to serious scholars) ridiculous books as *The Da Vinci Code* by Dan Brown.

The root of Gnostic beliefs is the fact that there are always people who think that God and/or events must be mysterious and controlled by an evil, secret power. For thousands of years, men have taken advantage of that concept to bring the gullible into secret societies, to sell secret books, and later to sell books and movie tickets. Gnosticism is warned of in the Bible by Paul in Colossians 2:8-9.

Christianity is open. The standard core beliefs of Christians have not changed significantly since Paul talked with Peter, James, and John in Jerusalem sometime around 40 A.D. Read the Bible in a modern translation, or learn Koine Greek and read it in the original. You will not find secrets held, but rather you will find the Truth proclaimed loudly and boldly. God has no purpose in hiding secrets from men. Only fearful men have secrets. An omnipotent God has no need to be secretive.

Jesus was a great Teacher.

Skeptical Beliefs

The human-only nature of Christ is still held by most non-Christians. In fact, in many ways it defines Christians from non-Christians. For example, in Japanese schools, the standard view of history talks about the "Great Teachers" - Confucius, Buddha, Socrates, and Jesus. But this is where Christians disagree most strongly with others. *Christians believe that Christ was both fully God and Man.*

Discussion Questions

1. Do you hold or have you held one of these beliefs? Why?

2. Do you have a friend who holds Gnostic beliefs? What are those beliefs?

3. Discuss the differences between each belief.

Standard Christian Belief

Christ was different from every other man who has walked upon the face of the earth. Let's look at some basic claims as documented by four separate books of the Bible with four separate authors - Matthew the tax-collecting apostle, Mark the young friend of Peter and Paul, Luke the Greek physician

Jesus was a great Teacher.

friend of Paul, and John, who considered himself the best friend of Jesus. Perhaps you don't accept the validity of the Biblical account – that's ok for now. We'll talk further about why the Bible can be believed.

- He was born of a virgin. Until artificial insemination was developed in the 1980's, this was not possible without a miracle. Joseph understood this completely, and initially planned to divorce Mary "quietly". This is detailed in Luke 1:26-34.
- He declared Himself in front of the authorities and friends: "I Am". In Hebrew, this is the name used for God. Go to Exodus 3, and you will find that when Moses asks God what His Name is, God replies "I Am That I Am". (In Hebrew, this is YHWH. In our English Bibles, our custom is to use "The LORD" (All Caps) whenever the proper Name of YHWH occurred in the Hebrew Bible.) When Jesus said "I Am", the Jewish authorities immediately declared a death sentence for blasphemy – Christ was claiming to be God. For details, see Mark 14:61-64.
- Jesus attracted thousands of followers during His Life, largely due to miracles that He performed in public. Matthew 21:6-11 is a good example of this.
- His claims of deityhood led Him to His death. Matthew 26:63-66 tells of this episode.

Jesus was a great Teacher.

As Oxford professor C.S. Lewis pointed out, we have a man with an incredible claim: Jesus claimed to be God!

And, as Professor Lewis also pointed out, there are only three possible interpretations:

1. Jesus was who He said He was.
2. Jesus was a lunatic.
3. Jesus was the devil.

Whatever else you may say, you cannot say that Jesus was simply a great teacher. For if He was only a man, then He was crazy and we shouldn't listen to a word He said. But if He was not crazy, then we must accept His words at face value. He was God!

To support His claims, we have several points of evidence:

- Of His 12 Apostles, all but one died violent deaths, maintaining to the end His Deityhood. (John died a peaceful death of old age). Peter was crucified upside down because he maintained that he was not worthy to be crucified in the same way as his Lord. Paul spent the last years of his life explaining about Jesus to men and women in Nero's household until he was executed. The other Apostles were either executed or murdered for their faith.

    It is easy to talk about a lie, but how many people will maintain a cover-up when threatened with death? Would you? Yet these Eleven continued to insist that Jesus

Jesus was a great Teacher.

was God until their death when a simple recanting of this statement would have released most of them. Clearly, the Apostles believed Jesus was God.

- No one in the early days of the church claimed lunatic status for Christ. Instead, the authorities treated Christ as a dangerous revolutionary -- not as a lunatic.

  Some have claimed that the claims of deityhood were not actually present. They claim that these are our misunderstandings of Christ's statements. However, the reaction of the priests, scribes, and antagonistic crowds was very clear -- every time Jesus said "I AM", they took His claim as a serious case of claiming to be God -- and attempted to kill Him! So we see that the Jewish priesthood of the time did not think that Jesus was a crazy nut. On the contrary, they believed that he was a dangerous revolutionary and blasphemer who claimed to be God.

- The common people did not believe that Jesus was a lunatic. Throughout the Gospels, we find that adoring crowds surrounded Jesus. People do not follow someone they consider crazy. As an additional point of evidence, the Jewish/Roman historian Josephus talks about the many people, both Jewish and Greek, who became followers of Jesus.
- We can dispose of the Jesus is evil hypothesis quickly. Do you really believe

- that His teachings were evil? And if so, then do you believe that Jesus was actually a supernatural but evil being? No, it doesn't make any sense. To maintain our intellectual integrity, we must exclude this possibility.
- Let's take another tack for those few of you who believe that Jesus was a supernaturally evil creature. If Jesus was evil, your system must be developed to include how His teachings are evil – and thus what truly good teachings would be.

His Miracles

- When we look at the Miracles of Jesus, we find that they are described in a different way from almost all descriptions of miracles in other literature. They are neither exaggerated in their character, nor reported in a skeptical fashion. Instead, they are reported as simple facts.
- Jesus does not call special attention to His Miracles, as a parlor magician might. In fact, He went so far as to ask people not to say anything about them.
- His Miracles are not the miracles that you might expect a miracle worker to perform. His Miracles don't involve fireworks and spectacular destruction, disappearances, speaking with the dead, or sleight-of-hand, as do the tricks of sorcerers, psychics, and modern magicians. Instead, they usually involve life and life processes or control over physical laws. He turns water into wine in a few minutes. He cures the sick. He heals the lame. He cures blindness. He feeds

Jesus was a great Teacher.

thousands with a little bit of bread and fish. He calms a storm and walks on water. And, most spectacularly, He raises His friend Lazarus from death - something only God can do. Then, to show it isn't an accident, he raises the daughter of the centurion who believes. The Gospels make it clear that He healed dozens, if not hundreds, of people.

When He performed His Miracles, no spells were cast and no special props were used. The furthest He goes with props is when healing a blind man He spits into the mud and rubs the mud on the blind man's eyes. (This indicates that a man can see because of the Truth that comes out of the mouth of God.) But no special tools were used -- no "magic wands", no advanced technology. In fact, we don't even have special gestures used. We simply see Jesus commanding that the Miracle occur -- and it occurred!

- Some of His Miracles are also meant to show control of the spirit world. Several demonic possession cases are brought before Him for healing. In those days, this was apparently a serious problem. Today demonic possession is not generally recognized today as a problem -- outside of Haiti and Jamaica. But in those countries, both Christian missionaries and voodoo practitioners agree that spirit possession occurs. (By the way, medical epilepsy is also known in these countries as a totally different condition.)

Jesus was a great Teacher.

- Just when His reputation for healing was beginning to spread and crowds were appearing, He did something that no self-respecting power seeker or money-seeker would ever do -- He withdrew from the cities to get away from the crowds. And the crowds followed Him outside of town.
- But were the ancients a group of easily duped rustics? No. These men and women were fully aware of the rarity of miracles. They were fully capable of determining death in a person, of telling the difference between wine and water, and knowing what could be healed and what could not. Peter was an experienced fisherman who knew his Sea of Galilee -- he understood when a storm was dangerous and when it would be considered a miraculous calming. But Christ also left the best for last...
- The final pieces of evidence for the Deityhood of Jesus were the events surrounding His death and resurrection.

Discussion Questions

1. Jesus claimed to be God. Why do you think He claimed this?

2. Of the three possibilities that Lewis pointed out, which do you think is true?

3. Support your assertion.

Jesus was a great Teacher.

4. How do you individually account for each of His Miracles?

4. Find all the Miracles in the Gospel of Mark. Assume the writer wrote what eyewitnesses saw.

5. For each Miracle, describe how that particular Miracle might have been accomplished.

6. Determine if any non-Divine man could have accomplished the list of Miracles.

His Death

There are roughly a half-dozen possibilities regarding the death of Jesus. This execution was recorded in all four Gospels. In addition, it is mentioned in most of the other books of the New Testament. It is mentioned in the Jewish historian Josephus' work *Antiquities 18.63-64*, by the Roman Tacitus in his *Annals 15.44*, and by several other non-Christian ancient writers. It is also mentioned or alluded to by over 20,000 manuscript

Jesus was a great Teacher.

commentaries or sermons which we have which date from ancient times. (In comparison, we have less than ten ancient copies of Caesar's *The Gallic Wars*, which is recognized as a definitive source for Roman history.) Many early works even mention Joseph of Arimathea, who buried Christ in his own tomb. More than anything else in history, it is certain that the Romans crucified Jesus Christ during Passover sometime around 30 A.D.

Over the years, several theories have arisen regarding his death:

1. He did not die, but fainted and revived later in the Tomb.
2. He died, but the Apostles stole His body.
3. He died, but the Romans or Jews stole His body.
4. The women got the wrong tomb.
5. The Apostles hallucinated about seeing the resurrected Jesus.
6. Jesus really died and was resurrected as described in the Gospels and Acts.

Let's look at these one-by-one:

Fainting

In this theory, everyone in the area was fooled because Jesus fainted on the Cross. His body was taken down too early, and He later revived in the cool air of the Tomb. Supporters of this theory point out that many crucifixion victims remained alive for several days. Let's look at some facts about the treatment Jesus received. (You might want to view *The Passion of the Christ* movie, which is generally

Jesus was a great Teacher.

accepted as an accurate portrayal of these hours of His life.)

- After a full day, He was arrested late on the evening before the crucifixion and endured the entire night being passed from one judge to another. During this time it is recorded that He was beaten by the Roman guards and forced to wear a crown of thorns, which likely caused a degree of blood loss and substantial internal injuries.
- At this time, if you were put into prison, your food and sometimes your water had to be brought by a friend. It is very doubtful that Jesus received any food or water during the time He was captive. Nothing is recorded as given to Him except some vinegar while He was on the cross.
- He was scourged. To be scourged meant that you were whipped with a cat-of-nine-tails, which was so-called because it was a leather whip with nine separate strands. In each strand were embedded many small pieces of sharp glass, nails, thorns, etc. The victim faced a post and had his hands tied around the post. His shirt was removed. Then, the whip operator would send the lashes around to the side of the victim and pull them back sharply across the back of the victim. After enough of these strokes, the victim's skin on his back would be essentially cut into fine ribbons or even diced. And not only the skin on the back was affected -- the skin on the abdomen was also horribly torn.

Jesus was a great Teacher.

Scourging was often fatal by itself, since 39 lashes was the common measure. If the victim didn't die from blood loss, the system shock that occurred due to general fluid loss would kill. Massive infection almost always occurred, which killed many victims over the next few days. And in some cases, the damage to the skin and connective tissue was so severe that the stomach and intestines could not be held properly to the back as the back ripped open.

- Jesus was too weak after his scourging to carry His own Cross. Simone of Cyrene was impressed by the Romans to carry His Cross.
- Roman records report that crucifixion was considered too extreme for Roman citizens. At this time, only slaves and foreign rebels could be crucified. With good reason -- it is perhaps the most barbarous death known.
- Our pictures of crucifixion are sanitized. In real crucifixions, the victim was often hung facing the cross. As archeological evidence shows, the victim's heels were fixed in place together by a single long nail driven through the heel or ankle area. The legs were thus bowed uncomfortably. Nails were truly driven through the wrists. This was for two reasons. The first reason was to support the body in a much stronger way than the weaker hand bones could. The second reason was to enable an expert crucifier to drive the nail into the carpal tunnel nerve, creating additional pain.

Jesus was a great Teacher.

- Despite all of this, the method of death for most crucifixion victims was slow suffocation. If you are supported solely by your arms and heels, sagging down will cut off your air. Thus, you must unbend your cramped and bowed legs to keep you up sufficiently high to breath.
- Meanwhile, the victim's body fluids gradually move into his legs, in a way similar to the problem of standing at attention for a long time. This leads to further weakness. In the case of Jesus, He had also lost considerable blood from the scourging, which would have weakened Him further.
- As reported in the Gospels, the Jewish Sabbath was approaching. Jewish law forbade someone's body be hung overnight, but the body must be buried that day. In deference to this, the Romans commonly sped up the process of crucifixion in Palestine by breaking the legs of the victim so that he would die very quickly through internal bleeding in the legs, and through an inability to lift oneself to breath. Archaeological evidence supports this.

The Gospels report that the Romans broke the legs of the two thieves who were crucified with Jesus. Then, because Jesus was apparently dead, a Roman soldier stabbed Jesus in the side with a spear and "blood and water came out". This is exactly the proper result if the lungs of Jesus had filled with fluid due to the severe beatings that He endured and the spear punctured

Jesus was a great Teacher.

those lungs. A large crowd that had watched the execution apparently observed this.

The Romans had a strong motive in testing if Jesus was dead; if He lived and escaped, according to Roman law, the soldiers would be executed in His place!

- Satisfied, the Romans allowed Joseph of Arimathea to take His Body to a tomb that Joseph had previously prepared for his own family. This tomb was apparently just a few feet away from the site of the Crucifixion. After mummy-wrapping the body in linen and spices, the friends left. The Tomb was sealed with a large boulder. Soon, a guard was set, and Pilate's official seal was placed upon the Tomb because the Jewish authorities were afraid the body would be stolen.
- Violating Pilate's seal was punishable by death. Also, Roman guards who fell asleep were punished with death.
- Tomb-blocking stones were large wheel-shaped 2000 lb stones. They were easy to roll in front of the Tomb, where they fell into a ditch carved for the purpose. They were very difficult to remove from the ditch. We have many examples of tombs of this sort dating from the 1st century in Palestine.
- A couple of days later, Jesus began to appear to many people - not as an apparition, but as a touchable Man who has wounds and eats with the Apostles. Later, some 500 people saw Him.

Jesus was a great Teacher.

Analysis

The supporters of the fainting theory would have us believe each of the following items to avoid a supernatural explanation:

1. The Romans -- the best executioners of the ancient world -- didn't recognize a living body when they saw it.
2. They made this mistake with the execution of a major public figure.
3. After the beatings, scourging, nails, and spear wound caused a terrible loss of blood, Jesus still was able to wake up in the Tomb.
4. Despite being mummy-wrapped, He was able to remove the linen wrappings by Himself.
5. Despite living in the First Century, He was able to stop the blood loss from the spear wound and heal the rest of His wounds, including the pain from the nail holes through his ankles.
6. He somehow replaced His body fluids and His lost blood.
7. Next, He rolled the heavy stone up out of the ditch...
8. He then sneaked past the guards, who had not noticed all of this...
9. and soon cheered up Mary and the other women by saying, "Rejoice!"
10. Within a couple of days, He had recovered enough to look very happy and walk to Galilee - an eighty mile journey on recently nailed ankles - where He met with Peter and several other disciples and looked inspiring -- not beaten and bedraggled.

Jesus was a great Teacher.

This doesn't seem too likely without some form of supernatural intervention.

The Apostle's Body Theft

This theory holds that the Apostles stole the dead body of Jesus and hid it, never to be found again. Then, they made up the stories of His Resurrection. This theory has several holes, however.

1. The Apostles, with the exception of John, died martyr's deaths for Jesus. (John died of old age.) While many people may lie, almost no one will die for a lie.
2. In many political scandals, we see that even three or four people cannot successfully keep a conspiracy secret. Think about Watergate, for example.
3. Large conspiracies are hard to keep. In one of his letters (I Corinthians 15:6) written about 20 years (roughly A.D. 56) after the event, Paul points out that over 500 people saw Jesus alive after His Resurrection. He further challenges his readers by pointing out that of these witnesses, "the greater part remain to the present". In effect, Paul said, "Don't take my word. Go and talk to the witnesses!" What is more, many scholars see this section of Paul's letter as a repetition of an early Christian creed that may date from within 5 years of the Crucifixion.
4. There were no ancient books that put forth this theory. Clearly, there were many people who had a solid reason to prove this theory as true, but none did: Neither the Romans, nor the Jewish priesthood did.

Jesus was a great Teacher.

5. A body has never been found that is supposed to be the body of Jesus. (No, not even Cameron's tomb contained a body.)
6. No proposed resting places for the body have been put forth. Even union boss Jimmy Hoffa's disappearance has generated many, many theories about where his body ended up.
7. The Roman guards would not have allowed it to happen. They were posted for the very purpose of preventing such an occurrence.
8. Other Messianic movements existed. But after the death of their leaders, the movements fell apart. This began to happen over the first couple of days after the arrest of Jesus. But after the Resurrection, the group of Apostles came back together. Why?
9. Peter's entire attitude changed. On the evening before the death of Jesus, Peter was a cowardly figure, slinking around the temple and denying any relation to Christ. But a few weeks later, Peter was standing boldly before the crowd at Pentecost proclaiming the Resurrection. Something significant had changed his outlook.

Could the Apostle's have stolen the body? It doesn't seem very likely.

The Roman or Jewish Theft of the Body

In this theory, the Romans or the Jewish priesthood stole the body. (Notice that no one denies that the Tomb is empty!). But this theory fails quickly.

Jesus was a great Teacher.

1. There were no motives for the Romans or the Jews to steal the body.
2. Both groups knew that the apparent Resurrection of Jesus would be a major political problem:

   - Jesus and His followers would replace the Jewish priesthood.
   - The Romans would likely see another Jewish revolt, something that occurred all too regularly.

3. Perhaps the body was stolen to prove that there was no Resurrection?
4. However, the body was never shown. After all, a public display of the body of Jesus would be a very effective rebuttal to early Christian preaching, wouldn't it?

Thus, this theory fails.

The Lost Women

The theory has been advanced that the women got the wrong Tomb.

1. It is highly unlikely that they would have lost the Tomb where they laid such an important personal friend and political figure.
2. It is also highly unlikely that Peter and John would also have lost the Tomb later that day.
3. Finally, surely someone would have finally said, "You've got the wrong Tomb. He's over here!" If not one of the Apostles, then

Jesus was a great Teacher.

> perhaps Joseph of Arimathea, who had spent considerable money having the Tomb carved out.

Not a likely theory.

The Hallucination Theory

In this theory, the five hundred or so people who saw the Risen Jesus actually saw a hallucination.

Only one objection is needed for this theory:

Didn't a member of the Jewish priesthood think to produce the body? After all, if everyone was hallucinating, then the body actually existed, right?

Discussion Questions

1. Pretend that you are on a jury. What theory do you prefer? Why?

2. Which theory do you consider the weakest? Why?

The Conclusion

Thus, looking at the facts, we see that the only explanation that makes sense is that Jesus truly died and was truly resurrected – despite the unique and miraculous nature of this event. Notice that if this

Jesus was a great Teacher.

happened, then the essential Truth of Christianity is proven. The rest of the entire religion hangs on this one point. (Notice that it also makes interesting, but false novels such as *The Da Vinci Code* very pale beside the Truth.) But how was He resurrected?

- Not through the science of the time. Everyone then understood that this was a Miracle. Bodies simply do not rise up from the dead. People in the 1st Century understood this completely. In fact, they were more aware of death than we, since most parents could expect to lose half of their children to childhood illnesses. These people *saw* dead bodies – how many dead bodies have you seen other than made up in a funeral home?
- Not through some advanced technology. Science fiction writers may talk of fantastic medical advances coming in the future, but no serious scientist talks of resurrection - only repairing the body before death occurs. Even the wishful thinkers of the 1970's that hoped for scientific resurrections knew that freezing the body was vital to avoid decomposition. And there were no opportunities for a 1st century Dr McCoy to get to the body quickly enough to save the brain from a real death. For reversing death is not just a matter of restarting a stopped machine. The chemical and biological processes that occur with death are not simply reversed -- decay begins within an hour of death. How could technology possibly reverse the oozing decay of a brain?

Jesus was a great Teacher.

>   (This is an important line of thought for me personally. I had read Erik von Daniken's *Chariots of the Gods* when I was a teen. I always wondered if Jesus was really a high-tech astronaut or alien. So one day I began to read the Gospel of Mark with an eye toward explaining each of the Miracles with high technology. About the time that Peter walked on water toward the Lord, I gave up. Although I could come up with a plausible explanation for many of the Miracles, taken together they were completely impossible to explain and the astronaut theory completely fell apart.)

- Another science fiction idea is the idea of immortal men, as shown in the movie "Highlander". Even if Jesus Himself was a member of a race of Highlander-type immortals, there is still the problem of His other Miracles. Perhaps Jesus and His relative Lazarus were immortal, but was the daughter of the centurion also? And what about the other Miracles: Wine, blindness, weather, etc.?
- No, we are left with the concept of Divine Resurrection. We are faced with the conclusion that a supernatural Being exists who controls life and death. Uh-oh! There's God again!

But couldn't Jesus have been a man Resurrected by the Father instead of being Deity Himself?

Yes. And the Father may have resurrected him. But Jesus claimed to be Deity. Would a just and good

Jesus was a great Teacher.

God have raised a liar from the dead? Surely not! Not to support a lie about Himself! Thus, we are led to the conclusions as follows:

1. The Resurrection actually happened.
2. Jesus claimed to be God and Man.
3. His Resurrection could only have occurred with Divine intervention.
4. God, who is just and good, would not raise a liar or a devil.
5. His teachings and the testimony of contemporaries prove He is good.
6. Jesus must have been who He claimed to be!
7. As the only proven Deity, claiming to be the *only* Deity, we should believe in Him and listen to what He said.

For More Detailed Evidence

Lee Strobel - *The Case for Christ* (Zondervan, 1998 ISBN 0310209307) and Professor Mark E. Moore of Ozark Christian College have both written extensively on the evidence for the Deityhood of Christ. Lee's book and a lecture by Mark at Corinth Christian Church in Loganville, Georgia in 2002 helped me immensely in the development of this chapter. I highly recommend their books.

Conclusion

Now, you understand why Evangelical Christians believe that Jesus is both God and man.

During the life of Jesus, He associated with many people considered to be unclean low-life by the Jewish priesthood - Romans, prostitutes, Roman tax

Jesus was a great Teacher.

collectors, beggars, lame, mute, blind, Samarians, and others. In the next chapter, we will see why modern Evangelical Christian churches are open to all.

Discussion Questions

1. Discuss the various theories for the Resurrection.

2. Why do you think people discount the story of the Resurrection?

Actions

1. Hold a friendly debate over the Resurrection with a friend.

2. Watch *The Passion of the Christ* movie.

Suggested Scripture Readings

- Matthew Chapter 27, Mark Chapter 15, Luke Chapter 23, and John Chapter 19 - These tell of the death of Christ.

Jesus was a great Teacher.

- Matthew Chapter 28, Mark Chapter 16, Luke Chapter 24, John Chapter 20-21, Acts Chapter 1, 1 Corinthians 15:3-8 - These tell of the Resurrection of Christ.

Bibliography and Suggested Readings

Lee Strobel - *The Case for Christ* (Zondervan, 1998 ISBN 0310209307)

Mark E. Moore - *A Humble Defense: Evidence for the Christian Faith* (College Press, 2004 ISBN 0899004865)

Suggested Viewing

The Passion of the Christ (DVD) (Fox Home Entertainment, 2004 ASIN B00028HBKM) (Caution: This R-rated movie is very violent and bloody, but is a very realistic approach to the Crucifixion. This is not a "family movie" and is not appropriate for children.

FAQ #2 – Why do Evangelicals Constantly Talk About God?

By now you understand some of the basics of Evangelical Christian theology. So we now look at one of the defining characteristics of the Evangelical – the tendency to relate everything in the world to God.

Sharing the Gospel

One obvious thing about Evangelical Christians is that they talk about God. Evangelicals are much more likely to talk about their religion than Catholics, liberal Christians, or Jews. Why is this so?

Let's look at a passage of the Bible that is extraordinarily important to Evangelical Christians. It is comes from the final 28th Chapter of the Gospel of Matthew, verses 18 to 20.

> **The Great Commission**
>
> And Jesus came and spoke to them, saying, "All authority has been given to Me in heaven and on earth. Go therefore and make disciples of all the nations, baptizing them in the name of the Father

Why do Evangelicals Constantly talk about God?

> and of the Son and of the Holy Spirit, teaching them to observe all things that I have commanded you; and lo, I am with you always, even to the end of the age." Amen.

This Great Commission is the heart of much of Evangelical action. Let's take it apart and see how it relates to the actions of individual believers.

Jesus is speaking just before He ascends into Heaven and leaves the Apostles behind. Evangelical Christians interpret that the command given applies to all Christians.

Make disciples...

The word disciple means student. We are instructed to make people students of Christ's teachings. Evangelical churches almost always have extensive Sunday schools and mid-week Bible study programs.

...of all the nations...

This is the justification for the worldwide missionary focus of Evangelicals. Evangelical churches today are even stronger in Africa, Asia, and South America than they are in America.

...baptizing them...

As we will see, baptism is how people become members of the church. And Evangelical churches are growing fast, with some churches exceeding 10,000 members in major cities.

Why do Evangelicals Constantly talk about God?

...teaching them...

Evangelical church services almost always have a very detailed, practical sermon that teaches the congregation about some aspect of Christian life.

So we have an understanding of the command given by Christ that sets up the outreach. But what is the personal motivation that leads so many Evangelical Christians to follow this command?

In Matthew's Gospel, Chapter 22, verses 34 to 40, a religious lawyer questions Jesus. "Teacher, which is the greatest commandment?"

Jesus said to him, "You shall love the LORD your God with all your heart, with all your soul, and with all your mind... And the second is like it: You shall love your neighbor as yourself."

This second commandment is the key to this outreach. An Evangelical thinks through the situation like this:

- I am to love my neighbor. Jesus made clear that my neighbor is anyone I know or meet.
- What can I do to show love to my neighbor? I can hug them, help them, feed them, give them money, and a whole host of different things.
- But what will help my neighbor the most? What has helped me the most in my life?
- The answer comes: help my neighbor gain eternal life. (If you have eternal life, you can eventually solve all the other problems.)

Why do Evangelicals Constantly talk about God?

- How can I help my neighbor gain eternal life?
- Help them understand the Good News message of Jesus Christ, that God wants to have a special relationship with every person, including you, and that a simple desire to gain that relationship by following Jesus and His teachings will lead us into that relationship.

And so this combination of Christ's command and our love for our neighbor makes it imperative that we tell you about Christ and help you understand His message.

Discussion Question:

- Have you ever felt the need to share a wonderful experience?

- How does that help spread the Christian message?

Myth #5 - Evangelical Christians Don't Let Sinners in Church.

> You who say, "Do not commit adultery," do you commit adultery? Romans 2:22

In the last chapter, we saw why Christians believe in the Deityhood of Christ. In this chapter, we will discuss another common Christian myth - that Evangelical Christians are an exclusive group.

The Myth Explained

My daughter has a friend who is a male homosexual. He knows that Christianity is opposed to homosexuality, but one day a friend was to be married. He told my daughter that he would go to the church wedding, but jokingly expected his "hand to fry" when he touched the church doorknob.

What exactly is the Evangelical Christian position on sinners? Are they welcome in church? Or can you be "too bad" to go to church?

Sin

Christians believe that there is such a thing as "sin". In the Evangelical Christian vocabulary, a "sin" is an offense against God. In many ways, sin is a parallel concept to "crime", which is an offense against the government. Thus, a "sinner" is a person who has committed a crime against God.

God is good and just. He established a set of laws for us to follow and dictated these laws to Moses. Most of this is in the Book of Leviticus, the third book of the Old Testament. Some of the laws are specific to the priesthood, some apply only to Jews, and others apply to all men and women. This set of laws is referred to as the Mosaic Law.

A special general-purpose subset of the Mosaic Law is the Ten Commandments, which were discussed in some depth in Chapter Two. The Commandments are very simple, but very difficult to follow, since Evangelical Christians believe that not only overt action is covered, but also covert thoughts. In Matthew 5:21-29, Jesus specifically points out that the Commandments apply to thoughts as well as deeds. In other words, you have broken the commandment if you have even thought about committing adultery. You have broken the commandment if you have even thought about murdering someone, or stealing something.

Because of this, Evangelical Christians believe that *all people* are sinners. Christians also believe that all people deserve death at God's hands. Breaking even the slightest part of the Law is sufficient grounds for God to choose not to associate with us. Why do Christians hold such a strong position?

Evangelical Christians don't let Sinners in Church

How God deals with Sin

Look at a child. Let's assume that your very young son looks up at you one day and calls you a nasty name. "Daddy, you are a ------!" The child does not understand the seriousness of what he is saying, and the temptation is to laugh. Such a big nasty word coming from such a small mouth! You didn't even know he had ever heard the word. But you know that if you let him off the hook this time, he may begin to call other people that nasty name, and this will lead to two consequences: First, he will eventually get himself into a fight when he calls the wrong person that name, and secondly, his use of the word in public will reflect poorly upon your reputation. So you correct your son. If he uses the word again, you punish him. And thus, you lovingly teach your son that that word had better not be used.

Now let's look at sin from God's perspective. You are now God's little child. You decide to drink too much and become a drunken bore. God looks at you and understands that this behavior will harm you if continued. You will eventually loose your family and perhaps kill people. In addition, if you are a professing Christian, this reflects badly upon the reputation of God.

A story is told of the czar Alexander of Russia. It came to the czar's attention that there was a man in the town, also named Alexander, who had become an accomplished pickpocket with a bit of a reputation. People were beginning to compare the taxes of the Czar Alexander to the petty thievery of the pickpocket Alexander. So the Czar had the pickpocket brought before him and said "Alexander,

Evangelical Christians don't let Sinners in Church

you are possessed of a very fine name. That name must remain spotless in its reputation. Therefore, you must change your occupation or change your name!"

God is perfect, and is very concerned with His reputation. In the Bible and in Evangelical Christian circles, this is referred to as His "Name". God is concerned with the reputation of His Name. Thus, God responds to your sin with a correction based upon the dual needs of your long-term best interests, and His reputation. He makes you feel absolutely vile the morning after you were drunk. If you continue to get drunk, he takes away a few friends, and gradually turns up the pressure until you die or cry "Uncle!". He takes His reputation -- and your needs -- very seriously and has the power to make your life miserable until you kill yourself with the bottle, or learn self-control.

Imagine that you are a United States Senator and that you have a friend who literally is a dirty, filthy, stinking, drug-addict who eats from trash dumpsters and never brushes his teeth, combs his hair, or washes his clothes. He's also widely known to be a lying, cheating, sexual pervert who has been convicted of spying for our number one national enemy. Now imagine that you decide to eat lunch with him at the best restaurant in town. Rightly or wrongly, is it possible that being seen with him might stain your reputation? Of course.

Now imagine that your daughter joins a gang of scantily clad, heavy-drinking, pot-smoking girls who regularly use strong language. Is possible that she may take up some of the aspects of those girls? Of course.

As I said earlier, God is perfect. Part of His perfection includes a need to stay perfect -- and the power to do so. This is His ballgame and He will play only with those who acknowledge that it is His game. A perfect God has perfect standards, and will not associate with imperfect creatures -- unless they are willing to be perfected.

"Willing to be perfected" means that those creatures have voluntarily joined God's self-improvement class for creatures. Those creatures have acknowledged that God has the answers that they don't have. That self-improvement class begins when you become a believing Christian.

The only alternative to joining God's class is death. We are imperfect creations, imperfect through our own choice. As an imperfect creature, we must ultimately be perfected or die. One of the marks of perfection is eternal life. Since we have no way to permanently avoid death ourselves (accidents happen!), we must look to God for that gift of eternal life. His price is that we acknowledge that He is God and we are not. The neat thing about his bargain is that we can do that simply by accepting the gift. By that action, we have implicitly accepted that God is God and we are not. At that point, He can begin working with us.

Which Sins are Worst?

Many people think that some sins are worse than others. This is contrary to Evangelical Christian belief. From God's eyes, you or I are essentially just as bad as Hitler. Hitler killed many people -- there is no doubt that he was evil. You and I have both killed many people in our minds - is there any real doubt that we are evil too? The only difference between Hitler and us is that Hitler had the ability – and the lack of inhibition - to accomplish what he wanted to do. We are too cowardly to do what we have thought of doing. (If you protest that you never killed anyone in your mind, remember back to when you were a child. Wasn't there *anyone* you imagined dead? Your parent who had just punished you? Your "mean-old" teacher? The bully in class? The girl who took the guy you had a crush on?)

Which is worse? The man who slept with 50 women before AIDS caught up with him? Or the man who mentally slept with 500 women by looking at Internet pornography?

Which is worse? The woman who stole her friend's necklace? Or the woman who stole her friend's good reputation through gossip?

Which is worse? A man who kills a young family in anger but becomes a believing Christian and works prison ministry for twenty years? Or a man who never acknowledges the existence of God and lives a hermit's life, doing no good for anyone until he dies?

Jesus was very clear. He said that thoughts are the same as deeds to God. God looks to the heart. And in God's Law, a single liar who harms another is as worthy of death as a mass-murdering serial pedophile rapist. God will not associate with either.

However, if either one repents (literally "turns away") from his sin, asks forgiveness, and puts his trust and belief in Jesus as the Son of God, then God will accept him into His house.

The Reason for the Prayer of Salvation

God knows that there are essentially two types of people in the world. There are those who can be taught and those who can't be taught. God, being very wise, has developed a simple test to see if you can be taught.

God knows that if you are able to acknowledge your wrongs and accept that you are not capable of fixing them yourself, then you are capable of being taught -- given enough time. And God has infinite time that He can give to you.

However, if you will not acknowledge that you have caused many of your own problems - you can't be taught. You will continue to blame others for those problems, and thus you will never be able to fix your inherent problems. In addition, if you will not admit that you need help fixing those problems, you will not be able to fix those problems. And thus, you are hopeless. No amount of time will ever fix you.

When you sincerely pray the Prayer of Salvation – you tell God that you are teachable. He will then put you on the Spiritual Training Course and you will be given eternal life. Your progression on the Course will be up to you.

The Prayer of Salvation is words similar to these:

Evangelical Christians don't let Sinners in Church

> *"Father, I have done wrong. I cannot fix those wrongs -- nor myself. I need your help. Please forgive me for what I've done wrong and help me. I will follow you and Your Son, Jesus Christ. Please help me."*

Only one thing ultimately determines whether God accepts you into Heaven -- your relationship to Jesus. He completely forgets any sin you've committed if you are right with His Son, because He knows that this means that in the long run you will be proper to associate with. Without that relationship, you will be a wild animal -- a feral cat -- always scratching and clawing.

When you sign up for the Spiritual Training Course, you are given a helper -- the Holy Spirit. The Holy Spirit is the third person of the Trinity. The Holy Spirit, which arrived on earth in Acts Chapter 2, inhabits Christian believers. Non-believers sometimes talk about part of Him as "the conscience". He guides us in moral decisions; He also helps us connect with God. If we listen to Him, we will develop a Christ-like character. If we ignore Him, we will stagnate.

The Trinity

The Trinity is a difficult concept -- Christians believe in One Being with Three Personalities. Many people are confused by this concept. Some people understand it in this way:

> Imagine we are in a swimming pool. I hold my hand under the water in front of you and lift three fingers.

Evangelical Christians don't let Sinners in Church

What am I holding up? "Three fingers", you say.

"How many objects am I holding up?" I say.

"Three", you reply.

Next I raise my hand above the water. "Now how many objects am I holding up?"

"One", you reply.

This is how Three can be One. We don't see well enough spiritually to see the Union between the Three. But the Three are One when we look deeply enough.

The Trinity and Software

An analogy to help computer-savvy readers understand the Trinity is this:

> In the Beginning, a Program appeared. It consisted of three parts: a Server, an Installer, and a Client. The Server was originally on the Net. It communicated with its operator, but the operator sent the Server illegal requests that violated its Protocol. The Server locked out the operator.
>
> Over time, various operators tried to communicate properly with the

Server, but to no avail. Finally, the Server chose an operator to whom He published a file full of a communication Protocol for various operators and programmers to use to communicate to the Server. This key operator even published a detailed User's Manual explaining the Protocol. But the chosen programmers would not stick to the Protocol or read the Manual, and kept trying other protocols and sending illegal requests to the Server. The Server would not allow access because of this, and responded by crashing their systems.

Finally, the Server sent the Installer program. The Installer was sent to the programmers and operators to show them the proper way to communicate with the Server and never have system crashes, but by now the lead programmers and operators wouldn't listen. So they deleted the Installer, assuming that it was a malicious virus.

Shortly thereafter, the Installer re-appeared, un-deleted by the Server. The Installer went to several key programmers and operators who had listened to it and proceeded to install the Client on their systems.

The Client remains and has become
widely used throughout the world.
People who use the Client and study
the Manual experience trouble-free
communication with the Server.
These people also know from
reading the Manual that the Installer
will return from the Net some day
with a new Version that will usher in
a new and wonderful age.

- The Server is God the Father.
- The Installer is the Son -- Jesus Christ.
- The Client is the Holy Spirit.
- The Manual is the Bible.

All are necessary. The Father is the Creator and Supreme. Belief in The Son is necessary to establish proper communications with the Father -- belief shows proper respect. The Holy Spirit is within us for guidance in life and in those communications. And the Bible is the instruction book for understanding the Trinity and developing a Christ-like character.

Developing a Christ-like Character

One of the goals of an Evangelical Christian believer is to develop a Christ-like personal character. This is a gradual process, which we all strive for. It is a journey that takes more than a lifetime to accomplish. Yet, we can often see major improvements in just a few weeks. As the Holy Spirit is given more and more control over our actions by us, we stop being a natural man and become a Spiritual man.

Paul wrote that the difference between the natural man and the Spiritual man is like the difference between the flesh and the Spirit. (The following quote is from *The Bible, New King James Version, Galatians 5:19-26.*)

> "Now the works of the flesh are evident, which are adultery, fornication, uncleanness, lewdness, idolatry, sorcery, hatred, contentions, jealousies, outbursts of wrath, selfish ambitions, dissensions, heresies, envy, murders, drunkenness, revelries, and the like; of which I tell you beforehand, just as I also told you in time past, that those who practice such things will not inherit the kingdom of God.
>
> "But the fruit of the Spirit is love, joy, peace, longsuffering, kindness, goodness, faithfulness, gentleness, self-control. Against such there is no law. And those who are Christ's have crucified the flesh with its passions and desires. If we live in the Spirit, let us also walk in the Spirit. Let us not become conceited, provoking one another, envying one another."

The "fruit of the Spirit" is what Christians crave. But we all start with "the works of the flesh".

Evangelical Christians don't let Sinners in Church

Evangelicals believe that all men can eventually achieve this Christ-like personal character -- if they submit to the rule of Christ in their lives. This is a key reason that mature Evangelical Christians are accepting of all people -- even if new Christians may not be so accepting. The new Christians have not yet harvested the fruit of the Spirit.

Discussion Questions

1. How can a perfect God relate to people?

2. How does God's perfect love differ from our human parental love?

3. How does God's perfect discipline differ from our human imperfect discipline?

4. Discuss the Trinity. How does viewing It depend upon your perspective?

5. Discuss other ways to understand the Trinity.

6. Which of the "works of the flesh" afflict you?

7. Which of the "fruits of the Spirit" can you see in your own life?

8. How does the Holy Spirit affect you? How can you know His Presence?

The Crowns

One of the items mentioned in the Bible is that our good deeds will store up treasure in heaven. I once had a daydream as follows:

> I dreamed I visited Heaven and I was shown into a special room on tour. Here were all sorts of artisans fashioning beautiful crowns with wonderful gems. I noticed that some crowns were small with only a couple of gems. Others had hundreds or even thousands of gems. I noticed a few were on display and asked my guide about the crowns.
>
> "Each gem represents each soul won by the person for Christ," he answered.
>
> I noticed a beautiful crown on display with a thousand or so gems. "Saint Paul's", my guide pointed out.

Another had about fifty thousand gems and was still being worked on. "Billy Graham's", explained my guide.

I looked in puzzlement at two huge crowns. Hundreds of thousands of diamonds, emerald, and rubies glittered on each of them. But the crowns were apparently being disassembled. The artisans were very clearly coming to the crowns and carefully un-soldering the gems. Each gem was being moved to a different crown.

"What is going on here?" I asked my guide.

Tears came to his eyes. "We had every hope up to the very end. We hoped to present them with their crowns when they arrived. They were responsible - albeit indirectly responsible - for bringing more people to Jesus than any other men. There would have been great celebrations when they arrived. But they never welcomed Jesus into their own hearts. So we have to disassemble the crowns. They won't ever wear them. You see," he paused, "these are the crowns that were prepared for Hitler and Stalin".

Yes, God used even Hitler and Stalin. And God's Word states that even such evil men could be accepted into God's Presence if only they had repented of their evil deeds and accepted the Lordship of Jesus over their lives. You simply cannot be too bad for Christ to accept you -- *if* you truly are sorry, accept the control of Jesus over your life, and attempt to change. For proof of this, Evangelical Christians read about the deeds of the man named Saul, starting in the Book of Acts, Chapter 7.

Saul was a key leader of the first persecution of Christians. He drug people from their homes and threw them into prison. He participated in the stoning death of Stephen, the first martyr. He even received letters from the high Jewish council allowing him to go to Damascus to pursue fleeing Christians.

Yet, on the way to Damascus, Jesus and Saul met. And Saul was forever changed. He even changed his name – to Paul, known today as one of the greatest Christian writers of all history, and as the author of more of the New Testament than any other man.

Our Sins

We've covered one point about sin – *no sin is too great for Jesus to forgive*. But as Evangelical Christians, we also point out the other, corresponding point: *All people, including all priests and ministers and outspoken Christian*

Evangelical Christians don't let Sinners in Church

politicians and writers, are sinners. We've all committed a huge list of sins – just as you have.

So what does Christianity say about the ordinary man and woman, and the most common sins of the twenty-first century?

Addiction and Sex

These two areas are what most people think about when the concept of sin comes to mind.

Alcohol

Drinking alcohol is not a sin. Almost everyone in the Bible, including Jesus, drank wine. This was largely because the alcohol in the watered-down wine kills harmful bacteria. However, the Bible specifically commands us not to become drunk and not to become a drunkard. And an Elder of the church should not be too fond of wine. The original Greek text of 1 Timothy 3:3 literally says to "not lay down with a wine jug".

Different Christian groups treat this differently. Most of the oldest groups, such as Catholics, Orthodox, Lutheran, Episcopalian, Anglican, etc. use real wine at Communion, and will often have wine with certain church meals. Baptists and Disciples of Christ frown heavily on the use of alcohol, maintaining that men who live in a society with safe alternatives to alcoholic beverages should avoid the possibility of becoming alcoholics or of becoming drunk by avoiding the temptation. Let me emphasize that no Christian groups will tolerate an alcoholic who does not wish to change. But if you

Evangelical Christians don't let Sinners in Church

want to change, well -- that's a totally different matter. Christ is about changes.

If you have a drinking problem, go to a church. Tell the priest, minister, or pastor of your problem, and ask him if he can help you. He will. Many churches can assist you by connecting you with an Alcoholics Anonymous group. AA and your pastor can help you combine the help of Jesus with the help of Christian friendship to defeat the pull of alcohol on you. Alcoholism is such a common sin that almost every pastor has helped multiple Christians deal with the problem. He'll be happy to help you, too. And the people of the church will love nothing more than to help you defeat the bottle.

If you drink occasionally, the reaction of Christians will depend upon the group. The groups I've listed above will likely accept a modest amount of drinking without the slightest discussion. But other groups, such as many Baptists, will consider you a dangerous influence as long as you drink the slightest bit. But other Baptist groups may be found drinking beer as a group at the local football game. (Baptists are such a diverse group!)

And so, you see that *drinking to excess* is the real Biblical Christian issue. But drinking alcohol may keep you from fitting into a particular church.

Now, there is a point to consider: If you are making the acceptance of modest drinking a factor in your choice of church, what really controls your life? Your relationship with Jesus? Or your relationship with your "modest drinking"?

Evangelical Christians don't let Sinners in Church

You must decide.

Drug Use

If you use illegal drugs, or use drugs for the recreational effects, Evangelicals believe that you are sinning. Christians believe that the body is a temple for the Holy Spirit, and needs to be kept clean and pure. So how will Christians react to you if you smoke pot, take speed pills, or smoke crack?

The question is your willingness to change. Christians will not accept a persistent drug user permanently into their fellowship. But if you would like to leave the drugs behind, any Christian pastor or priest will help you kick the habit. Most pastors have dealt with other people with your problem before, and can help you in many ways. And after you go through withdrawal, you will begin to experience the natural joy of fellowship with Jesus. Christianity is about the freedom from addiction -- not about rules to constrain you.

Something worth noticing: In the 2000 election, George W. Bush talked about his excessive drinking and possible drug use as a young adult. But he pointed out that he had become a committed Christian later in life and this changed his behavior. Others remarked about this change that had occurred in his life.

The Evangelical community accepted and embraced Bush – his story was familiar to us. We all have experienced problems early in our lives. Most of us understand that learning to lean on Christ to overcome those problems was a major, positive experience for us. And so, we welcomed Bush. Evangelical Christianity is about positive changes – and honesty.

Cigarette Use

Evangelicals believe that any Christian believer who smokes should try to wind down and stop smoking. You are polluting the Holy Temple, which is your body. Another issue is the First Commandment -- You are to serve One God, not nicotine. Almost all pastors can help you kick the habit.

That said, few Christian groups would be upset at you for smoking. They understand the difficulty of quitting, but will gently be "on your case" because they love you and would like you to live a long time with them. Show your love for them back by quitting your sin.

Homosexuality

A plain reading of the Bible in both Old and New Testaments teaches that homosexuality, lesbianism, adultery and all other forms of sexual activity *except* heterosexual marriage are sins. In almost all Christian groups, the congregation rejects people who continue to have sexual activity outside of heterosexual marriage. We are commanded to do so.

Notice that this is very broad. Yes, certain high profile television politician/preachers have made statements that are very anti-homosexual. But God's

Word is very clear. You are also committing a sin in *any* of the following situations:

- You and your unmarried girlfriend sleep together before marriage.
- You have a heterosexual affair with a married man or woman.
- You commit rape of anyone.
- You even *think* about having sex with the rock star Madonna -- who is, after all, a married woman.

Christians will look on people who do these things with a combination of disgust and pity. The Congregation and Elders are ordered to love all people -- they will make the attempt. But the Church is commanded in the Bible to reject people who *continue* in sexual sins -- the specific examples used in the Bible include gays, lesbians, a young man who was sleeping with his stepmother, adulterers, and others who are "lewd".

Why is homosexuality looked upon as a sin? Because, like all sins, homosexuality keeps men and women from accomplishing God's purposes in the fullest manner. A drug user is not capable of accomplishing as much work as a sober person. A homosexual does not reproduce as a homosexual, and thus does not accomplish as much of God's work. In addition, multiple Biblical passages point out explicitly that homosexuality is considered a sin by God.

Most homosexuals have a long list of associated sins to deal with even before we deal directly with the homosexuality itself. Most other people have a long list, too.

Try this sin checklist:

1. Have you ever wished to have sex with a married man or woman?
2. Have you ever had sex with a man or woman outside of marriage?
3. Have you ever been disrespectful to your parents?
4. Have you ever lied about your sexual behavior?
5. Have you ever hated a heterosexual - for *any* reason?

This is a list that few heterosexuals can pass, and homosexuals can't either.

If you are a homosexual, here's the Evangelical program:

1. First of all, commit your life to Christ. This is the key.
2. Read Romans 1:18-32.
3. Begin attending church. "Metropolitan Community Churches" are a group of churches that specifically welcome gays, lesbians, and bisexuals. But you can attend any church.
4. Begin reading the Bible. Begin working on the sins in your life. (Everyone has a very long list to work on.)
5. Eventually, Jesus will begin to show you things - difficult things. He will have you

begin changing your activities. You will become happier.
6. This is a fair warning: Jesus will eventually require you to stop homosexual activities, and He will *help* you stop. You will no longer *wish* to be a practicing homosexual. This will *not* be a message from "the Church". This will be a message from Jesus.
7. You will stop homosexual activities and be happier for it.

Why do I say that this is the program? *Because it is the program that works for any sin.* And Jesus works very hard on His People to get them to stop behaviors that cause them problems. Homosexuality is no different from any other sin. Jesus will point out how it harms you and help you stop the sin. (If you are a homosexual you can probably list some of these harms already.)

One of the key aspects of homosexuality that makes it a difficult sin to stop is that it has become a religion to many people. Do you worship "homosexuality" as others worship Christ? Is your "gayness" your god? Have you tied up so much of your identity in your homosexuality that you don't feel that there is much else to you?

Evangelical Christians believe that there is infinitely more to you than your sexual orientation. You are a unique individual with whom God would like to have a friendship. Can we Christians do any less?

Other Sexual Sins

Let me make sure that I've been clear about the Evangelical outlook -- God doesn't like *any* sin. But some sins are more apparent in our culture than others.

- If you are a prostitute, you are sinning.
- If you patronize prostitutes, you are sinning.
- If you have sex with your neighbor, you are sinning.
- If you look at pornography, you are sinning.
- If you have sex with your boyfriend/girlfriend, you are sinning.
- If you have sex with your wife, you are doing as God asks, and He is pleased.

So what should you do?

Re-read the Gospel of Mark. You should notice – as Evangelicals have - that Jesus continually visited sinners. He said that it was much more exciting to help a sinner turn away from his sins than to talk to a righteous man. *Most Mature Evangelical Christians agree.*

Just as with the other sins, you should visit a church. Today. Ask for Jesus to help you avoid the sin. He will. He will send someone into your life at that church who can help you. But you have to ask for help.

Money

Is money "the root of all evil"? No. Or is it "the love of money that is the root of all evil". No. God expects us to be successful and have abundance. The problem occurs when you focus your life upon finding money instead of finding God's Will.

Sam Walton, the founder of Wal-Mart, was a very rich man and is in heaven today. Why? Because Sam knew that God was more important than all of Sam's stores and billions of dollars. "Mr. Sam" was focused upon God and people, and helping people. His success was a blessing from God for following God's Commandments.

On the other hand, there are many entrepreneurs who would steal a grandmother's purse if it held the telephone number to another venture capitalist. There are men and women who are addicted by money. Ted Turner of CNN allegedly said that "Life's a game and money is how you keep score." Ted could learn some things from Sam Walton.

The great sin question about money is this: Who is in control -- you or the money? Does the pursuit of money control your regular daily decisions?

Now, I'm not talking about the mind of the man who has just been laid off from his job. That is a different issue. I'm talking about the man who has enough money to spend and save after he buys his basic food and shelter. I was this way when I had recently graduated from college. I was saving $500 per month, yet I needed more money. And God finally led me to make some stupid decisions to try to get more money, which gave me debts that have taken over fifteen years to pay off.

It was only when I began to care more for God than for money that I began to be financially successful again.

If you have an addiction to money or another money sin, talk to Jesus or a pastor about it. They will help you. That's what Evangelical Christians are supposed to do – help one another.

In certain Christian groups, the "prosperity gospel" is preached. This is the idea that if you simply have enough faith, God will give you the material things that you've prayed for. But most Evangelical Christians take issue with this concept and have a slightly different view on it.

To most Evangelical Christians, the actual idea is that if you will talk with God about your material needs and wants, your needs will be met. Your wants – well, that's a different matter. In most cases, a maturing Evangelical Christian will be taught – through listening to God in prayer, reading the Bible, and through experience – that most of those material wants are unnecessary for happiness. The Evangelical believes that we will be "prosperous", which means that we will be free from the fear of want, and relatively happy. And occasionally God will bless us with more money than we need. Then, the question will be: How shall you handle the money God has given you?

More Common Sins

Evangelicals know that it's easy to look at the first few sins I've listed and feel pretty good about yourself. Most people don't have those problems to worry about. But now it's time to examine some other sins that are just as disgusting to God. Go back and re-read that "works of the flesh" list. Add to that the list from Romans 1:28-32.

Anger and Hate

Anger and Hate are often the equivalent of murder in God's eyes. Most of the time, when we demonstrate anger we are reacting to an emotional or physical attack on ourselves. Jesus said that we should respond with quietness and pity for our attacker. Proverbs says that the rebuke of a friend should be graciously accepted as a gift. But to respond with anger is sinful. Angry men end up with short lives.

We logically relate this to the effects of anger. Angry men get into fights, which can lead to injury or death. Also, angry men harm people whom they love - children and spouses. Anger can lead to excessive speed on the highway, leading to accidents. And medical science has related anger-prone personalities to a higher incidence of heart attack and stroke.

There is truly righteous anger that is not sinful; Jesus demonstrated that anger when He cleansed the Temple of the moneychangers and merchants. In this episode, though, the anger of Jesus was focused upon the blasphemy of the men toward God. They were not properly respectful of God's Temple. Jesus was showing proper respect toward God by his anger. But few people get angry for that reason today. Most of the time, our anger is a reaction when *we* aren't shown "proper respect", or we are "dis'ed", or someone assaults our sense of honor.

Once again, coming to understand the Gospel is the cure for anger. When you know that you will live forever, you begin to put events in their proper perspective. A great cure for anger is simply realizing that the situation that would make you so angry will be forgotten in ten thousand years. And ten thousand years is just the beginning of eternity...

Angry men are welcome in church - provided that they are ready to work on their anger. In fact, this is one of the most common signs of difference in a man's personality before he is saved and after he becomes a believing Christian. "Do you see Jim?" the old preacher says. "Before he attended church he was angry and always getting into fights. Today he's a smiling fellow." I've heard that story many times -- only the name has changed.

Gossip and Back-biting

These two terms appear in the list of sins. Why? Because "Thou shalt not bear false witness against thy neighbor." Gossip and backbiting often spread false tales. If you do these, you are also a sinner -- welcome in church, but asked to repent.

Unfortunately these sins are not well understood by many people. So let's have a few definitions:

- Gossip - when you pass along negative stories about other people.
- Backbiting - when you imply or create negative stories or motives to other people and pass these thoughts on to others. In other words, you are damaging their reputation.
- Legitimate information - when you tell positive stories about other people, or provide factual accounts of problems people are having for the express purpose of helping those people.

A good rule to follow is this: Would Sarah be upset if she overheard you telling your friend about Sarah's problem? If so, you are gossiping or backbiting.

In other words, Evangelicals believe that you should only tell stories in private about other people which you (and they) would like to hear told in their presence.

Let's look at an example. Let's say that Harry has lost his job. If you hear that John's company is hiring workers like Harry, it is quite proper for you to tell John that Harry is looking for work. It is *not* proper to pass on the rumor that Harry lost his job because he made an improper advance toward a co-worker.

My wife and I have been in many churches. In some of them, gossip was common and caused problems. In one, there was a no-gossip policy. Unfortunately, the policy was so strong that no one knew what was happening with each other -- legitimate needs that the church could assist with were silenced. So it is important to understand the difference between gossip and passing along legitimate information.

Gossip and backbiting can harm people - both the nominal victim and the gossiper. When I was a manager at one company, I knew the best way to get word informally around the company was to talk to one particular engineer. He would spread the word quicker than any formal meeting I could call. He had developed the reputation for being the company gossip.

Another engineer had the reputation for being a backbiter. He was always putting down this manager, that manager, various engineers, and various projects. Gradually, he lost his audience, as he became known as "Mr. Negative". He also made the "layoff list" when times got tough.

Once again, Christians will accept anyone who wants to reform himself. We've all known the sins in our lives and are willing to accept you as you are. But we will expect you to try to remove sin from your life and improve. After all, that's what we're trying to do to ourselves....

The Specific Sin Doesn't Matter

Mature Evangelical Christians understand that everyone has sin. We understand that some sins are more shocking and lurid than others, but that God hates all sin. And we understand that all sins can be overcome with the help of Jesus. A statement common in Evangelical circles is "hate the sin, love the sinner". Most Evangelical Christians try to follow that concept.

But Repentance is Necessary

But the idea of repentance is necessary. You must be trying to remove your sins from your life. Few Christians will tolerate a serial adulterer in their midst. Nor will they tolerate an alcoholic on their Board of Elders.

The recent pedophile scandal in the American Catholic church is a result of Christians trying to follow their teachings, but incompletely. Priests who engaged in inappropriate behavior were not kicked out of the church, but were counseled and helped. Unfortunately, some of those priests did not learn their lessons -- they sinned again, some repeatedly. And also unfortunately, the behavior of those priests and the bishops who were trying to be kind to them led to a major scandal as non-Christians desperate for revenge and financial windfalls created a bonanza for trial lawyers. Perhaps in retrospect, those bishops should have followed the teachings of Paul regarding the Corinthian church. Read 1 Corinthians Chapter 5.

In the Corinthian church, there was a young man who was sleeping with his stepmother. The Corinthians were proud of their tolerance of him. Paul rather strongly suggested that they should not be proud, but should toss the young man out of the fellowship, comparing him to the leaven (yeast) that affects an entire loaf of bread. Paul was concerned with the reputation of the Christians and the negative effect that this young man would have on their behavior.

Paul goes on to discuss sins in general. His instructions were to be friends to non-Christians who were sinning. God would judge those who were outside the fellowship. But after the person became a Christian, if he fell back into his old ways, the sinner was to be removed from the fellowship. The Elders and the Congregation were to judge the person. The sinner was entitled to "due process", for Paul wrote to his protégé Timothy (regarding another sinner) to "admonish [a sinner] once privately, then a second time. But if he does not stop, then remove him from [the Church]."

In this way, Christians are to be very accepting of sinning non-Christians. New people in the faith are constantly compared to "little children". But Christians are to uphold a high standard of behavior in their own fellowship. Please note that this applies to adults. A child or teenager is not expected to uphold the same standard of behavior as a mature man or woman. But Evangelical Christian parents will still try to hold their children to a higher standard of moral behavior than is common in the community. And that is why many Evangelicals dislike Bill Clinton – a man who constantly put on the words of a Christian, but whose behavior indicated a low standard of morals.

This being said, remember that all people who claim to be Evangelical Christians are not Mature Evangelical Christians. And all churches are not filled with mature Christians. Thus, many Christians do not behave in accordance with the ideal.

Evangelical Christians don't let Sinners in Church

What about Hypocrites?

The word "hypocrite" comes from a Greek word meaning "behind the mask". It specifically compared certain people to Greek actors that held a mask in front of their face as they performed. Throughout the ages, there have been hypocrites in all parts of society, including the Church. Hypocrites are very concerned with complaining about your sins while they commit their own public sins. Entire groups of people are turned away from church life because they want to be morally superior -- they won't associate with "hypocrites". Are you one of these people?

If so, then you are also a practicing hypocrite. You claim to be morally superior, but will not help those who are your inferiors. Instead, you simply stay snobbish and aloof. What should you do?

A properly moral person should work both on his own sins and help -- not force -- others to overcome their own sins. If you once had a drinking problem, you are probably a good person to help another who currently has a drinking problem. But you must be very, very careful not to communicate with an air of snobbery. Otherwise, your "help" will do nothing except offend your student. It is very easy to forget how things were before you were saved and how difficult your road was.

Hypocrites are always found in every group of people. But Evangelicals know that if you focus on Jesus -- while they focus on you -- you will grow past them in wisdom and maturity. Then you can help them.

Evangelical Christians don't let Sinners in Church

What should you do?

If you are not yet a Christian, don't let a major sin problem stop you. Jesus specifically said that He "did not come to save the righteous, but to save the sinners." Talk to a pastor about your problem - he can guide you to help. Christianity has been called "God's Self-Improvement Course". With Him as your counselor, the Bible as your textbook, and Mature Christians to help, it is possible to leave any sin behind.

But what if you *like* the sin?

Evangelical Christians maintain that most sins control the person. For example, it is not the fact that you *drink* wine occasionally that is a sin, but the fact that you *can't avoid* drinking wine that is the sin. It isn't the fact that you occasionally get angry that is the sin, but the fact that you can't avoid getting angry. That is the way that sins control us. Evangelical Christians talk of being enslaved by sins. Do you want to be free or be enslaved? What sin enslaves you?

Sins destroy people. Most of the time, we can see how our particular sin is destroying us. And if we want to leave that sin behind, Evangelical Christians are ready to help. If you think that you are in control of your sin, go a month without committing that particular sin. If you can, you are probably free. If not, then the sin controls you and you need help.

If you are a Christian, remember to welcome and help the sinners. But avoid a condescending

Evangelical Christians don't let Sinners in Church

attitude. On the road to remove the sin in our lives, we all have farther to travel than the distance we have come.

And so another myth is dispelled. The truth is that sinners are welcomed by Evangelical Christians.

Discussion Questions

1. What sins have you overcome in your own life?

2. What sins are present in your life today?

3. How do you recognize sin in your own life?

4. Why do you think that the Christian "Pros" become humble?

Actions

1. Invite a disgusting sinner to dinner. (How to determine "disgusting"? That's up to you.) Be nice to them and don't mention Christ unless they bring Him up.

2. Focus on one single sin in your life. For example, are you prone to yell at your children? Or do you overindulge in chocolate? For the next month, pray every morning that opportunity to commit that sin will be taken from you.

Suggested Scripture Readings

- Romans Chapter 1 tells us of the nature of Sin.

- Ephesians 4:17-32 gives more advice about sins.

Myth #6 - Christians Who Die Become Angels.

> I saw still another mighty angel coming down from heaven, clothed with a cloud. And a rainbow was on his head, his face was like the sun, and his feet like pillars of fire. Revelation 10:1

In the movie "*It's a Wonderful Life*",[1] Jimmy Stewart's character George Bailey is rescued from despair by Clarence, an angel who is trying to get his wings. Clarence has been dead a hundred years or so -- he used to be an ordinary man on this earth. And, as everyone who has watched the movie knows, "Every time a bell rings, an angel gets his wings."

This story is silly. Everyone knows that when you die you go to Heaven, where Saint Peter will fit you with a pair of wings and a harp during your first day. Right? Wrong.

While this belief is very common in Hollywood movies, TV shows, and Madison Avenue commercials, it has no Biblical basis and is not believed by Evangelical Christians.

You will never become an angel. Your fate can be so much better. As Paul said in his letter to the

Christians who die become Angels.

Colossians (2:18) "Let no one cheat you of your reward, taking delight in false humility and worship of angels..." What could be better than becoming an angel? We'll look into that later in this chapter.

However, angels are interesting to study. So, let's first examine what the Bible says about angels.

Angelic Appearances

In the Bible, man's first encounter with an angel is as Adam is leaving the Garden of Eden in Genesis 3:24. Angels and a flaming sword are placed to guard the entrance to the Garden to keep men from re-entering.

A second encounter was in Genesis 16, where Hagar, Abraham and Sarah's maid, encounters the "angel of the Lord" in the desert. He gives her a message and sends her back to her master.

Next, we see two men and the Lord visiting Abraham, on their way to destroy Sodom and Gomorrah in Chapter 18. Abraham is able to plead with the Lord to spare Sodom if he finds enough good men. In the passage in Chapter 19, the two angels visit Lot in Sodom, where we get a clue that the angels are strikingly good looking, for the Sodomites want to "know" them, an expression which means that they desire sexual intercourse with them. The angels blinded the men, and then destroyed the city. (It is interesting to note that the angels were sent to destroy the city -- here it does not say that God directly destroyed the city.)

Christians who die become Angels.

There are other appearances where the angel of the Lord talks to Hagar and Abraham at different times "from heaven".

In the Book of Daniel, we see some of the most impressive appearances of angels. One angel, who says his name is Gabriel, talks with Daniel about some dreams that Daniel is having. Then, in Chapter 10, Daniel has been praying for 3 weeks. An angel appears clothed in linen with a belt of gold. His face is like lightning and his eyes are like two fires. Interestingly, the first thing he does is apologize to Daniel for being delayed for the last three weeks because the "prince of the kingdom of Persia" delayed him. The angel explains that after he got help from "Michael, one of the chief princes", he was able to come to deliver his message to Daniel. A couple of chapters later, Michael is described as "the great prince that protects your people" (referring to the Jews.)

New Testament

In the New Testament, the angels get many assignments.

Before Christ's birth, the angel of the Lord talks with Zacharias, the father of John the Baptizer. Gabriel visits Mary, and Joseph also receives an angelic visit. And, of course, an angel announces Christ's Birth to the shepherds.

Later, an angel appears to Jesus in the Garden of Gethsemane to "strengthen Him". A few minutes later, Jesus points out that He could call upon more than "twelve legions" (roughly sixty thousand) of

Christians who die become Angels.

angels if he wanted to be rescued from the soldiers who were arresting Him. Peter is later released from prison by an angel.

In the Book of Revelation, angels are all over the place, blasting trumpets, destroying people, and generally having a grand time using their God-given powers.

Real Angels

But Evangelicals know that nowhere in the Bible do we see or hear about people being turned into angels. Instead, we see that angels have certain characteristics.

- They are created beings who have a very long life-span (probably immortal). We know this because Gabriel visited Daniel around 450 B.C., and then Mary around 4 B.C.
- There are more than sixty thousand angels.
- Mankind is created a little lower than the angels, but will move into a position higher than the angels.
- Angels are beautiful and wonderful to look upon. See Genesis, Daniel, and Revelation. Although they can fly, most don't have wings. They appear generally as beautiful men. Female angels are not mentioned except in Zechariah 4:9, where two women with wings carry away Wickedness.
- Angels bring you messages from God. Since angelic messages come from God, they should be carefully noted, since angels have a one hundred percent accuracy rate.

Christians who die become Angels.

- We are told that people may entertain angels unaware. Thus, they must sometimes appear as ordinary people.
- However, angels are also terrifying. Most of the time that an angel stops by for a chat, the first thing he has to say is "Don't be afraid!", because the person visited has fallen prostrate. Of course, since angels are sometimes used to nuke cities (see Sodom, etc.), a person visited by angels probably should show proper respect.
- Angels don't want to be worshipped. This is important. In the Book of Revelation, one specifically tells John to "worship only God".
- Cherubim and seraphim are types of created beings that may be angels or may be something altogether different. These creatures have wings.
- There are "good" angels and "bad" angels. Most theologians agree that the "princes" mentioned by the angel in Daniel 10, and by Paul in his writings, are powerful, high-ranking angels. Michael is the "prince" who watches over Israel. We also hear from Daniel's report that there is an antagonistic prince who controls Persia (today's Iran).
- It is generally thought by Evangelical Christians that Satan (Lucifer) was the most beautiful and powerful angel. He did not want to be a servant any longer, so he led a rebellion, was defeated, and took a third of the angels with him to Earth, where he has become the temporary ruler. He is also described as "the lord of the air". The "fallen

Christians who die become Angels.

angels" are sometimes known as "devils", a word which means "deceivers".
- Unlike what Hollywood says about devils, there is no biblical evidence that they are red and have pitchforks, tails, or horns, or that they live eternally tormenting souls in a flaming Hell. Instead, they are fallen angels, and probably are difficult to distinguish from "good" angels. Satan is said in the Bible to wander the earth looking whom he might devour. He is also constantly visiting God in Heaven where he accuses men of sin.

So What is the Purpose of Angels?

In essence, angels are the servants in God's household, while we are the children of God. While children are young, the servants protect them, advise them, and send them messages from the head of the household. Later, though, the mature children, who are the heirs of the household, give orders to the same servants.

> What is man that You are mindful of him,
> And the son of man that You visit him?
> For You have made him a little lower than the angels,
> And You have crowned him with glory and honor.

The above is from Psalm 8:4-5. This is also quoted in Hebrews 2:5-9 with a detailed argument about the position of angels, Jesus, and men.

Christians who die become Angels.

Discussion Questions

1. Discuss Hebrews 2:5-9.

2. Look in a bible with a concordance or index. Look up "angels" and follow as many references as possible. What do you discover?

3. Read Daniel Chapter 10. How does this angel differ from common Hollywood presentations of angels?

What Really Happens to Dead Christians?

If you don't become an angel, then what really happens to you when you die?

Some of the details are fuzzy and *are disputed* by different groups, but most Evangelical Christians believe something close to the following, although the timing of events is subject to considerable debate:

1. You "die". In general, it appears that most Christians sleep in death until the events of the Second Coming begin. (I Thessalonians

Christians who die become Angels.

4:13) You are probably *not* sent directly to heaven where you watch all the comings and goings of your friends and children. However, some Christian groups believe that you *do* go straight to Heaven on the strength of a few specific passages. Others argue that Heaven and Hell operate outside the timeline of our earth, and thus it is impossible to relate events in Heaven and Hell in strict time sequence compared to this world. In any event, Christians believe that the next few steps are as follows:

2. At the last trumpet, the dead will be raised in a new immortal, incorruptible body. (I Corinthians 15:51)
3. Christ pulls aside those who have accepted Him as Lord. These people are placed in another area separate from the rest. (This may occur immediately after you die -- or it may not happen for another few hundred years. It's really not that important how long after your death it occurs. It will be the next event that happens that you will be conscious of.) To see what happens to believers, jump to point 8.

One thing that is clear is that, contrary to Hollywood and a thousand jokes, you will not be standing in front of the pearly gates awaiting a question-and-answer session with Saint Peter. The reality is much more spectacular -- you will see the LORD himself.

4. All that remain go before the judgment seat of Father God. This is a grim procession.

Christians who die become Angels.

5. Non-Christians are judged according to their earthly sins. Satan is the prosecutor. God the Father is the Judge. A trial is held. The charge is violation of God's Law. Those who do not follow Jesus must mount a defense:
    - "You didn't warn me." - You were warned by all of the Christians in the world. This very book you are reading is warning you again.
    - "I didn't commit any crime." - You broke every commandment -- even one is enough for a conviction.
    - "I didn't believe you existed." - Yes, you did. But you knew that acknowledging that would be inconvenient. So you chose to ignore Him.
    - "I don't want to live under your authority." - That's fine. He will grant you that wish. You can fight out a government with all the others who didn't want to live under His authority. Machiavelli, Hitler, Napoleon, Stalin, Pol Pot, Chairman and Madam Mao, Nero, Genghis Khan, and many others will be forming that government. You see, God will ultimately respect your wishes.

The only defense is to be on the Son's list. And now it is too late. All who are judged are convicted and are sent "into the outer darkness". (Matthew 8:11-12)

The "outer darkness" was a reference to the situation in 1st Century Palestine. In those days, lighting was very expensive. If a wedding party were to be held, everyone in the village would bring a candle or oil lamp to the village center or the house where the party was to be held. The party would run late. However, there were no streetlights or front porch lights. When you left the party, it was *dark*! This was the outer darkness.

In essence, God will say to the unbelievers, "You didn't want to follow my rules in your life. That's ok. Now, you can live without me in this life. See if you can make it outside the party -- alone in the dark with the others that rejected me." (Some believe that you will truly be alone.)

6. Later, as part of the final cleanup, unbelievers will be tossed into the eternal lake of fire described in Revelation 20:15. Satan and the Antichrist will meet them there. There is some question as to whether unbelievers will simply vanish in a wisp of smoke or will be tormented forever, as are the definite fates of Satan, the Antichrist, and the beast of Revelation.

7. Is a literal Hell real? Christians split on this issue. Some argue that it is a figurative concept. Others argue that the lake of fire is another name for Hell. Please keep in mind that a significant portion of the concept that

Christians who die become Angels.

we hold of Hell (Devil with pitchfork, etc.) is a medieval creation and not found in the Bible.

The vast majority (over 90 percent) of Evangelical Christians affirm that there is indeed a literal Hell because it is mentioned by Christ Himself several times. But just what that means is unclear. Regardless of the answer, part of the reality is clear – you will be required to live without God's help after your normal death if you do not agree to follow Christ.

8. Meanwhile, Christ holds His own judgment for the purpose of distributing rewards and positions to His followers based upon their works on behalf of His Kingdom. This is a cause for great celebration for many. Notice that the works don't get you into Heaven -- but they are important to determine your position in the New Jerusalem. Christ cares that you spend time working for Him.

9. About this time is the Marriage Feast of Christ, a huge party held to reunite the Church with Christ.

10. After the rewards ceremony, we live on the new earth in the city of New Jerusalem ruled

Christians who die become Angels.

by Christ. Notice - we don't float in the clouds; we don't flit around. Instead, we live forever under Christ's Divine and Just Rule.

The New Jerusalem described in Revelation 21 is a huge city. It is a cube 1400 miles (2000 km) to a side. Allowing for 10 billion believers gives each believer over 2000 acres (about 900 hectares) of land and headspace of about 500 feet (160 meters) high. Note that this is the estimated space for each believer - not each family. That should be plenty of space for all the flowers, fruit trees, waterfalls, and patios that anyone could want, as well as enough time to do any gardening, reading, or inventing that anyone would like.

Isn't Hell Unfair?

Many non-Christians look at the concept of Hell and say, "I can't believe in a God that gives eternal punishment", or give some similar argument. Let's look at this idea for a minute or two.

Imagine that you have a rebellious teenage son or daughter. Further imagine that you repeatedly set a curfew for your teenager and repeatedly warn him about it. But your teenager insists that he or she is an adult and should be treated as one. If the teenager stays out late at night – past curfew – is it proper for the parent to lock the door at some time and require that teenager to find other lodgings after enough warnings?

Or, let's look at it another way. God is infinitely good. Part of that goodness is that He – unlike us –

Christians who die become Angels.

respects each person's right to make his or her own decisions. However, God – the Creator – did build the system a certain way. In the end, He lets a person make the decision to spend eternity with Him or not. He simply asks you to make that decision before your death. If you decide not to spend eternity with Him under His rules, then He allows that. He is quite gracious, actually. It is totally your choice.

Unfortunately, there are other people who want to make the rules for how people live under those circumstances, such as Hitler, Ted Bundy, Saddam Hussein, Stalin, and other people who chose not to live under God's rules. Hell does not need the Devil to be Hell. It only needs a collection of people who choose to make their own rules.

The real problem that many people have with the concept of Hell is that it requires them to accept that they don't control what will happen to them after death. Just as most people, I'd love to be able to decide that I can do whatever I want with no consequences. But the Universe exists with rules – and we don't control those rules. We are not in control of what happens to us. At least God has revealed to us the options.

Conclusions

The problem with Hollywood views of Heaven and the afterlife are that they lead to a series of mistaken ideas. When one believes that men and women will become flitting angels, it is easy to trivialize angels, devils, Heaven, and Hell -- or conversely, you can

Christians who die become Angels.

begin to worship angels and forget the One who made the angels. We can begin to believe that our actions in this life will make us a type of godling, like Hercules in Greek Mythology. And soon, we believe that ultimate lie, that being "better" than other people will "get us into Heaven".

Instead, Evangelical Christians cling to the basic concept that Christ died for our sins and only by acknowledging Him as our Lord will we gain access to an eternal, beautiful life.

Discussion Questions

1. Discuss your thoughts on the afterlife. Support them with Scripture.

2. What possible additional defenses can you think of? What do you suppose the prosecution will say to those defenses?

3. Some Christians argue that there is no need for Hell to have devils -- the inhabitants will create their own tortures without any outside help. Imagine a jail without any jailors -- just one big open cell. What do you think of this concept?

Christians who die become Angels.

4. What proportion of your normal day do you spend on Christ's payroll? How can you improve that?

Actions

1. Go to the Book of Daniel, Chapter 10 and draw or paint the angel described there.

2. If you are a believer, make a list of unbelievers you know. For one solid week, plan to mention Jesus to at least one person on the list each day. You don't have to give a detailed testimony. Just mention Jesus "in passing" to them. Later, write down their reactions -- and your reactions.

Christians who die become Angels.

Suggested Scripture Readings

- Psalms 9:17, 55:15, Proverbs 7:27, 23:14, 27:20, and Isaiah 14:9 are Old Testament references to Hell.

- Matthew 5:22, 18:9, 23:33, Luke 12:5, James 3:6 are New Testament references to Hell.

- Revelation 20:11 to the end refer to the Judgment and the events of the end of time.

Notes

1) *It's a Wonderful Life*, (Copyright 1947, DVD 2004 Lions Gate Home Entertainment ASIN B00062J00S)

Myth #7 - Christian Denominations Believe Radically Different Things.

> Now I plead with you, brethren, by the name of our Lord Jesus Christ, that you all speak the same thing, and that there be no divisions among you. I Corinthians 1:10

It is an article of faith among many ethnic Christians and others with little in-depth knowledge of Christianity that Christian denominations are radically different. And to the casual observer, there are great differences between the very formal services of Catholics or Anglicans, the high-energy services of some AME congregations, and the informal meetings of many independent groups. But these are all surface differences. Let's look at the reality.

Basis for Comparison

When we look at different Christian groups, we will find that there are five significant ways in which they differ from each other:

- Worship Style
- Baptism and Communion

Christians Denominations are Different.

- Social Beliefs
- Personal Background
- Theology

Worship Style – The Visible Difference

Christian groups differ most from each other in worship style, which is probably the least important but most visible way of understanding a group. I use the word "style" intentionally, for worship styles go in and out of fashion in the same way that hemlines go up and down. Certain things are common to almost all groups. With few exceptions, Christians, (including Evangelical Christians) do the following things in worship:

- Pray
- Read from the Bible
- Sing songs of praise
- Take Communion
- Give gifts to the church
- Listen to a lesson

The order varies from congregation to congregation. In some groups, there is a rigid order and prescribed words. In other groups, every service is new and different.

Evangelical Christians cannot be pigeonholed into a single worship style, since this is not a core part of what distinguishes Evangelicals. Evangelical Churches may use any of the styles mentioned in this section or even create new styles or blends of styles of worship.

Christians Denominations are Different.

This diversity is because Evangelicals understand that worship is an act that can occur in many different ways. Evangelical Worship services usually have a four-fold purpose.

- First, there is the act of paying proper respect and thankfulness to God for who He is and His Grace.

- Second, there is the act of teaching about God to both Christians and seekers.

- Third, there is the opportunity for new Christians to join the church.

- Fourth, there is the opportunity for fellowship between the Christians.

Currently, there are several principle worship styles found in the US.

Liturgical High Church Worship

This style is most commonly found in the Catholic, Anglican (Episcopalian), and Eastern Orthodox churches. In addition, many Methodist, Lutheran, and Presbyterian congregations use this style. It has its roots in the formal worship of the late Middle Ages used in many large cathedrals of Europe. About 10 percent of Evangelical Christian congregations use this style of worship.

Liturgical worship refers to the following of a formal plan of worship. The regular Sunday order of worship is rigid. The Biblical readings are planned on a three or five year rotation, and the

Christians Denominations are Different.

lesson revolves around those readings. Prayers are also largely formal and pre-planned. Even the songs may be planned far in advance of the actual service. At least that is what most people think.

In reality, many liturgical plans have considerable flexibility. "Pick two readings from these five" is how one plan works. The lesson often reflects the needs of the congregation with only a slight tie-in to the reading. It all depends upon the personal style of the priest or pastor who leads the worship.

High Church is the name given to a style of worship where most or all of the participants wear robes, there is considerable use of gold and silver, classical music is usually played by professional musicians and sung by an excellent large choir. Beautiful paintings and sculptures adore the very large marble church or cathedral with high ceilings (hence the name, "high church") that is lit through stained glass windows. Everything impresses the attendee with God's wealth and power. Once again, that is the stereotype, and is the reality in a very few churches.

In many of these churches, the robes are about 10 years old, the "golden" vessels are brass, the organist makes most of her living teaching elementary students, and the choir is usually off-key. But they are trying to the best of their ability and funds to make the service uplifting.

High Church also has a theological meaning we will talk about later.

Christians Denominations are Different.

Advantages Claimed

Proponents of the Liturgical High Church Worship talk of three advantages. First, the entire Gospel story gets told to regular attendees every few years, whereas a less planned system may result in an inappropriate concentration upon certain aspects of the Bible. Second, the general effect of the traditional words and music used in the liturgy is to tie the listener to the other Christians throughout the previous centuries who listened to and recited those same words, creating an emotional feeling of tradition which can be overpowering. Finally, the architecture, decor, robes, acoustics, and light all combine to create a feeling of awe and reverence. High Church just says "You are close to God here."

Disadvantages Claimed

Many opponents of Liturgical High Church Worship do not feel comfortable in such a church. If you do not understand the rituals, when to sit, when to stand, and when to kneel, it can be disturbing. Thus, opponents claim that such churches are intimidating and can repel the non-Christian. Opponents also claim that the general formal nature of the service keeps the attendees from becoming friendly with one another. Finally, they claim that the rigid structure keeps the Holy Spirit from working in the service and in the development of the congregation. They claim that it is necessary for the pastor to be free to select which lessons the congregation that week needs.

Christians Denominations are Different.

Traditional American Middle Church

Many of the Disciples of Christ, independent Evangelical Churches, Baptists, Methodists, Churches of Christ, Presbyterians, and many smaller groups prefer this worship. This is the style used by most older Evangelical Christian congregations, as well as many newer ones.

This form of worship follows a regular Sunday worship order that is relatively rigid. For example, a particular church may use the following program Sunday after Sunday:

1. Hymn
2. Invocation prayer
3. Announcements
4. Hymn
5. Reading from the Bible
6. Hymn - Meanwhile, Children dismissed to Children's Church
7. Special music
8. Sermon
9. Offering
10. Pastoral Prayer
11. Hymn
12. Benediction Prayer

However, depending upon the style of the pastor, the reading and sermon may be prepared on Saturday afternoon -- or a year in advance. The pastor probably wears a business suit most Sundays and may wear robes occasionally.

Christians Denominations are Different.

In most of these groups, the music selected is either a hymn, which is a solemn, traditional song designed for congregational singing, most of which were written between 1500 and 1940, or is a Gospel tune, a more upbeat tune originally developed for a small group between 1920 and the present, which has been adapted to congregational singing. (There are two distinctly different Gospel song traditions - Southern Country Gospel and Soul Gospel.) In some groups, there is a movement toward easy-listening contemporary Christians music from the 1980's and 1990's. Most groups support the music with organ, piano, or both. A choir is usually present.

The church is usually a wooden or brick building without much decoration. In many groups, members of the congregation will participate in the service by giving prayers or performing readings. The sermon usually is focused upon the needs of the local congregation and often forms a series of lessons on a particular book of the Bible, a particular subject such as "prayer", or the life of a particular Biblical person such as Elijah. The congregation usually is quiet during the service -- talking by other than the worship leaders is discouraged.

Contemporary Folk-Style American Informal Worship

Beginning in the 1960's, a new style of worship began to spread in the USA. The goal was an informal worship style that would be less intimidating to the visitor and bring more people into direct worship. Less spectators -- more participants is the goal of this worship style. In this version, the worship service often begins with a skit -- a short 2 or 3-minute play that sets the tone for the service. Singing is by the congregation with several leaders who comprise a "praise team". One or more acoustic guitars often accompany songs. This is very common in newer Evangelical Christian congregations.

The meeting place may be a traditional church building, or it may be a meeting room rented or borrowed for the purpose. In many of these groups, the group sits in a circle instead of the more traditional auditorium-style seating. One person may act as moderator of the group, or the group may worship in a loose flow as five or even ten members present a devotional reading, a song, a talk, a skit, a dance, or a piece of artwork. Still, the traditional elements of biblical reading, songs, and lesson are still covered.

In this type of worship many people will pray during the service -- it is not usually limited to one or two leaders.

This type of worship is commonly practiced among teen-age and college age groups, as well as among some older groups descended from college study groups.

Contemporary Rock Charismatic Worship

At many Charismatic (Full-Gospel) or Pentecostal churches, the worship emphasis is on developing an emotional service that appeals to many younger Christians. This worship style includes electric guitar, keyboard, drums, and bass guitar as

Christians Denominations are Different.

instrumental accompaniment. A praise team of vocalists sings with the band, which is often professional quality. The order of worship is often very similar to the traditional American church style listed above, with a couple of additions to worship. (This Christian rock music and praise band style is present in many Evangelical Christian congregations. Some will identify themselves as Charismatic, while others will identify themselves as non-Charismatic.)

Charismatic churches practice two gifts during their services which most traditional churches don't. A key part of the services are the use of speaking in tongues and the gift of prophecy.

Speaking in tongues is discussed in Acts Chapter 2. At the Pentecost Festival, the Holy Spirit came into a prayer service that the early Christians were holding. People were gathered from around the Roman world that spoke many different languages. People began speaking to each other in languages that they did not know -- but those who heard understood. This "gift of tongues" led many to believe.

Pentecostal churches often have members who will speak in tongues during the service. Sometimes, the speaking in tongues is clearly intended for a foreign visitor. More often, the speech appears to an onlooker to be babbling. Sometimes, there is a person present who can interpret the babbling into a useful, legitimate message. Other times, the speech appears to be an ecstatic utterance -- someone who has become caught up in the emotion of the

Christians Denominations are Different.

moment. Is the gift of tongues real? Most Mature Christians will say: "sometimes".

The other part of a Pentecostal service will be prophecy. Someone will claim to have a message from God. He or she will give the message. Sometimes the message is relatively bland -- other times, the message will be a personal message that will knock the socks off of a visitor. Is the gift of prophecy real? Most Mature Christians will say: "sometimes".

The result of the music, tongues, and prophecy is that Charismatic church services are a highly charged, emotional affair. They are very different from most traditional services on the surface -- but the basic beliefs and practices underlying these churches differ only in details from those of other Christian churches.

Black Churches

This is another case where Hollywood has made a stereotype. Black churches vary across the country in their style of worship, from the high-energy services seen in the Whitney Houston movie *The Preacher's Wife* and in *The Blues Brothers* to quiet study groups where a dozen men quietly worship through Bible study.

Other Groups and Practices

There are other practices that have made their way into small groups of churches. Snake handling is practiced by perhaps a dozen tiny churches. These churches take their cue from a verse that says that

Christians Denominations are Different.

men will be able to handle snakes without danger from their venom.

A larger number of churches practice foot washing as a symbolic ritual of servanthood and humbleness. One who is willing to wash the feet of another is truly humble.

Prayer by the congregation is common in many smaller churches, where a leader starts a prayer and others add to the prayer. After anyone who wants to pray has prayed, a leader will close the prayer.

Many congregations of the Church of Christ adhere strictly to a policy of singing without instrumental accompaniment. At the other extreme are some large congregations that have complete orchestras every Sunday morning. I've also known of "Country and Western" churches that use steel guitar, mandolin, banjo, and guitar for accompaniment. Many Assemblies of God have professional level rock bands, while the best-trained classical organists can often be found at a local Episcopal Church. It all depends upon the local congregation and their "style".

The basic worship styles that I've detailed above are not hard and fast categories. For example, I know of one church that has four Sunday services: The 8:00 and 11:30 services use traditional hymns, piano, and organ. The 10:00 service uses a skit, praise band, and contemporary Christian Rock music. Finally, the 6:30 PM service is almost totally devoted to Southern Gospel songs accompanied by honky-tonk piano.

Christians Denominations are Different.

Another church I know tries to use a contemporary tune each week (using acoustic guitar) followed by two or three traditional hymns using piano and organ. Around Christmas, they will probably change to classical pieces from Handel's Messiah with piano, organ, and strings.

A third church that I know uses a formal liturgical service, but starts with a contemporary Christian song played from a CD over the sound system. The service is an interesting combination of the ancient and the modern.

The bottom line is that worship styles change with the preferences and needs of the church leadership and congregation. You should look for a church where you feel comfortable -- but don't expect perfection as long as humans run the church.

Discussion Questions

1. What types of music do you prefer in church? Why?

2. What type of church service are you most familiar with?

3. Which service do you think is most effective at bringing new visitors into the church?

Christians Denominations are Different.

Baptism – How to Join the Church

Baptism is an event practiced by all Christian groups. In most groups, it is the ceremony by which a new Christian officially joins the church. The precise details of the method, timing, and meaning of Baptism differ between groups, but all groups baptize.

History

The first overt mention of baptism as a rite is mentioned in the Gospel of Luke. John the Baptist (or as more correctly translated John the Baptizer) was the older first cousin of Jesus. He had become known for taking people, asking them to confess and repent of their sins, and then putting them under water to "baptize" them. The baptism represented a cleansing of sin, the death of an old life, and rebirth into a new life. John the Baptizer baptized Jesus. Later, in the book of Acts, we see the disciples baptizing many people.

The word "baptize" comes from a Greek word which means "to dye" in the sense of coloring fabric. There were two methods of coloring cloth which the word covered. First, you could take the cloth and immerse it in a barrel of dye. Secondly, you could pour the dye on the cloth. Both methods were covered by the word – according to one group of Greek scholars. Another group of Greek scholars maintain that only immersion is covered by the word. And this has led to many disputes between churches over the acceptable methods of baptism.

Christians Denominations are Different.

Major American Denominations

Name	Members	Congregations
Catholic	62 M	19,000
Southern Baptist	16 M	41,000
7th Day Adventist	12 M	51,000
United Methodist	8.2 M	24,000
Church of God	5.5 M	29,000
ELCA (Lutheran)	3.8 M	9,300
National Baptist	3.5 M	2,500
Assemblies of God	2.6 M	12,000
Presbyterian	2.5 M	11,000
Progressive Baptist	2.5 M	2,000
Lutheran (Missouri Synod)	1.9 M	5,200
African Methodist Episcopal	1.8 M	7,700
Episcopal	1.8 M	7,300
Churches of Christ	1.5 M	15,000
American Baptist	1.5 M	5,800
Greek Orthodox	1.5 M	500
United Churches of Christ	1.3 M	5,800
Christian Church	1.0 M	5,500
Primitive Baptist	1.0 M	1,500
Orthodox Church	1.0 M	725

(Source: Compiled from *The Complete Guide to Christian Denominations*, Ron Rhodes, Harvest House Publishers, 2005 ISBN 0-7369-1289-4)

Method

Evangelical Christians traditionally have *preferred* total immersion baptism. In this method, a candidate stands beside the Christian believer performing the baptism. The candidate may be

Christians Denominations are Different.

asked to answer a few questions or say a few words, and then the baptizer leans the candidate backwards under the water, says a few words, and lifts the candidate out of the water. This is often done in a river or stream, but many churches have constructed elaborate pools inside their sanctuaries for this purpose. It is commonly thought that the very best place to be baptized is in the Jordan River, but this is simply because of the historical nature of this. Many people (including your writer) have been baptized in backyard swimming pools. Others have been baptized in bathtubs.

Some groups insist that the only proper baptism is full immersion, with some groups even insisting that baptism must be conducted in a river or stream. However, other groups disagree.

In many areas, it was difficult or even deadly to find adequate clean water for a total immersion baptism. So, many groups adopted a method of putting water on the head of the candidate, by either sprinkling or pouring. Over time, this method became the standard method for these groups. The groups using sprinkling and pouring use three points to defend the practice. First, they point out the dual meaning of the Greek root word for baptism. Secondly, they point out that no method of baptism is clearly indicated in the Bible. Third, a first century Christian writing known as the *Didarche*, or *teaching*, says to preferably immerse, but to pour or sprinkle if necessary. These groups represent a very large proportion of Christianity, including many Methodists, Lutherans, Anglicans, and Catholics.

Christians Denominations are Different.

In most cases, words similar to the following are used:

> "(Candidate's name), since you have confessed your faith in Jesus Christ, I baptize you in the name of the Father, and of the Son, and of the Holy Spirit."

While it is most common for baptisms to be performed by a pastor, most Evangelical groups will agree that any baptized Christian can baptize another, since, according to the Book of Hebrews, we are all priests.

Purpose

Groups differ about the purpose of baptism. Some groups argue that it is necessary for salvation -- you are not going to Heaven without a baptism and your faith in Christ. Most groups, however, argue that baptism is a declaration to the world that you are a Christian, but it is not necessary for salvation. However, these groups also argue that you should get baptized as the appropriate manner to make that declaration.

Another point of dispute over meaning is whether or not a Christian sheds his sin nature when baptized. Most groups believe that this does not happen, although some argue that it does happen.

Many groups believe that the Holy Spirit enters into a person at the time of baptism, while others argue that this happens at the time of belief or requires a special ceremony.

Christians Denominations are Different.

One thing that is not in dispute among Evangelical Christians is whether or not baptism is sufficient to get you to Heaven. It is not. The act of baptism means nothing without your personal belief in the Lordship of Christ. You must have trusted in Jesus Christ as capable and worthy to be your Lord, or baptism has no value.

Symbolism

Baptism is filled with a variety of symbols. Full immersion baptism symbolizes dying and rising from the dead as a new, clean person. All baptisms symbolize the removal of sin and the cleansing of the soul. In many baptisms, the candidate wears a white robe to symbolize both the death shroud and the new, cleansed nature. The use of water for cleansing of sin dates back to Genesis and the Flood. Christ said, "I am the Living Water". Water also represents life in many places in the Bible.

Timing

The timing of baptism is another issue that is disputed between groups. The major older groups (Orthodox, Roman Catholic, Lutheran, Anglican, Presbyterian) believe that belief in Christ is an age-appropriate thing. These groups believe that a very young child can believe in Christ -- although he may not be able to express that belief in a coherent, rational way. Yet, many children know that Christ is good and will take care of them and somehow is involved in getting them to Heaven. An even younger child may have an even more elementary faith. Thus, these groups commonly baptize infant children of believing parents. When these children reach a maturing age of about eleven, the children undergo a confirmation ceremony where they take on the role of a Christian in their own name and of their own volition.

On the other hand, the groups that came from the Anabaptist movement of the Reformation (Baptists, Pentecostals, Mennonites, Amish, and many independent churches) believe that baptism is only something that a maturing or mature individual can undertake. They argue that infant baptism leads to a belief that baptism saves -- not belief. What does mature mean? We attended one church that had a minimum age of eleven. Another church we attended accepted younger children down to about age six who could express their belief in Christ well. Some other churches require that candidates be in their teens.

All groups regularly baptize older people who wish to be baptized. Some churches do this regularly in early January -- others baptize every few weeks. One church we attended had a policy that they would open up the church and baptize you at 3 AM on a Wednesday morning in the middle of an ice storm if you were ready to be baptized.

Knowledge

This is related to the age issue. Some groups require that a candidate for baptism have a detailed understanding of Christian belief, acquired through a class known as *catechism*. Other groups will baptize anyone who requests it, day or night, after a simple statement of faith such as "I believe that I am a sinner and want Jesus to be my Lord!".

Christians Denominations are Different.

Principles

As you can see, there is a substantial amount of disagreement over baptism. There is a principle of Biblical interpretation that is involved here. This principle is that when the Bible is vague about something, it is probably not very important to get it exactly right -- in fact, there may not be an exactly right way.

Biblically speaking, it is very clear that baptism is something that Christians should do. However, it is not true that there is a clearly defined method or meaning to baptism – the arguments between many very wise and well-educated men show this.

Therefore, the details of the baptism or its meaning are not that important -- but you should still get baptized because Christians get baptized. We may not agree about the why, the how, and the when, but we all agree that the ritual is something a Christian should do.

Sometimes it is simply necessary to show our obedience by doing something even though we do not understand it completely.

In the C.S. Lewis novel *That Hideous Strength*, a group of believers is asked to find a particular person one night. They spend the entire night on a futile quest for the person, never finding him, wandering across the field. They feel like they didn't accomplish anything, but what they did was show their obedience. Because of that, they accomplished much. Baptism is like that. It is truly

Christians Denominations are Different.

enough to know that Christians should get baptized, and thus we should do this.

A second principle involved here is that many disputes happen between Christian groups over hypothetical issues that are not relevant to the parties concerned. For example, what happens to unbaptized babies who die? Although this happens occasionally, it does not concern you about *your* baptism.

You are in control of *your* side of your relationship with God and you should get baptized if you have not already been baptized. If you *might* have been baptized, but you don't know, then get baptized. Nothing bad will happen and something good might happen.

Now, if you have an unbaptized child who cannot talk to you and discuss belief, then talk to your pastor. He will help you understand whether or not baptism is proper at this time.

Scripture Reference

Read Romans Chapter 14 to see the proper stance for a Christian to take on doctrinal disputes.

Discussion Questions

1. How were you baptized?

2. How much did you know about Christianity when you were baptized?

Christians Denominations are Different.

3. If you are not yet baptized, explain why.

Communion – The Lord's Supper

This is another of the rituals that differ in style from church to church. Communion -- also called the "Eucharist" or "Thanksgiving" -- is the ceremonial re-enactment of the last part of the Last Supper, which was the Passover Meal of Jewish tradition.

Jesus changed the traditional Jewish ceremony a bit when He broke matzo bread and gave it to the disciples, saying, "This is my body that you eat". Then, at the third cup of wine, he said to them "This is my blood that you drink". He commanded the disciples to always remember Him when they did these rituals. Communion is where Christians re-enact that ceremony.

In almost all Christian churches, Communion is celebrated. But there are substantial differences in that celebration.

Timing

Many churches have weekly Communion. Others, claiming that the performance of a ceremony too often trivializes it, celebrate Communion monthly, quarterly, or annually. But almost all churches perform the ceremony, and all claim that it is important.

Christians Denominations are Different.

Method

Methods also differ between churches. Many churches have the members visit the front alter rail, where the priest or pastor serves the bread and wine. Other churches pass the elements throughout the congregation. Some groups eat the bread as they receive it -- others eat and drink in unison. While most groups use wine, other groups use grape juice and still others use both, allowing the member to chose wine or grape juice.

The original meal was conducted sitting around a table, with the bread and wine being passed around. The bread was a matzo, a cracker-like piece of un-leavened (flat, non-rising, yeast-less) bread.

Today, many groups use Communion wafers. Others use broken matzo bread, and others use breadcrumbs.

Purpose

The purpose of Communion is disputed among Christians and is a major cause of the Protestant Reformation that occurred five hundred years ago.

The Roman Catholic and the Orthodox Churches believe that the purpose of the Eucharist is the renewing sacrifice of the body and blood of Christ again for our salvation. In the Mass, these groups believe that the bread and the wine actually become the body and blood of Christ, which is then sacrificed to God. This interpretation was rejected completely by the Evangelical, Reformed, and Baptist churches that came from the Reformation.

Christians Denominations are Different.

However, the new churches never were able to totally agree upon a purpose for Communion. The Lutheran and Anglican churches developed a view that the body and blood of Christ are symbolically present in the Communion elements and that the eating and drinking of the elements somehow strengthens us spiritually. In Communion, we also reaffirm our membership in the body of Christ, which is the church.

The Reformed and Baptist groups decided to emphasize more the idea of using the Communion ceremony to remember Christ's once-and-for-all sacrifice and to use the ceremony as an opportunity for reflection and reaffirmation of membership in the church.

Who can Partake?

There are three concepts that exist about who can take Communion.

- Many denominations hold that you must be a baptized or confirmed member of the denomination to take Communion.
- Other groups hold that you must be a baptized or confirmed member of the specific congregation.
- Many independent Evangelical Christian churches hold that any baptized Christian may take Communion with them.

Naturally, it is important that you understand the Communion rules of the local congregation before taking Communion.

Christians Denominations are Different.

Notice the common opinion about Communion. Where Baptism is in some measure a transitional ceremony whereby the participant joins the church, Communion is something that only Christians do.

Another subject of disagreement is the amount of knowledge and the age appropriate for first Communion. Some groups maintain you must first be baptized to take Communion. Others require a class before Communion. Still others have an open Communion, allowing anyone who is a believer to take.

For me, taking Communion was more of a decision point than my baptism. Our church served Communion monthly. Each month I would let the elements pass me, since I was not yet a believer. Finally, I remember the Sunday that I first took Communion. I was thirty-four years old. My wife was so-o-o-o excited!

As you can, Communion is another issue that has many opportunities for disagreement. However, there is no clear Scriptural guidance on many of these issues. About the only thing we can say for certain is that Communion is something that Christians do – and non-Christians shouldn't do.

When you take Communion, it is important to be reverent and reflect upon the various issues involved in Christ's death and resurrection. In essence, Christ said that He loved us so much that He was willing to have his body destroyed and his blood shed so that we might eat and drink and live. Communion is our remembrance of this.

Christians Denominations are Different.

However, Evangelicals do not get too attached to a single method of Communion. Although the Catholic Church requires a priest to perform the Eucharist, in many Evangelical Churches, a family can hold Communion around the dinner table. Keep the Purpose in mind, but don't worry so much about the style.

Discussion Questions

1. What methods of serving Communion have you seen?

2. What do you think of most when you take Communion?

3. When did you first take Communion?

Social Beliefs – Politics in the Church?

There are hosts of ways that churches disagree on social beliefs. The key reason for this is that social beliefs are generally questions about how Christians interact with and represent the greater society. Since the greater society is always changing, these issues are also changing.

An example is the question of proper dress. In the 1970's, a major source of debate in churches was the dress of women. Women's fashion had led

Christians Denominations are Different.

women to begin wearing slacks. Since this fashion change also coincided with the rise of the Women's Rights movement, it had political undertones, and led to major fights in many churches. Should women be allowed to wear slacks in church? Or simply should women wear slacks at all? Some denominations reacted against this fashion by developing dress codes for women, which often included long hair, dresses, and no makeup.

Another example from the same time was the wearing of long hair and beards by rebellious male students. This also became a political and religious issue, which led to debates within many churches about proper grooming standards for men and boys.

A third example is the ongoing debate over music styles used during worship. Some people were happy to see Christian themes appearing in rock-sounding music. Others were appalled. This issue still divides congregations. Different congregations favor different musical styles.

Congregations have settled other social issues in different ways.

Personal Background

Divorce has become epidemic in the last forty years. In the first half of the twentieth century, it was common to find congregations who rejected divorced people on the grounds that they were spiritually flawed in some way. However, as divorce has become more common, most congregations have many divorced members. Thus, most Evangelical congregations accept divorced

Christians Denominations are Different.

people today, although there are still some who consider them a source of danger. Many congregations accept divorced members, but may not allow them into leadership roles. Other congregations specifically hold recovery classes for divorced members to help them through the transition from married life.

There are other ways in which a member's personal background helps them be accepted or rejected in a church. Some of these ways include social status, income, race, nationality, language, marital status, dress, piercings, makeup, hairstyle, and behavior.

The key distinguishing feature that sets apart Evangelical Christians is a desire for everyone to know the Gospel and feel the love of Jesus. Thus, these churches have led the way in the integration of commonly rejected people into a dynamic, diverse congregation.

An upper-class church in Memphis we know is working to change their exclusiveness. They have intentionally started a free Sunday evening meal for the indigents in the neighborhood. A few of these people are now beginning to become regulars in the church, which is known for being primarily a richer congregation.

One of the other things that are beginning to change throughout Evangelical Christianity is the racial segregation that goes on during Sunday mornings. Whites go to white churches, blacks go to black churches, Asians go to Asian churches, and Hispanics go to Hispanic churches. But increasingly, churches are working to intentionally

Christians Denominations are Different.

integrate. Evangelical churches have recognized that we increasingly live in a diverse society, and accomplishing our churches' missions requires openness to all people.

Sometimes this change in attitude is caused by neighborhood changes when one group moves into the physical neighborhood of the church building while another group leaves. The predominately white congregation realizes that it needs to welcome new neighbors into the church if the congregation is to survive.

But there are other reasons, such as the situation with the Snellville, GA First Baptist Church. There, the congregation is dedicated to bring everyone in the community to church. The leadership realized that many Hispanic families were moving into the area and then established a Spanish language service expressly to attract those families to the church.

Just down the road in Between, GA, the traditionally white Praise Center Assemblies of God church found an aggressive black leader to head the Sunday school program. The church is now slowly integrating.

The church we attend is developing a ministry to international (mainly Chinese) students who attend the local college. We are working to bring them to church through outreach programs such as a Thanksgiving dinner and a Mentor Student program. In this program, initiated by the local college, families "adopt" an international student and involve them in family activities. The student is

Christians Denominations are Different.

loved by an American family, improves his English, and learns American culture, including our Christianity that underlies all of our culture.

At many more churches, the congregations are still segregated. In some cases this is by choice, but in many churches it is not the congregation that is making the choice. Rather, the visitors make it. I have observed two dynamic white churches in Georgia struggle to bring non-whites into the congregation with poor results - despite a conscious desire on the part of the church leadership to integrate. In general, there are three reasons:

- A few people in the congregation hold racist attitudes, and aren't welcoming to the visitors. This is no longer a major reason in most churches, however, since these people tend to be older attendees rather than leaders in the churches. Besides, this is a non-Christian attitude that is regularly taught against in almost all churches today.
- More commonly, many people in many dying congregations are not welcoming of *anyone*. Visitors who are not comfortable in the first place may perceive this attitude as coldness or hostility.
- Most importantly though, even in the most dynamic white congregations, is the lack of critical mass. Non-white visitors do not feel as comfortable in an all-white church as they do in a non-white church of their ethnic group or in a mixed group. Even a handful of outgoing non-whites in a church open up the church to full integration -- whereas a

completely white church finds it very difficult to attract non-whites.

This is the reason why the church in Between, GA was able to succeed. The white pastor recognized these issues several years ago. When a family of non-whites visited the church, he reached out to make extra sure that they felt welcome. When the strong black leader visited, the pastor made sure that the leadership of the church recognized the strength of the man and put him in a very visible position of church leadership. Critical mass had been achieved and the church began to integrate.

Other Social Segregation

Racial segregation is just one aspect of modern American church social segregation. All smaller churches struggle with social segregation in one way or another. A church may be known as a blue-collar or a white-collar church. It may be known as a place where the rich attend, or where the very poor attend. It may be a farmer's church, or it may be a college student church. One church we attended was jokingly referred to by its congregation as "The Church of the Holy Introvert" because the congregation was largely made up of doctors, engineers, accountants, and programmers.

Another congregation was 70 percent public school teachers. One church had a private school associated with it. Another was a church full of home schooling families. A third had never had any home-schooled families.

Christians Denominations are Different.

People simply attend churches where they feel welcome. And that is most likely a place where your friends attend. Guess what? Your friends are mostly people of your age and type of profession.

For example, until about 2003, a church we know had become an "old-persons" church. The average age was about 70 and there were very few -- if any -- children in church on a typical Sunday. Younger families were not coming to the church. It was ready to die as the older members died off. Younger families who visited also felt uncomfortable.

In our case, two families visited the church at about the same time. One family had moved into town and visited the church because the father's parents attended. They stayed for a while. Another family visited a few months later and found the other family in the pews. Because of the ages of the children, they became good friends quickly. Since both families had three young children in attendance, critical mass had been reached. Other young families were attracted to the church. But let me tell you about another couple of church-hunting experiences we had....

A Visit to a Small Church

One Sunday morning my family and I decided to visit a small church near where we lived in the suburbs of Atlanta. Our family at the time was fairly typical for many in the suburbs at the time. My wife and I owned and operated a small business with a good income; we had three children, ages 10, 6, and 4. We had a history of working in the church -

Christians Denominations are Different.

Saundra in the children's Sunday school program, myself in the choir, and both of us in adult mid-week bible study classes. Looking back, we had a lot to offer to a church - early-forties youth, work energy, and finances.

We dressed in our "visiting clothes", which meant that we assumed there would be a formal dress code at the new church. I wore a suit - Saundra wore a conservative dress - the children were also well dressed. Having scoped out the service schedule the night before on the church sign, we arrived 15 minutes early for Sunday School and piled out, Bibles in hand.

We knew the church was small by the size of the parking lot and the building; that was one of the things that appealed to us. Little did we know what would await us as we walked into the building.

We walked into the nearly empty 100-seat sanctuary. The decor was paneling, circa 1970 (This was 1999). A print of a rustic stream was located on the wall behind the pulpit. One man was working on the sound system as we entered. He ignored us and continued to work on the sound system as we looked at the missionaries listed on the wall. A few minutes later an older couple came in, nodded to us, and hurried to seats on the right side of the sanctuary. We sat down on the left side.

Shortly after, another few people drifted in and someone noticed we were new. This probably wasn't difficult, since total attendance that day, including our five, was only 21 men, women, and children. A minute later a man introduced himself

Christians Denominations are Different.

as the pastor and asked us a bit about ourselves. Finding out that I played the piano, he grew excited, since they had not had a pianist for a year. But it was 9:30 and time for Sunday school, so he excused himself and moved to the right side of the church - where everyone else was sitting. I noticed that Saundra and I were about 30 years younger than anyone else in the church.

The Sunday school leader passed out the lesson booklet -- it was the beginning of the quarter -- and then began to read the lesson word for word to us in a voice that can only be described as "droning". He made one comment that I remember: Where the Bible literally said that such-and-such a man became king of Israel "at the age of 12", he indicated that this could not be so, since "the years printed at the top of each page in [his] Bible show a span of 20 years between the two pages, so he must have been 20 years old when he became king."

Saundra later said that I looked like the Sunday morning comic character Bill the Cat from Bloom Country. (Bill looks like a cat that has been washed and then thrown into a clothes dryer.) But there was more to come....

As we sat in the next-to-back left row between Sunday school and the main service, a few more people arrived to bring the congregation up to the complete 21 people. We noticed that a large, frowning woman had arrived, bringing 3 young children and her husband with her. They sat down behind us. At least there was some balance to the seating arrangements now!

Christians Denominations are Different.

During the break, one nice elderly woman asked us our names and where we lived. We told her, but she didn't seem to know where this was, apparently since it was a subdivision only 10 years old located about 2 miles from the church.

After the invocation, the pastor introduced us and asked if I'd like to play the hymns for the service. I declined, since I had no idea what hymns were on tap, nor do I normally play unknown hymns correctly the first five times. He spent a couple of minutes setting up the karaoke system for the first hymn. After we sang that hymn, he commenced to have a short business meeting to discuss the building roof. When the service continued, I became aware of a hushed argument proceeding behind me. I tried to ignore it, but it continued. We finally reached the sermon. The children left with the nice elderly woman, and the pastor opened his Bible.

Now, I'm don't know about you, but sermons are a high point of a service for me. For many people, the sermon is the best way for God to say in blunt words "I'm talking to you!" The best sermons combine solid Biblical teaching with an emotional harpoon that makes the message stick. This morning, we would not get that type of sermon.

The pastor, God love him, was clearly trying but had little training. We had found out that he was a part-time pastor who was holding down a full-time job while trying to minister to the little congregation. His sermon droned on and on, rambling from point to point. It was during this time

Christians Denominations are Different.

that I became aware of the plumbing situation at the church.

It seems that the church toilet had a plumbing problem. This was something that I could not ignore, since the toilet was located just behind the sanctuary, and had a door that led directly into the back of the sanctuary. Over the last half hour, a nauseating odor began to drift into the back part of the left side of the church. I began to understand the reason that the older members were all located on the right side of the church. I looked at Saundra - she had an interesting green shade to her face.

After the service, our children were retrieved, we asked about mid-week services (there were none), and we left, with little further conversation. Although we had filled out a visitor's card, we never heard from them again.

We Visit the Cool Church

The next week, we decided to try the Cool Church in town. This church, we had noticed, was always under construction. The church, though looking like a classic old white steepled church, had received a recent facelift -- or maybe it was very new. We drove into one of the large, full parking lots. As we piled out of the van, we discovered a dilemma -- we didn't know which door to enter. I mentally flipped a coin, said in my best "Dad" voice -- "This way!", and we entered into the fashionably decorated back lobby *behind* the sanctuary.

We had timed things wrong, probably because there was no church sign announcing times of services.

Christians Denominations are Different.

Apparently, we had entered in that terrible 15 minutes before Sunday school lets out. We announced to a deacon-ly looking man that we were new, and where were the restrooms? He told us and scurried away. We kept the children quiet, visited the impeccably clean restrooms, and waited for people to greet us. No one did.

Saundra and I watched the ample crowd for a while and quickly discovered why the church was the Cool Church. Apparently all the "IN" teenagers from the town attended the church. The girls were all wearing their best mini-skirts, makeup, and jewelry. It looked like a fashion show from Rich's Department store! The teenage guys were dressed more modestly, but still looked like they were headed out on the town with a date. We watched this for about ten minutes. We still had not been greeted. I said to Saundra privately, "Do we want the boys to be around this much skin?" "No. That's exactly why we left the old church," she answered. "Then why are we standing here?" I asked her. "I don't know," she said. "Let's go," I announced. And we left.

Country Time

We drove a mile down the road. There was another church with a large parking lot. The old brick building had definitely been there a long time, as evidenced by the large cemetery across the street and the even larger oak trees growing around the building. The back of the building had been expanded in the 1960's, judging from the brick style. People were apparently leaving the first

Christians Denominations are Different.

service, while others were pulling into the lot for the second service. We decided to give it a try.

As we entered the lot, we followed the crowd to the door, where a heavy-set man introduced himself as "Lester, the Assistant Pastor". Lester took charge of us - "little one to the door on the right, your daughter into this room, and your oldest goes to Sunday School in the basement. Follow me to Will's class". We noticed that there were people of all ages, from infants through elderly. The teenagers were dressed modestly, but not Victorian -- comfortable blue jeans or slacks, mostly. Lester took us straight into a Sunday school class made up of a dozen or so married couples our age.

"Will" introduced himself to us immediately upon entering. We were asked to introduce ourselves, which Will followed by introducing everyone in the class to us. The class was composed of people from all walks of life, from literally a ditch digger to a schoolteacher to the owner of one of the largest pest control companies in Atlanta. By making a priority of introducing us around, Will subtly made us understand that people were more important here than the lesson of the day.

Will proceeded to run one of the most interesting classes I've been in. He was a member of the class, toward the older side of the group, and he operated on a question, feedback, and discussion basis. The topic was Daniel, and he liked to talk about Neb the Nose (The literal translation of Nebuchadnezzar.) The class ended with prayer for everyone's needs.

Christians Denominations are Different.

After the class, Will took charge of us and took us to the sanctuary, where he introduced us to about 10 other people. We sat down beside an elderly couple -- who immediately introduced themselves. The couple in front turned around and introduced themselves. The men across the aisle did likewise, as did the ladies behind us.

The service began, with a singing of "When We All get to Heaven", led by the very young Music Minister. After the invocation, the Senior Pastor stood up and said, "Wasn't that a great song! Let's sing the chorus again!" and proceed to lead the chorus himself.

Don, the Senior Pastor, later gave one of the tightest sermons on "Salt of the Earth" that I've ever heard. On the way out, he greeted us and talked with us a couple of minutes. On Tuesday, he showed up at our office and talked with us for about an hour, inviting us to "Family Night" on Wednesday evening, where we shared a great meal, followed by a great Bible study.

Making the Decision

Now which church do you think we attended until we left Atlanta? All three of the churches were Evangelical Churches. But the Country Church was where we went. And the reason was simple -- we felt welcome and comfortable there. But many things were involved in making us feel welcome and comfortable.

In our opinion, there are three key things that are important in determining a church:

Christians Denominations are Different.

- Warm atmosphere. Are the people friendly? A proper church is welcoming to newcomers. Churches aren't simply places you attend on Sundays. In the Evangelical Christian concept, church is a place where you can make lifelong friends. It is a place where you will be comfortable with your family because there are other people there whom you trust and love -- and who love you.

  A church where newcomers are not welcomed is a dying church. Look elsewhere.

- Good teaching. Evangelical Christians believe that a key role of the local church is teaching. And the teaching should be soundly based on the Bible. If your church quotes twentieth century leaders more than the Bible, then the teaching is suspect. If you feel paranoia, isolation, or fear in the church's teachings, then the teaching is suspect, for Christianity is strong and outgoing. Damaging cults fear to face the world. Christianity does not. Oh yes, there are dangers in the world. But Christ is strong enough to protect the wise man who meets his neighbors in friendly discourse.

  Beware in particular of groups that claim a value other than Christ as a god. Some groups worship Tolerance; Others worship the Bible rather than its Author; Others worship a set of behaviors as their god. All of these groups miss the real freedom and joy of worshipping Christ. Look elsewhere if the teaching is poor or not Biblically based.

- The third determinate of a good Evangelical Christian church is a sense of outward mission. The pastor should be able to describe what makes his church special. After visiting a few times, you should be able to describe what the church stands for. For example, is the purpose of the church to bring local people to Christ? Or to support foreign missionaries? Or to help suburban families? It doesn't matter much what the mission is, as long as it spreads the Word and Love of Christ in some way it will fit the concept of being an Evangelical Christian church.

On the other hand, I have seen a church that had the purpose of providing the pastor with a living. I've seen churches that were more concerned with "developing diversity" than in saving souls. And I've seen churches that had become a group of people more concerned with church politics than any sort of outward-focused mission. These churches may have purposes -- but they are not God's purposes. These churches are dead or dying. Look elsewhere, for they do not live up to the ideals of the Evangelical movement or to Christ's commands.

Christians Denominations are Different.

> **The Great Commission**
>
> In the 28th Chapter of Matthew, Jesus gives one last command, which Evangelical Christians call "The Great Commission".
>
> *Go, therefore, and make disciples of all the nations, baptizing them in the name of the Father and of the Son and of the Holy Spirit, teaching them to observe all things that I have commanded you.*
>
> The Great Commission is the driving force behind most of Evangelical Christianity. Not only are we to learn about Jesus, God, Holy Spirit, and improve our own behavior and thoughts, but also we are to actively spread these teachings. How? Not by the sword, as some have done in the name of religion, but by teaching the Truth.

The Pastor Effect

When interviewing a church, keep one thing in mind. As he becomes established, a church will take on the personality of the pastor. If the pastor is an introverted, thoughtful, and deep man, his sermons will reflect this and lead the congregation down that road. This has certain advantages -- and disadvantages.

If your pastor is an exuberant extrovert who could sell used cars with ease, the congregation will become outgoing and boisterous also. This also has certain advantages -- and disadvantages.

Christians Denominations are Different.

There are many, many ways that a pastor can lead a successful church. However, if your pastor is a fearful man who is suspicious of newcomers, the congregation will also become suspicious. Interview the pastor if possible. (If you can't meet with the pastor, that will also tell you something about him and his church.) These comments apply equally well to possible media interviews as well as to interviews you may hold for the purpose of understanding a church you are considering attending.

Theology

In English-speaking countries, there are a handful of major theological groups. These groups represent different ways of interpreting the information found in the Bible and in church tradition. Each theological group has a distinctive approach to understanding God, Christ, the Holy Spirit, and Their interaction with mankind, as well as our roles in the Universe. Some of these Theologies are recognized as Christian -- others are seen as non-Christian.

Catholic

I put Catholic Theology first because it is the largest of the groups. This group also includes some of the Anglican/Episcopalian groups with very minor disagreements. There are several major disagreements between Catholics and the majority of other Christian groups, including Evangelical Christians.

Christians Denominations are Different.

- First, there is the issue of Authority. Catholics believe in the Authority of Scripture and of church tradition, especially as given by papal decree. Most Evangelical Christians believe that Scriptural authority overrides that of church tradition. Catholics respond by saying that many people have created cults by mis-reading the Scriptures. The Thirty Years War and another hundred years of minor wars were fought over this issue five hundred years ago.

- Secondly, there is the issue of the importance of Mary, the mother of Jesus. Most Catholics revere Mary as the Mother of God. Catholic doctrine maintains that Mary was a perpetual virgin, and was sinless herself.

  Most Evangelical Christians disagree and believe that Mary was simply a good woman, chosen by God simply because she was willing to do what God asked. Most Evangelical Christians believe that Mary gets far more respect and even worship by Catholics than she deserves. Many Non-Catholics despise Catholics for "Mary-worship". Catholics respond that they do not worship Mary, but only treat her with the respect that she deserves.

- Catholics believe that there is a need for a priest to help man come to God. This is reflected in the Catholic interpretation of the

Christians Denominations are Different.

various ceremonies such as Baptism, Confirmation, Communion, Marriage, and Last Rites.

Most Evangelical Christians believe that all believers belong to the priesthood and can directly come to God, with no intercessor needed other than Jesus Christ. Catholics also believe that the priesthood can remove a man from fellowship with God through the act of excommunication. Evangelical Christians believe that the issue is between the man and God directly, and no other man can interfere.

- In the same way, Catholics believe that praying to Mary, or one of the canonized Saints is perhaps more useful than praying directly to God. It is believed that the Saint, who is seen to be in the presence of God, will ask favors on the believer's behalf. Evangelical Christians believe that a person should direct his prayers directly to God, needing no other justification than the sacrificial death of Jesus on his behalf.

- Finally, Catholics believe in the special position of the Pope as the "Viceroy of Christ". Evangelical Christians do not believe in a special position for the Pope, other than as a respected Christian. Anglicans and Episcopalians simply

Christians Denominations are Different.

> substitute the special position of the Archbishop of Canterbury for the position of the Pope.

Many Non-Catholics – particularly Fundamentalists - hold a special prejudice against Catholics. This is largely a leftover from the wars of five hundred years ago, but has been kept alive by the identification of the Catholic Church with several evil characters in the Book of Revelation by Seventh Day Adventists. Bob Jones University also continued anti-Catholic teaching in the twentieth century. I have even heard an otherwise mature pastor talk about "Christians and Catholics".

Most Evangelical Christians disagree. To Evangelicals, such hatred of brother Christians is not...well...Christian. Let's take a good look at this point.

A key point of Non-Catholic belief is that a priest is not necessary for salvation. Instead, belief in the Deityhood of Christ and acceptance of his rule over your life are the key issues. By these very measures, millions of Catholics are saved. Using these Non-Catholic arguments, I believe that it is fair to say that the following represents Evangelical belief:

> It may be more difficult to come to the proper relationship with Christ while attending Catholic services, but it is much easier to come to that relationship than if you do not attend any Christian services.

Christians Denominations are Different.

It is not fair to say that Catholics are non-Christians. The extra baggage of Catholic concepts of Purgatory, of the Immaculate Conception, and of canonization may be distractions to the Gospel message, but they are not denials of that message.

High Church versus Low Church

A key difference between most Evangelicals and other groups, including Catholics and "mainstream" denominations, is in the understanding of the role of the Church.

In the section on worship styles, we briefly discussed high-church worship style and mentioned that there is a theological difference between high church and low church, as well as a difference in worship styles. Let's look at that briefly, since it is a key to understanding Evangelicals.

Most Evangelicals – and let me emphasize that this applies to *most*, not *all* - have a low-church concept. The difference is as follows:

In the high church, the Church is thought of as the official organization of priests, ministers, pastors, bishops, friars, monks, nuns, and other full-time professionals that have given their lives to the Gospel. The Congregation is something distinct from this organization. The ministry is seen and talked about as "a Higher Calling", and those who are involved are commonly "ordained", or set apart through a special ceremony, to perform God's work. Only the ordained can perform certain functions.

Christians Denominations are Different.

In a low church, the Church is thought of as including the ministers and pastors, as well as the congregation. All believing Christians are part of the Church. And the minister or pastor is simply the guy who is paid to make sure the sermons get preached and people are baptized. Yet, in the low church understanding, all members of the Church are fully capable of performing all the functions of the Church, including evangelism, preaching, teaching, baptizing, and other functions, if they have the appropriate gifts.

Now, as with everything, this is more a continuum than two discrete camps. Some denominations believe in the low-church concept theoretically, but still ordain their full-time, trained ministers and the average congregational member does little. Other groups, even Catholic churches, are increasingly using "lay", or non-ordained, leaders in more and more roles. But there is a distinct difference in outlook.

Evangelical Christians are strongly affected by the low church concept. And that is a key theological idea that leads to a cultural difference. A Catholic who believes that saving the lost is the job of the priest is unlikely to do more than introduce a hurting person to the priest. An Evangelical Christian who believes that saving the lost is the job of every member of the church will likely learn detailed biblical knowledge so that he can answer questions from his seeker friends. And the Evangelical will be more likely to bring the subject around to Jesus and God when talking to a hurting friend.

Christians Denominations are Different.

Many times, I have been asked if I was a minister because of my knowledge and conversation. I have answered, "No, it is simply that my church believes that helping people to understand about Jesus is everyone's job. And yes, I guess that makes everyone at my church a minister."

If your church is not growing, it may be because the church has a high church outlook on this point. Is it the job of the minister to talk about Jesus? Or does your church believe that it is everyone's job? This simple point makes a tremendous difference in the vitality of a church.

Evangelical and Reformed Theology

Evangelicals and Reformers are a large group of Christians, including many Lutherans, Anglicans, Presbyterians, Methodists, Baptists, and Pentecostals. These groups agree on the major points I've outlined in this book. Dallas Theological Seminary (www.dts.edu) is one of the leading proponents of Evangelical and Reformed Theology today. Evangelicals represent over 80 percent of non-Catholic Christians. (The word "Evangelical" and the word "Reformed" often have overlapped in their meaning, but are slightly different, with true Evangelicals following Martin Luther's teachings more and Reformed churches accepting some of John Calvin's teachings. These differences are relatively minor for most purposes except to a relatively advanced student.) As a practical matter, other than a very strict definition of theology, "Evangelical" and "Reformed" can be used interchangeably.

Christians Denominations are Different.

Fundamentalist Theology

Three major points distinguish fundamentalism:

- A pronounced emphasis on a literal interpretation of the Bible, particularly the first few chapters of Genesis and an aversion to modern science.

- A tendency toward maintaining a congregation that is separate from the world and avoids interaction with more liberal congregations.

- A worldview that equates liberal theology with Communism and the gradual encroachment of satanic values upon society as a whole. Hence, Fundamentalists tend to be very conservative in their politics.

In *most* ways, Fundamentalists agree with Evangelical Theology. Fundamentalists have no disagreements with Evangelicals about the nature of God, of Christ, or the Holy Spirit.

However, Fundamentalists historically have focused upon the literal inerrancy of Scripture. Fundamentalists have a strict look at the reading of the Bible. For historical reasons, the evolution/creationism debate is of particular emphasis for fundamentalists, peaking in the Scope's "Monkey Trial".

Fundamentalists are found in many Baptist or Bible churches, as well as in many small groups throughout the world. Bryan College

Christians Denominations are Different.

(www.bryan.edu) in Dayton, TN and Bob Jones University (www.bju.edu) in Greenville, SC are the leading founts of Fundamentalist thinking today.

Be careful here -- Christian Fundamentalism is not nearly as widespread as the TV News would have you believe, since many people confuse conservative Evangelicals with Fundamentalists. However, Fundamentalist congregations are found in almost every denomination and in every location, despite being more likely to be found in the Southeastern United States. Fundamentalism developed in the early years of the twentieth century.

> Note: The Southern Baptist Convention is primarily an Evangelical group rather than a Fundamentalist group.

A key distinguishing factor between Fundamentalists and Evangelicals is in their focus:

Fundamentalists tend to be focused upon keeping the congregation's members on the right course. As part of this, many Fundamentalist congregations work very hard to define "Christian" behavior, establishing standards of dress, speech, and lifestyle which congregational members are expected to adhere to. Lapses are dealt with by unofficial shunning of the lapsing members.

Many Fundamentalist groups believe that certain behaviors inherently make a person "unsaved". In other words, a particular group might look upon watching movies as evidence that a person is not a

Christians Denominations are Different.

Christian, since the group might define avoidance of movies as "Christian" behavior.

In many of these groups, there is a theological difference with the remainder of Christianity. This difference is that many Fundamentalists believe that a person can very easily lose their salvation through "non-Christian" behavior or thoughts. Other Christians either believe that a person who has been "saved" cannot lose his salvation, or else that it is a very rare and difficult thing that requires a conscious effort on the part of the person. This theological difference creates a distinct difference in behavior. The Fundamentalist viewpoint creates a mentality of fear, where the "once saved, always saved" creates an attitude of confidence.

In contrast to the inward focus of many Fundamentalists, Evangelicals tend to be focused upon spreading the Word of the Gospel. Standards of behavior are much looser, with more allowance made, particularly in dress style, to fashion. Lapses are more likely to be tolerated, with a gentle movement toward a proper standard of behavior seen as appropriate for a new member, rather than an abrupt change.

> Another Note: The terms I'm using are not rigid terms like "black" and "white". Rather, they are slightly fuzzy terms that overlap in many cases, like trying to define the difference between "taupe" and "beige". There are Fundamentalist Evangelicals and Evangelical

Christians Denominations are Different.

> Fundamentalists who share characteristics of both camps.

Fundamentalists often have associated conservative political ideas with theology. During World War II and the Cold War, Fundamentalist theologians identified Satan first with Hitler and Nazi Germany, and then with Stalin and the other leaders of the Communist Soviet Union and China. The United States was seen as having a special role to play in the end times as the guardian of Christianity. Thus, any political program that resembled anything ever put forth by Nazi's or Communists was seen as Satanic in nature.

Up through the early 1960's, most fundamentalists voted as conservative Democrats. The 1970's and 1980's were a period of transition, with most Fundamentalists voting conservative Republican today. True Fundamentalism is slowly dying in the United States as the congregations stagnate and turn inward.

In contrast, Evangelicals, although generally conservative in their politics, have always distinguished between a primary allegiance to Jesus Christ as leader, and a secondary allegiance to the United States government – or whichever national government they reside under. In the Evangelical mind, the performance of the United States government needs to be judged against Christian standards – we do not let a 1940's government and culture be the standard by which we judge Christianity. Evangelicals also look at governments as being reflective of the spiritual state of the people rather than vice versa.

Christians Denominations are Different.

To an Evangelical, a government that is immoral is immoral because the people allow it to be. To change the government's point of view, we must first change the hearts of the people. To a Fundamentalist, an immoral government is immoral because it has been taken over by Satanic forces.

Finally, in contrast to Fundamentalists, Evangelicals are much more likely to support programs traditionally seen as "liberal", such as assistance for the poor, care for the environment, and assistance for HIV-positive persons – all within moderate limits.

Strict Calvinist Theology

Calvinist Theology has influenced many groups of Christians – some more than others. The mild form of Calvinism has had an effect on the vast majority of non-Catholic Christians, by speaking of such ideas as "God is in control", and "God is working on you." These ideas have influenced most Baptist, Reformed, and Presbyterian congregations somewhat.

The other form of Calvinism is much more strictly limited. Two major tenets of Strict Calvinism are that there are a limited number of "elect" that will be saved (sometimes limited to 144,000 people), and that you are chosen by God to be saved -- your free will is a complete misunderstanding of reality. Strict Calvinism is relatively rare today in America, but is very important historically, having developed in the 1500's in Geneva under the guidance of John Calvin. Most "Calvinist" churches in America today are hybrid churches, following some tenets of

Christians Denominations are Different.

Calvinist teaching while following many of Luther's teachings.

Non-Calvinists argue that anyone can be saved -- in fact billions will be saved. In addition, although God is in control of your destiny and knew your choices from the beginning, He has given you free will and you may refuse His gift of eternal life. Alternatively, some Non-Calvinists argue that even though you don't have free will, you should act as though you do.

Social Justice Theology

Unitarians, the United Church of Christ (UCC), and certain groups of Anglicans, Presbyterians, and Methodists are likely to hold to this theology. In this theology, which developed in the late nineteenth century, the primary purpose of man is to create a heaven on earth now. As such, we are to strive for "social justice", which usually means helping groups that are historically poor or weak in political power achieve more power and financial strength through political action. These churches descend from the liberal theology of the late nineteenth century that the Fundamentalists reacted against.

The Social Justice view of Authority is derived from a philosophical rather than a Biblical view. First, the believer should determine what is Just. Then, he should check the Bible to provide a basis for this program. One assumption made by these groups is that the traditional interpretations of the Bible are suspect, having been written by a male-dominated society several thousand years ago. Thus, Social Justice theologians disagree with

Christians Denominations are Different.

traditional Christian groups on many social issues. A few Social Justice concepts follow:

- Homosexuality was not the crime of the Sodomites. Rape was. To a Social Justice theologian, homosexuality is not a sin.
- Because power flowed into the woman who touched Jesus' garment, women have the right to abortion on demand.
- Mary Magdalene was an apostle every bit as much as the traditional twelve.
- It is wrong for American companies to produce products with workers in poor countries unless we pay them American wages and provide OSHA protections to them.
- Wild trees and groves are more worthy of protection than orchards and farms.

As you have probably guessed by now, most Evangelical Christians see Social Justice theology as an aberration and in its worst case as anti-Christian teaching. However, there is an undercurrent that flows through most Evangelical Christianity of support for the less fortunate in society. And this is a key difference between the "mainstream" liberal Christianity, and Evangelical Christianity.

Social Justice Christians see the poor as a result of intentional oppression on the part of richer people. It's all about power struggles.

Evangelical Christians see that God puts most people through life phases in which we are occasionally needy to teach us to better depend upon Him – and to allow people in more fortunate situations to learn the joy of being generous.

Social Justice Christians believe that women are "oppressed". Evangelical Christians believe that women have generally chosen a different course for their lives that lead to differences in average income and lifestyle than men. Evangelical Christians believe that women – just as men – need to listen to God to find purpose in their lives, instead of listening to society's definition of success. An Evangelical woman feels that it is just as wrong to climb the corporate ladder because our society expects it, as it was for a woman to become a nurse instead of a doctor in the 1950's – because society expected it. Evangelicals try to focus upon God and what His Holy Spirit is suggesting to us.

A good place to understand Social Justice theology is on the UCC website, www.ucc.org. Look under the "Justice" tab.

Styles and Substance

In this chapter, we saw that there are many styles to churches. More importantly, the lesson is that worship styles are just that: STYLES. The substance of Christian belief is relatively standardized, and has been since the early church councils defined what was standard and what was false teaching over 1500 years ago. The only major upheaval in theology occurred in the 1500's when Martin Luther launched the Reformation -- which removed a thousand years of added interpretations to go back to the simpler beliefs of the early church.

Christians Denominations are Different.

Discussion Questions

1. What current social issues are on your mind?

2. Why did you choose to attend the church you are now attending?

3. Which barriers does your church present to the new visitor?

4. If you haven't attended a church, why not?

Actions

1. If you don't regularly attend church, go visit one this Sunday. Or even visit a mid-week service.

2. The next time you can, such as when you go somewhere on vacation, visit the most popular growing church in town. Investigate what they are doing right.

Christians Denominations are Different.

Suggested Scripture Readings

- John Chapter 3 tells of our need to be reborn in Christ.

- John Chapter 14 discusses the Deity of Christ and the coming of the Holy Spirit.

- In Luke 12:13-34, Christ talks about the relationship of earthly money, heavenly treasure, and a focus on God. How does this prioritize our concerns for our lives and the lives of those less fortunate than us?

FAQ #3 What Are the Major Evangelical Denominations?

> So continuing daily with one accord in the temple, and breaking bread from house to house, they ate their food with gladness and simplicity of heart, praising God and having favor with all the people. And the Lord added to the church daily those who were being saved. Acts 2:46-47

At some point it is helpful to be able to quickly find and visit an Evangelical church. Denominational labels are always difficult, since a church can belong to a typically Evangelical denomination and yet not have the characteristics of Evangelical Christianity because of the personality of the pastor, or the traditions of the congregation. And the opposite is true. A church can be a member of a denomination with leadership that is opposed to much of the Evangelical concept and yet be a vibrant Evangelical church. Let's see if we can help understand this.

Key ways to find an Evangelical Church

First, we should look at growth. An Evangelical Church has an interest and a focus upon growth compared to the area. Naturally, a church located in fast-growing Phoenix will grow easily while a

What are the Major Denominations?

church located in a farm community in Ohio will likely have a difficult time growing at all.

Now some people will say that I am equating Evangelical churches with growth. Yes and no. Growth alone is not sufficient for a good church. But Evangelical Churches understand that the mission of the church includes growing the number of people attending church – among other things.

So the first clue that you have an Evangelical Church in the area is whether the church is experiencing strong growth.

Second, we look at teaching. Evangelical Churches are known for having strong teaching by the pastor and, in larger churches, by a series of other teachers.

Third, Evangelical Churches usually are pro-technology. Many Evangelical Churches use PowerPoint software to create sermon notes that are projected on a screen during the service. Not all – but this is an indicator of the Evangelical mindset.

It may not be possible for you to identify such a church if you don't have connections. So we fall back on denominations. The following denominations' churches *usually* fit the definition of Evangelical Christian.

Southern Baptist

Not all Baptists are Southern Baptists. The Southern Baptist Convention is the largest non-Catholic denomination in America. A few clarifications: Southern Baptists aren't all southern, and they

What are the Major Denominations?

aren't all located in southern states. They took the name when the Baptists split at the beginning of the Civil War.

Today, around 16 million people are members of SBC churches. And almost all of those churches, especially the newer ones and the larger ones, are Evangelicals.

Southern Baptists tend to have a combination of traditional services and "contemporary" services, which use electric guitar, bass, keyboard, and drums. This is solely to attract a younger membership.

In addition, you will usually find at the end of any Southern Baptist service a section called "the invitation", where the pastor encourages anyone in the audience who wants to become a Christian to come forward. It makes it much easier to join these churches.

Some famous Southern Baptist Churches include First Baptist Church of Atlanta, Second Baptist Church of Houston, and Rick Warren's Saddleback Church of Orange County, CA. But you can always find an SBC church – they are everywhere.

Church of God in Christ

The Church of God is a Pentecostal Evangelical denomination. These traditionally African-American churches usually dispense with the traditional church service and go straight to the praise band, which is an integral part of the denomination's style. This denomination is noted for speaking in tongues, healing services, and an aggressive ministry towards the poor.

Evangelical Lutheran Church in America

The ELCA is the largest American Lutheran group, and leans toward a formal worship service, although many churches are developing contemporary services. The politics of the ELCA tends to be more liberal than with most Evangelical churches, but this is not necessarily true of the many very conservative member churches that exist. Women may be pastors in the ELCA.

The Lutheran Church – Missouri Synod

This Lutheran group is more conservative than the ELCA and has a closed communion. In other words, most Missouri Synod churches insist that you be a member of a Missouri Synod church to take communion with them. Women may not be pastors in the Missouri Synod.

The Assemblies of God

This group is a Pentecostal Evangelical denomination and practices speaking in tongues and healing, along with dynamic praise band-style services. Women may be pastors.

United Methodist Church

The Methodists were the prototypical English-speaking Evangelical church in the early 1800's, but the fire went out of the church in the middle years of the twentieth century. The UMC became the great traditional church of middle America, but gradually has been losing membership. However, this has changed in the last few years. A new movement has swept the church and many of the congregations have adopted the ideas from *The Purpose Driven Life* and *The Purpose Driven Church*, both written by Pastor Rick Warren. And now, increasing numbers of Methodist denominations are adopting Evangelical concepts and styles, and have begun growing rapidly.

Independent Evangelical Churches

There are literally thousands of independent Evangelical churches that are "non-denominational". These churches may be aligned with the Community Church movement, the Christian Church/Church of Christ Restorationist movement, or simply be totally independent.

Emergent and Convergent Churches

These two movements are perhaps the fastest growing sections of the Evangelical movement. Let's see if we can try to capture the essence of these concepts.

The Convergent Church

The Convergent Church looks at three great streams of modern Christianity and tries to "converge" them. First, there is the traditional liturgical stream, coming from the Catholic Church, the Lutheran church, the Methodists, and the Anglicans, with rich robes, extensive symbolism, majestic organ music, and ancient words that have changed little in hundreds of years. This stream focuses upon the worship of God.

The second stream is the strong stream of extensive Bible study, personal Bible knowledge, personal evangelism, and personal relationship with Christ that flows from such churches as the Southern Baptists, the Adventists, the Brethren, and the Church of Christ movement. This stream focuses upon the relationship between the believer and Jesus Christ.

The third stream is the Pentecostal stream that emphasizes the gifts of the Holy Spirit, such as discernment, tongue-speaking, joyous emotion, healing, and prophesy. This stream focuses upon the impact that the Holy Spirit makes in our lives.

The Convergent Church is an idea more than a denomination, but is becoming more and more common in a variety of churches.

The Emergent Church

The emergent church is the name given to a group of concepts that are best detailed in Brian D. McLaren's book *A Generous Orthodoxy* (Zondervan/Youth Specialties ISBN 978-0310258032).

McLaren points out that there are wide ranges of things that each Christian denomination does very, very well. He sees a new type of church emerging from a synthesis of these various groups and ideas, borrowing the best from each group.

What are the Major Denominations?

An emergent church would start with the ideas of the convergent church and add ideas from many other smaller streams of Christianity, including the Christianity-is-a-way-of-life concept found in the Amish, the moving-toward-perfection concept found in the Methodists, the blending-of-ideas concept found in the Anglican church, the intentional use of symbols found in the Orthodox church, and other concepts, blending ideas into a new, vibrant, growing twenty-first century church.

Discussion Questions

Which denominations are you familiar with?

There are dozens of other, smaller Evangelical denominations. Can you name some of them?

What are the distinguishing beliefs of these denominations?

What common aspects of Christianity do they all affirm?

To what denomination does your church belong, if any?

Read Romans 14:1-4. How does this apply to denominational disputes?

God is a Matter of Opinion.

Myth #8 - The Existence of God is a Matter of Opinion and Personal Faith.

> For since the creation of the world His invisible attributes are clearly seen, being understood by the things that are made. Romans 1:20

A common viewpoint today is that all religions are based upon personal opinion. This view may be stated as "Christianity may be true for you, but it's not true for me."

This view is totally foreign to Evangelical Christianity. Evangelical Christianity does not require that we detach our brains and logic. Instead, it is the most logical philosophy and religion–indeed, the only logical religion. And a good Evangelical Christian pastor is ready to prove it.

Proof of a Religion?

Now get ready to follow some detailed logic about the differences between Opinions and Facts:

Facts

Some areas of study are clearly about *Facts*. The field of mathematics is about provable Facts, about

God is a Matter of Opinion.

what you can prove and what you can't prove. If you can't prove it, mathematicians call it a Conjecture. If you can prove it, then it is a Theorem. A Theorem is a proven Fact.

I once knew a young girl who had difficulties with math. It turned out that the main cause of this problem was that she felt that the answers to math problems depended upon the opinion of her teacher. When someone would ask her "what is 3 plus 4?", she would search the eyes of the questioner, searching for the answer the questioner wanted.

When I finally figured out what her problem was, she began to make steady improvement. Her problem had been that she really didn't understand the *absolute* nature of facts. Her parents had been divorced, and for several years she had spent alternate nights with each parent. She had come to the unconscious conclusion that reality depended upon what the person she was talking to thought reality was.

Opinions

Other areas of study are clearly about *Opinions*. Much of the fields of Literature and Poetry are about what seems to pull the emotion in one person versus another. Each person holds an Opinion as to whether or not a particular book is a "good" book. Politics is another area. Everyone holds an Opinion as to the best way to govern the country.

In some areas of study, many people are equally confused. Many people think that because there are

God is a Matter of Opinion.

various Opinions about religious practice and God, the field is about Opinions. But that is not so.

Despite what your Opinion about God is and what my Opinion about God is, there is a real body of Facts that we call *Truth*. Ultimately, God either exists -- or He does not exist. This is a Fact.

Ultimately Christianity is True -- or it is not True. This is another Fact.

Our purpose here is to understand these Facts. For if Christianity is True, its claims make it the most important thing in the Universe. But if Christianity is not True, then it is simply a big waste of time, for its claims are then reduced to nothing more than an interesting sociological case study.

Reality means Truth

Reality and Truth are intimately tied. Reality is what exists -- and what does not exist. Truth is also about what exists. Start with Reality; add the logical deductions that can be drawn from Reality and you have Truth. Both Truth and Reality are Facts. Everything in Reality either exists or doesn't exist. This is key to understanding God and Truths about Him.

For example, it is clear to me that you – the Reader - exist. Or perhaps it is more accurate to say that I *hope* that you exist. If you did not exist, then you would not be reading this material. You would not purchase this book and my publisher would not pay me. (I would be very unhappy about this. However, my happiness is immaterial to our discussion. I

God is a Matter of Opinion.

might be unhappy, in which case you would not be the least concerned, since you wouldn't exist. Of course, this might make you unhappy. Therefore, to keep us both happy, I suggest that it is best that you exist. OK?)

(It's ok to reread the previous paragraph. I had to reread this five times and I wrote it!)

So I am not really sure whether or not you (the Reader) exist. I hope that you exist. I hold the *Opinion* that you exist -- but this might be different from the *Fact* of your existence or non-existence.

I have a way to determine if my Opinion is True or False. My paycheck -- or lack of paycheck -- will be proof of the Fact of your existence or non-existence. In a few months, I will be able to determine Truth. But today - the day I am writing this book - I don't know if you exist or not.

However, I already know something. I have one Fact. I have narrowed down my ideas about you to a simple question. "Do you exist or not?" I know that you either exist or you do not exist. *One or the other is true*. This is the one Fact. Your existence or non-existence is not a matter of Opinion, but a matter of Fact. Either you exist -- or you don't exist. No in-between state is allowed.

I am writing this because of my Opinion that you exist. My Opinion is definitely true or definitely false. My paycheck or lack thereof will be my key proof. One way or the other, I will eventually know the Truth. But that Truth already has been decided.

God is a Matter of Opinion.

You either exist – or you do not. That much is a Fact and not an Opinion.

Now, my Opinion of whether or not you exist is independent of the Facts. I may be right or I may be wrong. But you either exist or don't exist -- and my Opinion doesn't affect your existence in the least. My Opinion doesn't control Facts.

Let me put it another way. I flip a perfect coin. I keep my eyes looking up and let the coin fall to the flat ground beneath me. I hear a "thunk!" and know that the coin has landed. When I eventually look down, I know that I will either see *heads* – or *tails*. (There is also the extremely rare chance that the coin landed on its edge, but we will ignore that for the sake of this example. Also we will ignore the much more likely chance that my small puppy has stolen the coin.)

Therefore, *even before I look down*, I know that I will either see *heads* – or *tails*. I will not see *both* or *neither*.

My son may look at me and say, "Dad, what side is up – heads or tails?" I do not know. But I am sure of one thing – the answer is either heads or tails. I can only hold an *opinion* that "heads" landed up. But I can be sure of the *fact* that either heads or tails landed up.

No matter whether I answer my son with "heads" or "tails", the fact is that that particular coin toss resulted in tails. My opinion given to my son didn't affect the answer one bit.

God is a Matter of Opinion.

How do I know the answer was tails? After guessing, I looked down and saw the answer. Fact.

God

In the same way, God either exists or He doesn't exist. We may have an Opinion -- that Opinion is either right or wrong. If God exists and I believe this, then my Opinion is correct. If God does not exist and I believe He does exist, then my Opinion is wrong. But in the same way that your existence does not depend upon my Opinion, God's existence does not depend upon my Opinion. He either exists or He doesn't exist. My Opinion doesn't make a bit of difference.

So, you see, we must dispense with this baloney about debating God's existence as if it is like the question of "who is the best female vocalist". His existence is and always has been a factual question – not an Opinion question.

The question now becomes whether or not we can determine whether God exists or not. What is the Fact? Does He indeed exist – or not?

There are several ways to determine whether God exists or not. Let's look at some of them:

Logic

Evangelical theologians such as Francis Schaeffer taught that we could use logic to determine the existence of God. Historically there are a half-dozen common proofs of God.
- Universal belief in the Existence of God.

God is a Matter of Opinion.

- Cosmological: The Argument from Cause.
- Teleological: The Argument from Design.
- Ontological: The Argument from Being.
- Anthropological: The Argument from Morality.
- Consistency: The Argument from Congruity.
- Biblical: The Argument from Scripture.

1. *Universal belief in the Existence of God.* If we look at all primitive cultures, there is a belief in God. Atheism is something that only develops in decadent, dying civilizations. Civilizations where people have to face nature everyday understand the Truth much better than our civilization where people are isolated from the natural world and are surrounded with man-made objects. Thus, we see that the people who are in closest touch with the natural world believe in God. It is only the ignorant man of the protected man-made environment who is an atheist. This generalization also applies even in our civilization. Farmers, engineers, foresters, medical workers, soldiers, and miners usually believe in God. Academics and entertainers tend toward atheism. The more we depend upon God, the more we believe in Him. The less we depend upon Him and instead depend upon the largess of other men, the less we believe in Him.

It is like a group of men who are meeting in a rectangular building. Inside the building is a corridor that goes around the building and

God is a Matter of Opinion.

has windows to the outside world. Inside the building is a room.

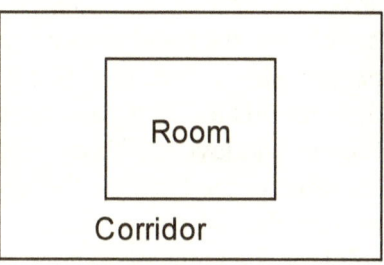

Those men who are standing outside the building discover that it is lightly raining. Those men in the corridor can look through the windows and see the rain. They can also see the evidence brought in by the men coming from outside who drip upon them. The men who are in the inner room cannot see the rain, nor do they see the dripping men who have just entered the corridor. They only have their own eyes for evidence, which tells them that it is not raining. They talk to men who have come from the corridor, who may testify that they saw wet, dripping men -- but that contradicts their own eyes, which does not see any evidence for the rain. Thus, they conclude there is no rain. They do not know any differently until they at least go into the corridor, or better yet, into the rain.

Those in the room are the academics, protected from nature and God by the government's funding. Those in the corridor are ordinary men, the industrial workers, the merchants, the retail workers, and the other people who can see the effects of God on their friends through good times, bad times, booms, and layoffs. Those who go out into the rain are the farmers, the ranchers, the miners, the fishermen, the foresters, the soldiers, the medical doctors, the villagers, the primitive tribesmen, and the ministers who discover God through personal contact as every day they depend upon His blessings.

Indeed, every natural society is filled with people who believe in God. Only those who live isolated from nature do not. It does not matter whether we are talking about the United States, China, India, or Africa. The result is the same.

2. *Cosmological: The Argument from Cause.* We discover through investigation that everything in our Universe has a cause. And we discover that causes have causes. The chicken and the egg. When we trace those causes back to the Beginning, we find it necessary to find a First Cause. That Cause must be a Be-ing -- not a Creat-ion. Thus, whether or not you believe in Adam and Eve -- or in the Big Bang or string theory -- we

both come to the conclusion that someone who is self-existent must have started everything. What – or Who – was present before the Big Bang?

Interestingly, in the Old Testament Hebrew, God gives to Himself the Name of "YHWH", translated as "I AM THAT I AM". Even His Name proclaims self-existence.

3. *Teleological: The Argument from Design.* This argument is based upon the concept that some things are too complex to occur without a design. For example, the immune system and the human eye are commonly cited as examples of systems that are worthless if only certain parts were developed. It is pointed out that several things would need to have developed independently but at the exact same time to be useful. This also applies to certain eco-systems where some animals are completely interdependent upon other animals or plants. If both are not present, neither can exist. Thus, the semi-random effects of evolution are limited in what they can achieve. Although God may have used evolution to accomplish His purposes, there are at least a few things in the natural world that were purposely designed. The argument continues: If a design must exist, this points to the presence of a Designer.

God is a Matter of Opinion.

This argument is much more fully developed by the Intelligent Design folks. A host of books are available on the subject.

4. *Ontological: The Argument from Being.* Imperfect and finite creatures like us are surely limited in our conception of Reality to that which is either learned or is pre-programmed into ourselves. But how can we imagine a perfect and infinite Being? Surely He was either discovered by men, or programmed Himself into us. The very fact that we can imagine Him proves His existence.

5. *Anthropological: The Argument from Morality.* Men have a sense of Right and Wrong. Interestingly enough, we generally agree on the main points. People around the world agree that killing children for our pleasure is wrong. We agree that stealing is wrong -- as is lying. We may disagree over definitions of murder, theft, or dishonesty, but we all agree -- men and women from all cultures and all times agree -- over the main concepts. This implies that there is a Standard of Right and Wrong, which is programmed into us. A Standard implies a Standard Maker -- God. This argument is much more developed in the excellent book by C.S. Lewis – *Mere Christianity*

God is a Matter of Opinion.

(HarperSanFrancisco – ISBN 978-0060652920)

6. *Consistency: The Argument from Congruity.* If we find that all the facts are explained by a theory, then we say that the theory is True. As you discover more and more about Christianity, God, and Jesus Christ, you will find that this knowledge explains all the facts. Think that you have a fact not explained by Christianity? Investigate further. (Remember the archeological discoveries of the twentieth century that continually proved Biblical accounts to be correct.)

On the other hand, as we investigate a false theory, we will discover more and more facts that are not explained by that false theory. For example, if there is no God and everything is simply caused by semi-random movements of chemicals, then it is necessary to explain why you can be self-aware while you are reading this yet still believe that I am simply a reacting mass of biochemical blubber.

7. *Biblical: The Argument from Scripture.* Reliable witnesses may establish facts. As detailed in other places in this book, the Bible is composed of 66 books written over a period of some 2500 years by over thirty

authors -- and only collected together after those books had been written! The reliability of these accounts is established far beyond the reliability of any other ancient work. Indeed, the only thing that calls the reliability of the Bible into question is the Message that it contains, which seems fantastic at first. Those books contain written testimony of the presence of God on our earth -- and of His Son. Thus, by the eyewitness evidence of the historical Biblical witnesses, God exists. Of course this is so. If God exists, wouldn't someone want to write about Him - the biggest journalistic coup of the ages?

Yet even after all this, we often hear that "God may exist for you but He doesn't exist for me." This is just another way to avoid facing facts. In the strict sense of the words used, this statement is plainly impossible. After all, a person like George W. Bush either exists or he doesn't exist. God is also a Person. He either exists or He doesn't exist. Sorry. This particular way to avoid God is not possible. God either exists or He doesn't -- now you need to decide based upon the evidence. Which answer is Truth?

Were you avoiding this answer because you know that God exists? A lot of people try this particular dodge. The Existence of God is an inconvenient fact. If He exists, then I can't be God. Neither can you. You are smart enough to realize that this leads to all sorts of troublesome conclusions, such as the fact that you need to listen to His statements about right and wrong. You may have to face the fact that

God is a Matter of Opinion.

something you are very attached to in your life is wrong. But that's better than lying to yourself, isn't it?

You may evaluate the evidence and decide that God does not exist. That's ok. You've made a decision. But don't avoid the decision by trying to avoid logic.

Discussion Questions

1. Is it possible that the reason some people think "Christianity may be true for you, but not for me" is that they have decided that all religions are false? Or is it that they truly believe that the Truth cannot be answered?

2. Discuss each of the seven traditional arguments for the existence of God. What appeals to you about each argument?

3. Discuss how the seven arguments fit together to support each other.

4. Which argument is most powerful to you?

Is God just a Concept?

God is a Matter of Opinion.

Some other people make the statement "God may exist for you but He doesn't exist for me", mean something else. What *they* mean is that God is simply a concept to them. He is not an apparent Person to them. Instead, He may be a vague imagined Being, but these people have never experienced His Presence. And that's very sad.

Have you ever seen chicks in a store cage? Around here every spring, the local farm supply company brings in about 200 chicks to sell. Those chicks are put into a pen where they wander around under a heat lamp and other evidences of human existence. Those chicks have no idea that we are standing there watching them until -- all of a sudden -- an ARM reaches in amongst them and removes a chick. That chick experiences instant panic! Suddenly, it is face-to-face with a huge, powerful creature that is so loving, yet able to destroy the chick in an instant -- my twelve-year-old daughter. It is very upsetting to most of the chicks.

We are like those chicks. We walk around in our daily lives, blissfully ignorant of the Presence of God in the room. One day, He decides to make contact with us. Suddenly, we panic and the hairs on the back of our neck stand up! God always existed -- we had heard all about Him. We even had plenty of warning from other people and from the evidence of our own eyes -- rainbows, for example. But we ignored Him, hoping He would go away. Fortunately for us, He doesn't.

Personal Testimony

God is a Matter of Opinion.

We can use the testimony of eyewitness to establish various facts. My wife and I can testify these facts that that point to God's presence in our lives.

- The year after I first accepted Christ was a difficult year for us. I lost my job the morning after I accepted Him. Within a month, we had started a business. A few months later, we were in big financial trouble. I said to my wife, "Saundra, we need $6000 to make our bills this month and I don't know where it's coming from. We need to pray." That afternoon, we received an unsolicited increase on our credit line of $6000.
- The next spring, I was involved in an accident that destroyed a $5000 piece of equipment. On the way home, I prayed, "Lord, if you want me to stay in this business, you'd better give me some indication of that." When I got home, Saundra told me that we had received a check from a friend for $5000 to buy stock in our company.
- A few months later, we needed $751.48 by 4:30 PM. We prayed. That afternoon at 4:00 PM, the mail arrived with two checks that totaled exactly $751.48.

Yes, we have seen God put His Hand into our lives. Now, since we know His Love, it is no longer frightening.

- Saundra planned to have our youngest son at home. That morning, Debbie the midwife determined that he was sitting up in the uterus -- a dangerous breach presentation. When Debbie determined this, Saundra lost control. Her baby brother had been born breach and suffered injury to his brain because of it. Another friend, Nancy, who was present said, "I'll call the church to start the prayers." At that moment, the phone rang. It was the shepherding minister from our church, calling to see if everything was ok. "Were prayers needed?" This proof of God's presence immediately calmed Saundra down, they went to the hospital, and Andy was born just fine through a flawless Caesarian section. After we invite God into our lives, He shows up every time we need Him.

- Last year, we had made friends with a Chinese student who was interested in understanding Christianity. However, we didn't know where to get a Chinese language Bible. The next day, we received a call from a customer who publishes Chinese language Bibles.
- This year, in October a Korean customer sent us three Korean Bibles. On Dec 2, one of our student friends brought over a new friend who needed to understand Christianity. The new friend was from Seoul, South Korea!
- When Saundra was young, she would take lilac sprigs from the bush outside her window, put them on her pillow, and close her room. When she came back into the room to go to sleep, the wonderful lilac fragrance would fill the room.

God is a Matter of Opinion.

Many years later, we moved to Ohio and purchased our first home. We selected our home in early March while the snow was still several inches deep on the ground. It was a time fraught with worry about whether or not we were following God's will. The first week of May, during our twelve-hour drive to Ohio from Atlanta, Saundra told me her lilac story and asked me if we could plant a lilac bush by the house. I said, "Of course, we own the house, so we can plant what we want."

When we drove into the driveway, we saw that under our bedroom window a huge lilac bush was in full bloom. Across the driveway, beside our ink warehouse's door, bloomed another lilac. Saundra wept. God had confirmed our move.

- A month before we came to Ohio, a woman spotted my mother's car in a parking lot. My mother is a state senator in West Virginia. The woman said that, although she lived in Ohio, she wanted to thank my mother for her support of home schooling. My mother told her that we were moving to Ohio and would be home schooling. The woman gave my mother her business card and asked her to tell us to give her a call when we were settled.

Six weeks or so later, we met a woman at our new church, who introduced herself as Dina. Dina was a home schooling mother. At that point, Saundra remembered the business card and pulled it out of her purse. It was Dina's card. Consider the odds of attending this church out of the hundred or so in the county -- this church was about ten miles from our new home.

As we go through our lives, we now look for those little indicators of God's Will and support. To us and millions of other mature Evangelical Christians, He is a very real Person. He is a good Friend who calls us up every time we need help or guidance. Talk to other mature Christians -- all of us have stories of many unlikely coincidences that happened to us.

Go to the Christian section of a bookstore or library. In those books are recounted hundreds of tales of when God made Himself known to the authors of those books. Many times, that's exactly why they wrote those stories.

I once heard a preacher tell the story of General Jimmy Doolittle's experience during World War II; his plane went down in the South Pacific. The General and his men managed to climb aboard a small life raft that drifted slowly through the ocean. They had received some rain, but no food. After several weeks adrift, they were becoming very weak. General Doolittle read aloud from the Bible and prayed for help. As he finished praying, he felt something settle onto his head. It was obvious from the frozen stares of the other men that a bird had landed on the General's head. Doolittle slowly moved his hand up beside his ear and suddenly grabbed the seagull. The bird was immediately

God is a Matter of Opinion.

killed and split between the men. A couple of days later, they were rescued.

One missionary woman on the Focus on the Family radio show told of being imprisoned by the Japanese during World War II. She was fed a very bland diet of rice and rice. After many days in her small cell, she saw a guard eating a banana. She instantly wanted a banana and prayed to God for one. But she also realized the difficulties in getting a banana, so she fell asleep having decided that it was impossible. The next morning, her cell door was flung open and a large object thrown into the cell. When her eyes were able to focus, she found that an entire stalk of bananas had been given to her. She counted 93 bananas. God had reminded her that nothing was impossible for Him.

Your Personal Experience

You can also experience His Hand. But He is so polite, He will not reach in His Hand until you ask Him to. However, if you look back through your life, you will probably be able to find times when God was present beside you -- you will be able to find His Marks on your cage. Maybe His Hand has even touched you.

Discussion Questions

1. How have you been touched by God?

2. What stories can you tell of God's impact on your life?

God is a Matter of Opinion.

Actions

1. If you haven't done so yet, read the Book of Mark. Identify each of the miracles of Jesus.
2. This week, every morning, pray "God, I'm looking for you today. Help me find you." Every evening, think about the day's events and see where God stepped into your life.

God is a Matter of Opinion.

Suggested Scripture Readings

- In John 5:31-47 Jesus talks about the barriers that prevent people from knowing God.

- 2 Corinthians 3:12-18 shows us another way to know God.

- James Chapter 4 helps us understand yet another way to know God.

Myth #9 - Christianity is All a Bunch of Rules.

> But now we have been delivered from the law. Romans 7:6

My mother has been in politics for the last thirty years. I've observed her approach to the government and I've observed other people's approaches, including two of my friend's approaches. It turns out that there are three principle methods that people deal with "the Government".

1. Distant Power -- To most people, including my friend Paul, "the Government" is a distant powerful organism. Most people pay their taxes, see an occasional traffic cop, get interested in the details of an occasional law when it impacts them directly, and generally hope that "the Government" will mind its business while they mind their business.

   Most people work very hard to ignore "the Government" and hope that "it" will ignore them. Usually, they achieve their goal. Unfortunately, they don't benefit from using the power of "the Government" to accomplish good in their lives and communities.

2. Rules and Regulations -- To lawyers, such as my friend Linda, "the Government" is a

set of rules and regulations – like a game! Fill out a form here, have a hearing there, pay a fee over there, petition this court, file that brief, and the gumball comes out of the machine. Lawyers work very hard to understand the proper use of the legal procedures that "the Government" uses to get action. They usually accomplish this. But they go through a tremendous amount of work and conflict to get what they want from "the Government".

3. Personal Friendship -- To my Mom, there is no such thing as "the Government". Instead, there are some persons she knows. For example: Joe is the Governor. There is also Kathy, the Secretary of State. Earl is the President of the Senate. Sharon is the Governor's secretary who handles the Governor's discretionary funds. When Mom wants money for a program in her district, she calls Joe and tells him what she needs. If he likes the idea, he tells her to talk to Sharon and Earl. She tries to have a personal relationship with these people. Because of this approach, she is very effective in representing her district. And she has fun with what she does. But she spends considerable time and energy talking to these people in "the Government".

This is also the approach that many other veteran politicians take. I once heard Secretary of Defense Donald Rumsfield on television responding to a question about the war in Iraq." What is the Administration's view on the situation in Iraq?" a reporter asked. Rumsfield responded, "First of all, there is no 'Administration's view'. I have my opinion, the General has his opinion, and the President has his opinion." The Secretary's point was that Governments are made of individual people and don't exist as an organism.

Approaches to God

Christians approach God in much the same way as they approach "the Government".

1. Distant Power -- Most people who claim to be Christians "believe in God". They may attend church weekly and bring a donation, stop at communion, baptism, and weddings, and occasionally get involved in a church project. They generally hope that God will mind His business and allow them to mind their business. They work very hard to ignore God and hope He will ignore them. Usually, they achieve their goal. Unfortunately, they don't benefit from using the power of God in their lives to accomplish good in themselves, their families, and their communities.

2. Rules and Regulations -- To a large number of Christians, "God" means a set of rules and regulations. These Christian lawyers,

which we refer to as "legalists", believe that being a Christian means following a burdensome list of rules and regulations. Don't dance. Don't ever drink. Don't wear swimsuits. Give exactly 10 percent of your income to God. ("Here is how you determine income...") Wear hats. Don't wear hats. Pray using these exact words. Don't ever miss church. These lawyers are the modern day descendents of the New Testament Pharisees, a legalistic Jewish sect against whom Jesus directed some of his strongest words.

Legalists aren't doing anything that will keep them out of Heaven, but they drag a huge burden after them every day and miss the true freedom of Christ. Their churches go through a tremendous amount of work and conflict that is unnecessary. And worst of all, they keep other people from knowing the love of Christ.

3. Personal Friendship -- Joyful, mature Evangelical Christians have a different view of God. He is not exactly "Father God". Instead, He is "Dad" or even "Daddy" (The literal translation of "Abba" as used in Mark 14:36). These Christians talk with God person-to-person in an easy familiarity. Every day, they are talking with God, asking His advice, requesting help with their projects, and accomplishing much good for themselves, their families, their friends, and their community. This is because they have taken the time to get to know personally the

Christianity is all a Bunch of Rules.

> Creator of the Universe, the One who makes everything happen.

Let's take a closer look at this.

God is a Distant Power

If you are a person who believes that God is a distant power, you are still weak in your faith -- or you are not a Christian. The distant god who does not concern himself with people directly is the god of Islam -- not of Christianity. It is clear that the God of Christianity is intimately concerned with our day-to-day events. He is the Ruler of the Universe -- and our best Friend.

Read the Bible

My wife and I had much the same experience in the small Appalachian towns where we grew up. Since the dominant translation of the Bible was the old King James Version, few people read their Bibles regularly. Instead, almost everyone relied upon the ministers to explain what was in the Bible. Since most people in town attended church regularly, the focus of most ministers became either the transgressions of their flock or the minor differences in doctrine between their church and the other churches in town. Very little attention was paid to teaching members how to learn and interpret the Bible for themselves. Thus, most people came away with a distorted view of Christianity, the view seen through the lenses of their particular pastor and church.

Christianity is all a Bunch of Rules.

Imagine if you will, that the only chance you had to attend school was 1 hour every week. You listened to only 1 teacher. You never had any homework. You didn't have a chance to ask questions. Wouldn't it have taken you many years -- if not decades -- to learn how to read, how to do basic arithmetic, how to write? There simply wouldn't have been enough time to learn the subjects properly.

Yet that is the same way that many people try to learn about Christianity. They attend church weekly -- or even less often. They leave immediately after services and never read their Bibles. Then, many years later, they still don't understand why some people they know appear to be "fanatical" about their religion. These other people talk about God as though they actually talk with Him daily. They seem to be convinced that they "know" what Jesus would do or say in a given situation. How come these fanatics are like this?

The difference is that some people -- growing and mature Christians -- actually do read their Bibles nearly every day. (The percentage of these people is rather high in many Evangelical churches.) They attend extra studies on Sunday mornings and in the middle of the week. They read commentaries on the Bible and books about Christian belief by experts in the field. These people have decided to study Christianity for real. They want to understand more about God, Jesus, and the Holy Spirit. They are hooked on Him.

If you think you are a Christian, yet believe God is a distant power, you probably have not read your Bible much recently. You may have heard many

Christianity is all a Bunch of Rules.

sermons, but you are only getting a small trickle of the goodness that you can get from self-study. You can turn that trickle of goodness into a fire hose flood if you begin reading the Bible regularly on your own. If you don't have a Bible, or only have an old King James Version of the Bible, you need to purchase a Bible that will help you understand it. Our personal preference is *The Nelson Study Bible*, New King James Version (NKJV) (1997 **ISBN**: 0785257292), available from Thomas Nelson Publishers, Nashville, Tennessee, USA, or almost any Christian Book Store.

There are several reasons why we suggest this Bible. First, the NKJV translation is very precise, yet uses late twentieth century language, which is much easier to read than the Shakespearean English of the old KJV. Second, Study Bibles - in general - provide additional cross-referencing and additional information which help you understand the passages that you are reading. Third, this version of the Bible is available in editions costing as little as $19.95.

It is very important that Christians read the Bible on a regular basis. If you just rely on what you get in the Sunday sermon, it can take decades for you to get the meaning of the Bible. It takes years for a pastor to go through the Bible verse-by-verse, and many pastors don't have this as their plan. In addition, some pastors will take a particular verse out of context, which can result in a misunderstanding of the original intent of the passage.

Least you think that I do not support listening to pastors, let me take a moment to explain the role of

Christianity is all a Bunch of Rules.

the pastor. A pastor's purpose is to make sure that certain minimum standards are upheld. He makes sure that necessary prayers are said each week. He makes sure that the basic story of Christianity is conveyed to everyone. He makes sure that funerals are preached and people are baptized and married. But he is not a substitute for your own desire to learn. He can teach -- but you must investigate and teach yourself also, for even the best pastor will never have the time to devote to teaching you everything you should learn about Christianity. All he can do is ignite the spark -- you must feed the flame. If you plan to remain in Christian kindergarten, attend church only on Sunday mornings and let the pastor teach you in his sermon.

On the other hand, to move on, you will have to take charge of your education. If you are in the habit of reading the Bible yourself, you can get much more of the feel for the Bible. It is the difference between visiting the beach for a week every summer, and living there for a summer. You can find the less-known, but wonderful shops and restaurants which the locals love. In the same way you can sample the flavors of the individual chapters of Proverbs, read the details of the life of King David, be touched by the life of Ruth, go down the short alleys of Nahum and Micah, as well as check out the main thoroughfares of Acts, John, Romans, and Genesis.

Strange connections appear. Did you know that the veil of the temple was torn when Jesus died? A study of Deuteronomy tells us of the importance of the veil. Did you know that Jeremiah predicted the slaughter of the infant boys that Herod ordered?

Christianity is all a Bunch of Rules.

Jeremiah 31:15 tells us this. The symbolism refers us back once more to Genesis and Rachel. Later, in Jeremiah 31:31 we hear about the new covenant which Jesus declared at the Last Supper and which we celebrate as Communion. In Genesis 14, Abraham meets an obscure king named Melchizedek. In Hebrews 7, the writer brings out the significance of this man.

Reading the Bible in depth allows us time to reflect and gain new insights. We find that Jesus wept before raising Lazarus from the dead. Why? Ruth Bell Graham read and re-read this passage. Insight came to her. Jesus knew what He was going to do. So why weep? Was it because He had to bring Lazarus BACK after the poor man had died once? What does this say about Heaven?

Finally, reading the Bible yourself will help God become real for you. You may have read a series of stories about a hero, or seen movies about that hero. After a while, you know how that hero will react in different circumstances. If the author is good, you will find yourself thinking about the hero as a real person, with whom you could almost hold a conversation and imagine his responses. For example, you may have this feeling about Sherlock Holmes, Scarlet O'Hara, Laura Ingalls Wilder, Jack Aubrey, Han Solo, Jean-luc Picard, Nancy Drew, or Frodo Baggins. In the same way, the Bible is the story of the Godhead: God, Jesus, and the Holy Spirit. Supporting cast of Adam, Abraham, Moses, Elijah, John the Baptist, Peter, John, Paul, and "a cast of thousands". It is the story of your Master, your Big Brother, your Father, and your Lord. But

Christianity is all a Bunch of Rules.

some of these characters are still there to truly talk with. You need to read this story.

When you read the Bible, it is important to read it properly. The first time, don't start at Genesis. If you do, you'll get lost somewhere in Leviticus or Numbers and give it up. I know. I did that at least three times when I was young. Instead, flip over to the New Testament and read the Gospel of Mark first. (If you are familiar with Torah, then read the Gospel of Matthew first.) Then read Luke and John, followed by Acts. Next, try Romans. When you finish the New Testament, go back to Genesis and begin reading. Now you will know where the story is going. Feel free to skip to the next Book if a particular Book is putting you to sleep. You may not be ready for a detailed reading of Leviticus yet -- but someday you will be. Go on to Deuteronomy. Come back in a few months. If you don't enjoy reading, then get an audio copy of the Bible on CD.

A Brief Summary of the Bible Books

The Old Testament

Genesis	The Origins of the Tribes of Israel
Exodus	The Escape from Egypt
Leviticus	The Law of Moses
Numbers	A Census of the Tribes
Deuteronomy	Preparation to Leave Sinai
Joshua	Israel takes the Promised Land
Judges	History of Early Israel
Ruth	A Neighbor Woman
1 Samuel	The First King of Israel

Christianity is all a Bunch of Rules.

2 Samuel	King David
1 Kings	The Early Kings of Israel
2 Kings	The Later Kings of Israel
1 Chronicles	The Reign of David, Commentary
2 Chronicles	The Later Kings of Israel, Commentary
Ezra	The Return from Babylon
Nehemiah	The Rebuilding of the Walls
Esther	A Godly Woman Saves the Jewish People
Job	When God allows Bad Things to Happen
Psalms	Songs by David and Others
Proverbs	Wise Sayings by Solomon and Others
Ecclesiastes	Solomon's Musings on the Purpose of Life
Song of Solomon	A Poetic Love Story
Isaiah	A Great Prophet's Prophecies
Jeremiah	A Prophet foresees the fall of Jerusalem
Lamentations	Songs of Distress about the Fall of Jerusalem
Ezekiel	Troubles Coming and Foreseeing the new Temple
Daniel	Stories from the Captivity
Hosea	God is Faithful
Joel	Impending Doom
Amos	Repent and Reform
Obadiah	Bad Things will happen to Edom

Christianity is all a Bunch of Rules.

Jonah	A Man who disobeyed God - God will have Mercy on Many People
Micah	Jerusalem will be destroyed, but a Savior will come
Nahum	God will destroy Nineveh
Habakkuk	God is Righteous; He will Judge
Zephaniah	The Great Day of the Lord
Haggai	Build the Temple; God will be with you
Zechariah	A Messiah will come
Malachi	The people have disappointed God - but He will fix it

The New Testament

Matthew	The Story of Jesus (toward Jews)
Mark	The Story of Jesus (toward non-Jews)
Luke	The Reporter's Story of Jesus
John	Jesus - by His best friend
Acts	The Early Church
Romans	Sin, Faith, and Salvation
1 Corinthians	Instructions for a Congregation
2 Corinthians	The Problems of Ministry
Galatians	Salvation is through Faith, not works
Ephesians	The Body of Christ - Believer's duties
Philippians	The Joy of Serving Christ
Colossians	The Importance of Christ
1 Thessalonians	Basic Doctrines of the Faith

Christianity is all a Bunch of Rules.

2 Thessalonians	The Day of the Lord is in the Future
1 Timothy	Instructions to a Young Leader
2 Timothy	Encouragement to a Young Pastor
Titus	How to Develop a Good Church
Philemon	How to Treat one that does Wrong
Hebrews	The Purpose of Christ
James	How to deal with Life's Problems
1 Peter	Why we Suffer
2 Peter	Separating True Teachings from False Teachings
1 John	Love indicates a Relationship with God
2 John	Christ is Critical to having God
3 John	Separating Your Church from Others is Wrong
Jude	Don't Attack evildoers; Save Yourselves and Them
Revelation	Instructions to Churches and the End of Time

Read the Bible yourself. It will become a cherished activity for you. And the Person of God will become more real to you.

Pray

When I was in college, there was a girl that all the guys saw the first day she arrived on campus. She was tall, blond, well built, and always smiled. None of my friends nor I had the courage to talk to her. Finally, about a month after the semester had started my friend found out about her. We'll say here name

Christianity is all a Bunch of Rules.

was "Sarah". My friend was in the marching band with her and had overheard her name. None of us yet had the courage to talk to her. We watched her at a distance, wondering what she was like. We knew that she must be dating one of the popular guys on campus - a girl with beauty like hers must already be taken! We were intimidated.

Three years later, in my last semester at college, I walked into a diner near campus and Sarah took my order as a waitress. It was late at night and there were no other customers, so I began to talk to her. It turned out that Sarah had dated a guy her freshman year, but he had left campus and she hadn't dated since then. All this time and she would have loved to have dated any of us! So Sarah and I dated a bit that semester until she went to a job in one state and I went to a job in another state.

Many people see God as we saw Sarah. He is so "with-it" that He surely wouldn't want to talk to "little ole' me". Yet God has few people that are talking with Him -- at least compared to His ability to respond! Start talking to Him. He will be happy to talk with you.

Will you hear a Voice? Probably not. God rarely talks in an audible Voice to people. However, He can direct you to parts of the Bible that will answer your needs, and can give you messages through other people and through signs on the highway. Remember my wife's answer that came in the form of two lilac bushes (chapter 8)?

Christianity is all a Bunch of Rules.

First, you need to begin talking. Like a good friend, He will listen first. Then, He will begin directing you as you allow Him to.

This is a good issue to discuss with your Christian Pro. Ask him or her how they talk with God.

In many churches, including our current church, public prayer is something that only the pastor does. But our church has recently started a technique of prayer that is designed to help people become more comfortable in prayer.

1. The group that will pray sits in a circle or around a table.

2. The first step is confession of sins. The group leader says, "We all know that we have sinned today. So first, before we start, we will all silently confess our sins to God." The group silently confesses to God and asks for forgiveness.

3. The next step is to worship God. The group leader starts the prayer and prays an attribute of God. For example: "God, you are so holy." Each member of the group who wishes to pray then prays an attribute of God. The prayer thus jumps around the circle. No one is forced to pray who does not feel comfortable doing so.

Christianity is all a Bunch of Rules.

4. Now, we thank God for his help. The group leader now thanks God for something. For example: "God, thank you for giving John a new job." Once again, each member follows the leader in thanking God.

5. Next, we can ask God for our needs. The leader next asks something of God for another. For example: "God, please help Daisy with her knee pain." Again, the members follow the lead in asking God for something.

6. We then focus upon ourselves. The leader then asks something for himself from God. For example: "God, please give me time to do all the things I need to do tomorrow." The members follow.

7. Finally, the leader closes the prayer.

You can follow this basic technique yourself as well.

For example, you may find that every day you are alone for fifteen minutes in your car, in your shower, on the train, in the kitchen, or on your job. Spot that time. Instead of listening to the radio,

Christianity is all a Bunch of Rules.

watching TV, or talking on your telephone, take that time to talk to God. If you are inexperienced, follow the technique above. Learn to talk to Him the same way you would talk to your Father or another wise friend. Except there is one particularly nice thing: God won't hurt you. He may teach you, but He'll never hurt you. If you learn to talk with God whenever you have time, then He will begin to respond to you. Try it.

These techniques will work well for the person who has always seen God as distant. But what about people who see Christianity as a bunch of rules?

Discussion Questions

1. Is God a Person who you know?

2. How often do you read the Bible?

3. How much Bible have you read in the last week?

4. What books of the Bible have you read? Which ones have you not read?

Christianity is all a Bunch of Rules.

5. Have you ever prayed aloud in a group?

6. How often do you pray?

Actions

1. Begin reading a chapter of the Bible every evening. Begin tonight.

2. If you have children, begin reading a chapter of the Book of Mark to them every day. Take the time to explain words and actions to them and answer their questions. Watch them ask for more.

3. Pray to God. Right Now. Follow the plan above if you are inexperienced in praying.

4. Begin a habit of talking to God every day while you are alone.

Christianity is all a Bunch of Rules.

God is a Set of Rules

I have met many people who attended church in a legalistic church when they were young. I have also met many people to whom Christ is represented by the pastor who pronounces hell and damnation on you for all sorts of crimes. (Many times these are the same people.) In these situations, you never seem to measure up to what is expected. Worse, there are people who attend these churches, commit the same or worse sins, and yet continue to attend without blinking an eye. Is it better to avoid church than to pretend to be good and attend church?

Legalism harms people. If you look at Christianity from a legal viewpoint, it is impossible to make the grade. You do A, B, C, and D -- because that's what's expected of you -- and then someone springs E, F, and G on you that you were never aware of. You have to pray correctly, dress correctly, behave correctly, sing correctly, and... there's no way! Finally you give up and leave the church. You may not come back -- if ever.

Worse yet, those rules eliminate the fun! What do you mean, Christians can't drink, smoke, dance, cuss, gamble, party, or have fun in fifty other ways? What is the advantage of being a Christian anyway? If Heaven were filled with those people, wouldn't Hell be a lot more fun?

I have friends who consider themselves morally superior to their Christian friends. The reason? They

Christianity is all a Bunch of Rules.

don't go to church and "pretend to be good". Their Christian friends are "hypocrites".

Legalism is the same web whether or not it involves government or involves God. The web entangles you and removes your freedom and fun. Life becomes drudgery. Fun disappears. Following the rules puts on a burden we were not meant to bear.

No Rules, Just Right?

Thankfully, there is an answer. To Evangelicals, Christianity was not meant to be a series of detailed rules. He made it very simple as shown in the box below:

> Christ said: "The first of all the commandments is ...you shall love the LORD your God with all your heart...And the second, like it, is this: You shall love your neighbor as yourself. There is no other commandment greater than these." (Mark 12:29-31)

In other passages, Christ made it clear that He despised the Pharisees who were careful to observe the letter of the Law, but ignored the spirit of the Law.

Christ's key teachings for this life were encapsulated in the passage I quoted above. In essence, He said that if you love God first and then love your neighbor (EVERYONE ELSE!), then you are doing the right thing.

Christ did not teach about dress codes, drinking, smoking, or gambling. A few years later though, Paul taught that Christians should lead a moral and

Christianity is all a Bunch of Rules.

respectable life. Why? To attract people to Christ. Paul made this clear to the Corinthian Church. Christians who act poorly and immorally will drive people away from Christ. Isn't this the very same argument that my "morally superior" friends make, albeit indirectly?

But Evangelical Christians don't do this to be good enough for Heaven. As I've pointed out earlier, we can never be good enough to meet God's standards. We simply can't measure up. (In this way, you've recognized a critical point.)

But Christ the Son of God can measure up. And because of *His* capabilities, you get into Heaven on His credentials.

It's like visiting the President. It is nearly impossible to get to see him on your own. You have to use the credentials of someone you know. If you can legitimately claim to be the best friend of the son of the President, you can get into the Oval Office.

The best thing about the grace of God is this: *Jesus has promised that all people who accept Him as Lord get into Heaven.* You get in solely by His promise. You don't have to do anything except accept Him as Lord. Sign the loyalty oath. You don't have to quit smoking, drinking, cussing, dancing, or acting like a fool. Just accept Him as Lord. Really. That's all!

So why is there such a fuss about the RULES?

Christianity is all a Bunch of Rules.

Because most people don't really believe that it is that easy. Or rather, they have problems accepting a certain basic premise of Christianity.

The Basic Premise of Christianity

The Basic Premise of Christianity is this:

> *God is God. You're not.*

This Premise has certain consequences. Perhaps the most important is realizing that there really is *nothing* that you or I can do that will get us into Heaven without His help.

- God sets the rules.
- God referees the game.
- God made the playing field.
- God owns all the players.
- God owns the scoreboard.
- God is the League Commissioner.
- God made the book.
- God calls the plays.
- God controls the weather.
- God can put you into Heaven even if you don't want to go!

God lets you play simply because He likes you and thinks that you are cute. But He can call the Game whenever He wants and there is no appeal. Whenever He wants, He can send you back to the minor leagues or cut you from the team. No compensation. No appeal. He can even change the rules on you and there is nothing you can do about it. You simply have to trust in His Goodness -- in

Christianity is all a Bunch of Rules.

His Grace. (The Book of Job tells of one man's experience with this concept.)

All of the Rules are simply man's way of saying, "I want to *help* You decide that I'm good enough, God. So I'll sweep and mop the floors. I'll stop drinking and tell others to stop drinking, too. And that way you'll like me better and *I'll* have helped You get me into Heaven."

God's answer to this has been given through Christ: "Don't be a stumbling stone for others." Christ was very upset with the Pharisee's for putting extra burdens upon people. He just asked His people to "love one another".

Evangelical Christian teaching is that people should focus on loving one another. *Every* person commits sins. Each person sins in many ways. My sin may not be your sin -- or it may be the same. I may be perfectly able to go into a bar and spend hours without getting drunk. You may not. You may be able to hold onto your temper under all conditions. I may lose mine at the least provocation. We should help each other overcome our sins and focus upon becoming like Christ. But we must keep love for each other in the forefront.

Christ will help each of us overcome our particular sins. I have found that by praying for His protection from particular sins, my day arranges itself so that I do not sin in that way. Christians have found that addictions to drink, drugs, cigarette, food, sex, anger, and even video gaming can be overcome by asking for Christ's help. His concern is never whether or not you drink, eat, or smoke -- but

Christianity is all a Bunch of Rules.

whether or not you are under control of that addiction. Does the vice cause you harm? Does the vice harm others? Is this vice more important to you than God?

My Experience with Addiction

A person can become addicted to many things. I know. I was once highly addicted to caffeine. I felt it was under control -- I always took my hits in the form of colas, hot chocolate, or chocolate foods. I never touched caffeine pills or coffee. But I found myself terribly tired all of the time. I blamed it on lack of sleep. Of course, I couldn't sleep -- I was drinking five or six cans of cola a day! I stayed up till 5 AM and slept till 2 PM on weekends. During the week, I just felt exhausted. I started having stomach burning -- I told myself it must be stress-induced ulcers. Right! I started my workday at 8 AM with a cola and followed it up at 10 AM with another. I was alternatively happy when I was high on the caffeine and depressed six hours later when I came down. Finally, I had an attack of kidney stones -- another side effect of too much caffeine. My doctor told me to cut out all brown drinks. I did. I slept most of a week and went back to work a new man, drinking Sprite and 7-Up. A couple of months later, I noticed that my ulcer was gone.

Two years later, I was back on the addiction again. This time it was tea. Same results. I was exhausted all the time. I couldn't sleep. Now I was married and I zoned out when I got home, ignoring my family. I finally recognized the problem and broke the addiction again. This pattern has repeated itself over and over in the last fifteen years. I wish I could say

Christianity is all a Bunch of Rules.

that I was over it, but tonight as I write this I feel my day's caffeine hit (an iced tea and two chocolate cookies) beginning to die. I will need to break my addiction once more. Tonight I will include it in my prayers. And I will include it in my prayers tomorrow morning.

This is my problem, which with God's help I will break. I need to remind my wife not to buy chocolate cookies again -- but I will break the addiction by *praying* for God's help.

The Legalistic Effect

Our Christian friends can help us overcome our sins. And that is why many churches have fallen into legalism. Instead of encouraging each person to break his or her sin, a frustrated pastor who has just counseled his fifth alcoholic in as many weeks declares, "Nobody should drink!" The congregation misses the point and focuses on "not drinking" as the mark of a good Christian rather than on loving and supporting people who are trying to break from alcoholism. Thus, they turn away many decent people who drink a beer or two a couple of times a month.

No, if you have come from a legalistic background, you need to very carefully investigate the concept of Grace. Christ's salvation is a gift to us -- we don't earn a gift. The first man other than Christ to arrive in Heaven was a convicted thief -- see the Gospels for the story of the thief on the cross. Nothing is said about that thief other than the fact that he trusted in Christ's ability to save him -- and that he was a thief and convicted criminal. If he received

Christianity is all a Bunch of Rules.

Christ's direct and verbal promise that he would be in Paradise with Christ that afternoon, then why do *you* think that you need to act better in order to get into Heaven?

Why Good Behavior?

Our good behavior as Christians is to be a work done in gratitude to Christ. To Evangelical Christians, the purpose of good works is to attract people by showing Christ's LOVE -- not to chase them away by arrogance. If a man says that "Christians are too good to go into a bar to help someone", I'll say "Which bar, what time?" If I can lead a man to Christ by getting drunk with him, I will. But I have noticed that God does not often ask this of His servants. In fact, He's never asked it of me. More often, we run into the man who says, "I once knew a pastor who was a drunk, so all pastors are hypocrites."

It's a tightrope walk for Christians dealing with the world. If we try to behave extremely well, we can become arrogant. Outsiders mistake our costly, tiresome battles to eliminate sin in our own lives as a "holier than thou" attitude. Then they think we are too good to associate with if we are successful. If we mess up and sin publicly, the outsiders talk about what hypocrites we are.

So what should Christians do? Christians should follow the commands we have been given. Love God. Love our Neighbors. Try to live wholesome lives so people will want to know our secret. Work very hard to be known as moral people so people will want to associate with us.

Christianity is all a Bunch of Rules.

I'll translate "love your neighbor" into modern language. "Be nice." That's all. "Care for people." That's all we need to do.

- If your best friend needs you to wear high heels and makeup for the first time in your life so you can be in her wedding, do it. Have a good time and pray for her marriage. Five years later after her divorce take her to your church and introduce her to your Wednesday night Bible study group.

- If you visit Japan and your hosts want you to drink sake with them until midnight, do it. If you know you have a drinking problem, tell them that you cannot drink for health reasons. Later, when they come to visit you in America, invite them to church and share the gospel with them.

- If your Bengali friends invite you to an Islamic prayer service, attend and politely watch. Come to their cousin's wedding. Then, when they ask you why you are different from other Americans, you can engage them in a discussion of Christ.

There is no magic formula to free you from the chains of legalism. If you are avoiding churches because of the legalism, find a church that preaches Grace. If your existing church preaches legalism, find a church that preaches Grace. *Talk with God*

Christianity is all a Bunch of Rules.

more. Read your Bible. Pray. It's really quite simple.

Discussion Questions

1. What legalism is present in your church?

2. Were you misled about Christianity by legalism?

3. What is the most obvious way in which you try to be good enough for God?

4. Have you ever broken a "good behavior law" to love a friend?

Suggested Scripture Readings

- Acts Chapters 10 and 11 tell the story of Peter overcoming legalism to spread the Gospel.

- 1 Corinthians 8 contains Paul's advice about legalism.

Personal Friendship

Christianity is all a Bunch of Rules.

Talk with God. Read your Bible. Pray. This will lead you into that personal friendship with God that is most fulfilling. The more I talk with God and get to know Him, the more I understand my pets and how they must feel about me. I often feel so honored and blessed that the Ruler of the Universe has time to do the things He does for me. A few minutes ago, I was feeling a bit lonely writing this book, wondering if anything I could write could give anyone the joy I feel. I clicked onto the Internet and found that a major atheistic philosopher, Anthony Flew, now believes in God based upon scientific evidence. Mr. Flew cited two books - Gerald Schroeder's *The Hidden Face of God* and *The Wonder of the World* by Roy Abraham Varghese - as important in changing his mind. That proof that a writer can affect someone makes me feel like I have received a card from a Friend that says, "Just thinking about you." And now I've been able to share that feeling with you.

This personal relationship is the reason Christianity stormed the Roman Empire nineteen hundred years ago. It is the reason that Christianity is growing so fast in India, in Africa, and in China. If you have thought that Christianity was all meaningless ritual or overburdening rules, I understand exactly why you have been searching for something more. For something more exists. It is the friendship which I have on a daily basis with the One who is closer that anyone else. It is the blessings that I receive from my Friend when He tells me He is thinking about me. It is the wonderful Joy I feel when I need some money to pay my bills, and the money arrives just in time. It is a caring, loving Heart that is always near me.

Christianity is all a Bunch of Rules.

When I go out back of my house, I can walk among some trees I've planted in a little, beginning orchard. I look up at the sky and a brilliant blue shines back, with a red-tailed hawk circling high above, checking to see if I'm actually a big rabbit. In that moment, I realize that I am also a small, little, beginning plant of my Lord, which is beginning to bear fruit. Last fall, we had three apples total for forty trees. Maybe next year we'll have a few bushels. In a few years, we hope to have enough to sell. In the same way, I know my Lord is looking at me, expecting fruit in the coming years. He is also looking at you.

Are you a fruit tree? Or are you barren bush? Growing in my orchard is a bit of rootstock. It was shipped to me accidentally last spring with the trees. I planted it anyway, wanting to see if it would amount to anything. It has grown tremendously in the last year. Now, I want to graft a scion from a productive tree onto it. The scion is what determines the fruit of the tree. Without that grafting, the rootstock will grow up and produce very little, tiny, very poor fruit. But with the appropriate grafting, the rootstock will provide a firm basis for a wonderfully productive apple tree, bearing delicious fruit.

You may be like that rootstock. Left to your own devices, you would grow old, producing little, tiny, very poor fruit. But by grafting onto you the Holy Spirit of Christ, you will be able to produce wonderful fruit for the Lord. The scion is a gift that comes from the orchardist -- the tree does nothing to receive it. The tree tells me when it is ready by simply growing. The gift of eternal life through

Christianity is all a Bunch of Rules.

Christ is a gift that comes from God. You need do nothing to receive it. Just sit back and tell Christ that you are ready. Grow. Bear fruit. Love God. Love your neighbors.

Discussion Questions

1. Which approach do you have to God?

2. How has legalism affected your spiritual life?

3. Have you ever prayed in public?

Actions

1. If you are studying this book in a group, pray as indicated in the chapter.

2. Get together with one or two friends and pray for each other this week.

3. Read a book of the Bible this week. Each time you begin to read, before you begin, ask God to open your eyes to His Word. After you finish, thank Him for His Word and ask Him what you needed to know.

Christianity is all a Bunch of Rules.

Suggested Scripture Readings

- Acts 4:13-31 tells of an event in the early church where many people talked with God.

- Luke 13:6-9 tells of the last chance given each person.

- Luke 13:10-17 tells of Jesus and His encounter with a legalist.

- 1 John tells us that Love is critical to knowing God.

FAQ #4 – What Do Evangelical Christians Think About Current Social Issues?

> Speak the things which are proper for sound doctrine: that the older men be sober, reverent, temperate, sound in faith, in love, in patience; the older women likewise, that they be reverent in behavior, not slanderers, not given to much wine, teachers of good things – that they admonish the young women to love their husbands, to love their children, to be discreet, chaste, homemakers, good, obedient to their own husbands, that the word of God may not be blasphemed. Titus 2:1-5

The media has told us that Evangelical Christians are a political group, no different in any substantial way than any other interest group. And as such, we are supposed to be uniform in our desires for our political ideas to be met.

Unfortunately, we aren't nearly as uniform in our political beliefs as the media would have everyone believe. We didn't all vote for George W. Bush and we aren't all pro-war hawks. Yet, there are certain guiding principles that we follow when we want to understand an issue thoroughly. Let's look at some of those principles.

What Evangelicals Think about Current Issues

Guiding Principles – What our Pastor Teaches

Like most people, Evangelical Christians often have a rapid gut reaction to a new idea – we either like it or detest it. But then, unlike many groups, we have a built-in class of intelligent, thoughtful men and women who look at issues and analyze them from a Biblical perspective. These men and women are our leaders, and most of them hold earned doctorates in theology, divinity, philosophy, or counseling. All of these fields train people to look at the impact of ideas on people's lives. And that is why most pastors – the ones you never hear about that serve small to mid-sized churches throughout America – are known for their wisdom.

Wisdom. Let's look at that word for a minute. It seems to be going out of style in favor of two other words: *intelligence* and *passion.* Today we evaluate leaders on the basis of their intelligence and their passion. But there was a time when we looked at our leader's wisdom. What is the difference?

Intelligence is the ability to quickly analyze a problem and develop a workable answer. *Passion* is the bull terrier-like tenacity to stick with a problem until an answer is found. But *wisdom* shows through when you understand the really important things in life and come up with the answer that doesn't create the unintended negative consequences that harm people as much or more than the original problem did. The couple of hundred thousand Evangelical pastors and other Evangelical leaders scattered around our country constitute a wonderful resource, a tremendous stockpile of wisdom.

A three-fold process gained that wisdom. First, the pastor learned to think and analyze by going through a rigorous education that led to his doctorate. We should not too quickly dismiss the rigors of this education. After all, most of the schools in the Ivy League were originally founded to train the most promising Americans for the ministry.

Second, he learned valuable principles by dealing with the problems and joys experienced by the diverse people in his congregation, for we should always remember that a pastor is more than a lecturer on Sunday mornings – he is called in to be a pre-marital counselor when a young woman is considering marriage, a marriage counselor when things go astray for the couple, a financial counselor when jobs are lost or the debt load proves too much, an addiction counselor for the man or woman trying to kick a drug or alcohol habit, a prayer warrior when a child is deathly ill, and a grief counselor when Mother is put to rest.

Third, every week he looks into an ancient book full of deep, detailed knowledge about human nature and the way the world works. He is expected to take a page or so of this arcane writing, tear it apart, and put it back together in such a way that his congregation, composed of a diverse group of people ranging from young children to anxious teenagers to exhausted mechanics to brilliant lawyers, can understand the message that is presented and take away something that will impact his or her life positively that week, and which makes sense when tied into the message that he taught the previous weeks and in the weeks to come.

Yes, we should never underestimate the wisdom of these men and women. And Evangelicals do not. We are profoundly influenced by what our pastors teach us. And rightly so, for that is what we pay and pray for them to do: influence us to become better people by teaching us about what God would have us do.

Guiding Principles – Respect for Every Person

"God created man in his own image." That's what the Bible says. As Evangelical Christians, we believe it. And that leads us to a very deep feeling about the respect due to each person.

Evangelical Christians believe that when we look at a fellow man or woman, we are looking at the image of God. To us, that means that those other people are, in some respect, holy like God. To Evangelicals, we see a distorted picture of God whenever we look at another person. Distorted. But still, that picture tells us something more about God. And so we are profoundly disturbed when we see such things as the hanging of a man such as Saddam Hussein.

Don't get me wrong. Evangelical Christians generally support capital punishment, for death is not a terrible thing to a believing Christian. We know that it is only a step in a process – not the end of all hope. Although many Evangelicals oppose capital punishment, our internal debates over capital

What Evangelicals Think about Current Issues

punishment revolve over when a man or group of men – such as rulers – may legitimately take another man's life. What disturbed us most about the hanging of Saddam Hussein is the lack of dignity that was given to the man and his family.

In the same way, we use this principle to guide us in our views on many other issues. Many Evangelical Churches have adopted a method of giving which allows the recipient to maintain his self-respect. That is why we have Goodwill Industries, where people donate items that are then sold at very low prices. Likewise, Family Consultation Services takes donations of new toys at Christmastime that they sell at very low prices to needy parents, thus allowing them to maintain their self-respect.

This is also why we were disturbed over the Terri Schiavo dying case. Terri Schiavo was created in the image of God, yet she became a helpless pawn in a national political battle. Some of us opposed the original decision to keep her alive because we believe that God should control the manner of our dying. Others opposed the decision to let her die of thirst, for it also was a slow death and not respectful. Very few of us would have her killed outright through an injection. Yet we all agreed that involving national politicians in a media frenzy was wrong.

Self-euthanasia is something we generally oppose, once again because of a feeling that what God created we have no right to destroy simply because we feel bad. It is not only others, but ourselves that we respect because we are made in the image of God.

The Principle of Respect for the Law

Likewise, we have an opposition to mood altering drug use, whether legal or illegal, due to the negative long-term effects on our bodies. This opposition is heightened for illegal drugs because we tend to be law-abiding and accept that laws were put into place for a reason – usually a good reason. (This comes directly from 1 Peter 2:13 "Submit yourselves to every ordinance of man for the Lord's sake…") Thus, you will not find that Evangelicals are a source of support for pot legalization bill, both because of the current illegality of the product and the negative effects upon users.

In a milder way, Evangelicals are generally opposed to cigarette smoking because of the negative health aspects – it damages the Temple of the Holy Spirit. However, we are unlikely to be a source of support for draconian anti-smoking laws, because of our respect for each person. Generally speaking, we believe that everyone has a "right" to sin. However, we try to encourage people to come to know Christ so that these same people will no longer *want* to sin.

This explains our dual attitude towards alcohol. About half of us come from traditions which accept moderate drinking as ok – we even have real wine at our Communion services - while the other half are opposed to drinking at all. But all of us are opposed to drinking to excess. We are very likely to think that an alcoholic will continue to be an alcoholic until he becomes a true Christian – and then he will be able to stop drinking.

The Principle of Love

We have written extensively in this book about the Christian principle of Love. It has been simply said that we believe that we are to love the sinner and hate the sin. This applies throughout our lives. We are to do to others the way we would like the others to do to us.

And thus, when we see a friend having problems, we help. As we mature, our definition of friend stretches to include our acquaintances, then people we've just met, then people throughout our nation, and then to people throughout the world. We love; We help. Christian Love.

But sometimes we are misunderstood because we are abrupt. We see people doing things that we know to be self-destructive. We speak to them, kindly at first. Then, when we see that they are continuing and not getting the message, we lose patience and speak strongly. Our words are unguarded and may be reported adversely. But that is because we are still human – we are not Christ Himself.

And that is why you see us opposing groups of people for their behavior. Some of us are not yet kind enough; some of us are clumsy with our words and deeds. But after a certain point of spiritual growth, we cease to hate, begin to pity, and then we love.

What Evangelicals Think about Current Issues

The Principle of the Spiritual War

Evangelicals believe that there is a continuous warfare going on in this world. It is between the ruler of this world (Satan) and an invading army of Christians whom God has sent to change this world for the better. Ultimately, Evangelicals believe that Jesus Christ will return to defeat Satan and his forces and take over the world as His Kingdom. But until Christ returns, we – the Christian Church – are the beachhead of the invading army.

We fight on various fronts. Most importantly, each of us has his own battles against temptation, fear, anger, hopelessness, and self-destructive behavior. Christ helps us with those battles on a personal level. Additionally, however, we believe that there are "powers and principalities" against which Christianity wars on behalf of Christ. Hitler was representative of this enemy at one time. Pol Pot was another representative of this enemy. Saddam Hussein another. The men who killed Hussein in such an undignified way were also representatives of this enemy.

Sometimes this enemy is in our own country, when a leader or group of leaders wants to do evil. In this, we are cautious. We question each new leader – particularly those who claim to be strong Christians – as to whether they are truly Christian leaders or merely men and women covering their evil in nice words. For Evangelical Christians are taught that in the last days there will come men pretending to be of Christ – or even pretending to be Christ – and they will be terribly evil, just as Hitler developed a theology justifying himself as the savior of

What Evangelicals Think about Current Issues

Germany. We are cautious, very cautious, and we get out our Bibles.

And so when we are told that Iran is a center of evil, we are inclined to believe you, since ancient Persia was a center of evil in the Old Testament. We believe the same about Babylon, the ancient capital of Mesopotamia, modern day Iraq. But we are less clear about countries not mentioned clearly in the Bible, such as China and any country of the Western Hemisphere. But we have our examples of evil and the results of men who radically thumbed their noses at God. Sodom. Gomorrah. The captivity of Israel. Jezebel.

Least we become too taken with any charismatic leader, we have our pastors, who studied Hitler's takeover of the German church, and who will remind us if it appears to happen again. We understand that our spiritual warfare is fought by our own thoughts and actions, by our individual prayers, and by our desire to honor God.

Unlike those who would love to easily, simply categorize us as "the Moral Majority", or "The Christian Right", we are complex. We think, we talk, and then we form our opinions.

Every Sunday morning we learn how to think a bit better. Every Sunday morning we learn a bit more about how to tell good from evil. Every Sunday morning we learn a little more about our personal role in this struggle.

The Islamists talk about "jihad". We have our own jihad – it is to fight for what we know to be right in

What Evangelicals Think about Current Issues

our own personal behavior, in our own communities, in our national government, and in the world. And that is the legacy of the Evangelical Christian and his approach to life. Ultimately, it is those millions of serious Christians fighting for a moral and ethical life that has changed our world from the Roman world of the gladiator and the slave to the modern American world of peace and charity. But we still have a long way to go. Our war is not yet won and won't be until Christ returns.

Discussion Questions

How do Evangelical Christians apply their principles to homosexual couples?

Why do Evangelical Christians generally support Israel?

Why do you think that most inner city soup kitchens and rescue missions are Christian in nature?

Have you ever seen a non-Christian rescue mission?

Myth #10 - Scientific Evolution and Christianity Are Contradictory Ideas.

> Hypocrites! You know how to discern the face of the sky, but you cannot discern the signs of the times. Matthew 16:3

Evangelical Christians are often portrayed as leaders in the forefront of what have become known as Creation Textbook debates. Yet, this is another case where Evangelicals are confused with Fundamentalists. Although many Evangelicals feel passionately about the issue, Evangelicals have a much wider range of viewpoints than Fundamentalists do. Things are much more complicated in this area than they are commonly portrayed. If you want to understand Evangelicals, you will need to understand the nuances of this debate.

This is an important area for me personally. For many years I avoided Christianity because of this Myth. I believed that scientific research had proven that Christianity was false. When I was eight years old, I remember asking the question: "Scientists state that the earth is millions of years old. The pastor just stated that the earth is only 5000 years old, based upon the Bible. Which should I believe?"

Evolution and Christianity Contradict.

A well-meaning old lady riding home with us from church that day said, "Believe the Bible, honey. Believe the Bible." But she offered no proof --no arguments -- any reasons. It appeared to me that she had no real answer. I took me twenty years before I understood that this debate was irrelevant to the Truth of Christianity and that many Evangelical Christians are perfectly fine with many modern scientific concepts – but don't accept modern science lock, stock, and barrel.

Historical Background

Christianity and Science have had some memorable encounters. Most famous was the Copernican/Galilean Revolution of the sixteenth century, when the earth-based system was replaced by the sun-based system. This was a major controversy at the time. You see, the Bible clearly states, "the sun was down" (Joshua 8:29). It does not state "the earth rotated away from the sun". An advance in understanding how to read the Bible finally settled this controversy.

Inspiration

There are several approaches that men take toward reading the Bible.

1. ***The Bible is a mythical book of fiction.*** Less-educated atheists often adopt this position. Although this position had a strong following in the late nineteenth century, it has been refuted by twentieth-century archeological, literary, manuscript, and non-

Christian historical research. The evidence clearly shows that Bible history - both Old and New Testament - is correct wherever we've been able to compare it to outside evidence. This means that most well educated atheists adopt the second position below.

2. ***The Bible is a historical work with some inconsistencies.*** This position is usually adopted by atheists and some liberal Christians who have not read the Book themselves. However, anyone who reads a modern translation of the Bible at least twice and studies a bit about the origin of the individual books will understand that the Bible is an extraordinary work, very different from all other documents. Sixty-six books that span over 5000 years of history with over thirty authors -- yet are theologically consistent in all major ways -- this is extraordinary. There is no other example of a set of documents that spans so many authors and so many years that has such an internal consistency.

Furthermore, the Bible is a collection of different types of writing as well. In the various books you will find histories, prophecies, letters, theological tracts, advice to a young pastor, love stories, a census, a collection of songs, a collection of wise sayings, and an example of investigative reporting. Yet all of these are first class literature and are self-consistent – if you study the documents sufficiently.

3. ***The Bible is a document that is literally true.*** Some very conservative and Fundamentalist Christians adopt this position. Yet, it is clear that this is not so. For example, "the sun was down" is a literal statement from the Bible. Yet it does not mean literally what it says. So most mature Evangelical Christians today take the final position.

4. ***The Bible is an infallible God-inspired document that is true in the idiom of the day in the original manuscripts.***

Let's break this apart a bit. "God-inspired" literally means "God-breathed". This means that the writers of the Bible were advised by God and the Holy Spirit in their writing of the Bible. It does not mean that the writers took dictation from God, except where they quote Him. Instead, each writer wrote in his own voice, using his own words. But God gave strong "infallible" guidance to the writers. When all the facts are in, the Biblical position will be shown to be true.

Evolution and Christianity Contradict.

"True in the idiom of the day" means that the writer wrote as a normal writer does. For example, if I write, "people like that drive me up the wall", you and I both know that I mean literally "people of that nature disturb me greatly." I do not mean that I am a car that they drive up a literal wall! In the same way, talking about "the sun was down" communicates a time of day that we all understand, although it is not literally true. It would have greatly interfered with the message that the Bible was trying to communicate if Joshua had been forced to stop for a moment and explain celestial mechanics to his readers!

Finally, "the original manuscripts" means that we believe that the original Hebrew, Aramaic, and Greek manuscripts were inspired -- not a particular English or Latin translation, such as the King James Authorized Version of 1611. (It should be noted that there are a few Christian groups who make adherence to a particular older version of the Bible a matter of dogma. But they are increasingly rare.)

The best way to *fully* understand the meaning of the Bible is to locate the earliest existing manuscripts and read them in the original language. Of course, this has certain practical problems. First, the original manuscripts apparently don't exist -- although, in the case of the New Testament, we have fragments of copies made within a hundred years of the originals. Since these manuscript copies vary slightly, scholars have analyzed these early texts very carefully to determine the best consensus texts. (It is worth noting that there are over 5000 manuscripts of the Bible and over 20,000 manuscript quotations from the Bible that are

Evolution and Christianity Contradict.

catalogued. Because of this, over 98 percent of the Bible is firmly established. The few verses that have the precise wording in dispute do not affect the theological consensus of the Bible in the least.) These consensus texts are readily available in stand-alone versions and in interlinear versions that mix the original language with a literal English translation. For example, Baker Books of Grand Rapids Michigan publishes an *Interlinear Greek-English New Testament*. Contact your local Christian bookstore or online bookstore for details.

These original manuscripts were all written by the apostles or their close associates within seventy years of the death of Jesus -- unlike most of the New Testament Apocrypha, or so-called "lost gospels", which were written in the second and third centuries by unknown authors who attributed their works to famous names. We know the antiquity of the Biblical texts because we actually have partial copies of them, which date from between 100 and 200 A.D. Or, in some cases, we have quotations of the Biblical texts in works, which date from the same time. This is not true of the New Testament Apocrypha, which date from later times. (Incidentally, the Apocrypha were never "lost". The most important of these works are readily available in most Catholic Bibles. Others can be found on the web at http://www.comparative-religion.com/christianity/apocrypha/)

The second practical problem is that learning to read the original languages is a time-consuming task. Learning to read Greek is not that difficult if you already know Latin, Spanish, or French in addition to your English, but Aramaic and Hebrew

Evolution and Christianity Contradict.

are substantially different than Western European languages. So for most people, the practical answer is a good translation.

The King James Version (KJV) or "Authorized Version" as it is sometimes referred to, is the Bible that most people have encountered. The KJV represents about a quarter of all English Bibles sold today in the USA, rising to nearly 40 percent during graduation and wedding time. A large committee of scholars translated it from the original languages in the early years of the 1600's. This was the time that Shakespeare was writing his plays. The language reflects this. The KJV uses many archaic words and constructions. Today, the KJV is considered difficult to read and understand by most modern readers. And most Biblical scholars wince at a few translation mistakes that were made in the KJV.

But a more serious systematic flaw undermines the use of the KJV. Over time, words change their meaning. For example, the word "meat" in Elizabethan England meant "bread" - not "beef". "Corn" meant "wheat" - not "maize". The word "meek" meant "quiet, unassuming strength" - not "weak and timid like a mouse", which is today's common interpretation of the word. Thus, to understand the Bible well, it is necessary to get a modern translation that will appropriately use modern language.

We suggest two translations, depending upon your preferences. The New International Version (NIV) is very popular and uses the informal language of the late twentieth century. The NIV is easy to read for most people, including most teens. It renders

Evolution and Christianity Contradict.

most poetic lines in the Bible as poetry, and puts appropriate paragraph breaks into the text. Quotation marks make it much clearer who is speaking than the old KJV did. However, many have criticized the NIV because the translators will use a less precise but common word rather than a more precise but rarer word. This can subtly change the meaning. For example, what used to be translated as "Behold" is translated in the NIV as "Look". In addition, the NIV has intentionally attempted to be somewhat politically correct, using "all people" when the original would literally translate as "all mankind". However, this translation is very easy to read and is very popular, representing about one-third of all American Bibles sold. (Do not confuse the NIV with the TNIV or the NIVI, which are two later highly-politically correct versions that very much worked to remove almost all mentions of "man" and substitute "person" or something similar - even when the original Greek or Hebrew clearly intended to talk about a single male person. We do not recommend these later versions.)

The second translation that we suggest is the New King James Version (NKJV), which uses more formal language. The NKJV was developed around 1970 in an attempt to accomplish several goals. First, it was to provide a very precise translation into the educated vocabulary of the late twentieth century. Careful attention was paid to the choice of original texts and to the precise choice of word. Second, the translators strove to retain the majesty of the original KJV, but yet tried to be much clearer and more readable. Quotation marks, poetic style, and paragraph breaks are also used in the NKJV. This is the Bible translation that my wife and I

Evolution and Christianity Contradict.

regularly use for our studies. In particular, we use the Nelson Publishing *NKJV Study Bible*. This Study Bible has additional material that helps explain specific words that have tricky meanings in the context. The NKJV represents about 10 to 15 percent of the Bibles sold in America, and is - in our opinion - the most accurate Bible that is commonly available.

Another type of translation, increasingly popular among Evangelical Christians, is the paraphrase. Popular paraphrase versions, such as *The Living Bible*, or *The Message*, do not strive for a word-for-word translation, but rather strive to put the *meaning* of each passage into a modern, innovative style.

If you want to compare these versions of the Bible, all three versions and many others are available online at BibleGateway.com.

Thus, most mature Evangelical Christians look at the Bible as the Word of God, delivered through the pen of men to other men. What does this mean to the Creation debate? We'll come back to that in a few minutes.

Discussion Questions

1. What are the differences between "literal" and "God-inspired" writings?

2. Which Bible does your church use? Why?

Evolution and Christianity Contradict.

3. Have you read any of the Apocrypha?

4. Why do you suppose that some people read the Apocrypha more than the Bible itself?

5. How does the change in the meaning of the word "meek" affect your reading of the Sermon on the Mount?

Actions

1. Go to BibleGateway.com and compare several versions of the Bible.

2. Buy a NKJV or NIV Study Bible.

3. Ask a pastor friend to show you a section of the Greek New Testament.

Evolution and Christianity Contradict.

Suggested Scripture Readings

- Matthew Chapter Five contains the Sermon on the Mount.

- 2 Timothy 3:16-17 discusses the inspiration of Scripture.

- Joshua Chapter 8 contains several examples where the literal words of the Bible are not true, but idioms are used. See how many you can find.

Various Positions about Creation

When we talk about Creation, we must once again deal with facts. We need to return to the Reality Check -- our position about Creation must fit the facts -- all of the facts. Once again, we will gain if we will list some of the relevant facts that people have noticed.

- The Earth exists. It has layers of rocks.
- The Universe exists. So do stars and planets.
- People exist. So do skeletons of human-like creatures.
- People are self-aware.

Evolution and Christianity Contradict.

- Strong independent historical, literary, and archeological evidence exists for the truth of virtually everything mentioned in the Bible, especially the Deityhood of Jesus Christ and His Resurrection.
- Strong evidence exists for a widespread flood.
- Fossilized skeletons of extinct animals exist.
- Evolution has been observed in fast-lived creatures such as drug-resistant bacteria.
- Many credible witnesses have testified in ancient and modern times to the rare occurrence of miracles, which are defined as episodes that are not explained by the normal actions of physical laws.
- Very elegant, simple mathematical laws can almost always express our physical laws.
- Many credible witnesses testify to the presence of God in their lives.

Each of these facts needs to be accounted for by any proposed answer to the Origins question. So what do we end up with? Well, that depends upon where you are coming from.

The most interesting thing about the Origins debate is the total mis-understanding that most people have about the other side of the debate. In most cases, the problem is that people on one side of the debate completely devalue the evidence from the other side of the debate. In fact, what most people do not realize is that there are actually at least five separate positions on Creation. Three of the five positions are held by at least some Christians. In addition, there are actually several different questions and issues to be discussed. Let me list them and discuss

Evolution and Christianity Contradict.

each one from the point of view of an Evangelical Christian.

- *Pure Naturalistic Creation.* In this view, God is not necessary. The Universe just happens to exist, and came into being through the Big Bang or through the mechanisms of superstring theory. After the Universe began, natural physical processes suffice to explain the development of everything. For example, the laws of gravitation caused the formation of galaxies and then stars and planets. Lightning and solar radiation provide the energy for the gradual assembly of more and more complex molecules, until eventually a self-replicating molecule is assembled -- more or less accidentally. (Gerald Schroeder's *The Hidden Face of God* (2002 The Free Press ISBN: 0743203259) makes a particularly strong *scientific* argument against this viewpoint.) Then, these molecules gradually change through the process of natural selection.

In natural selection, it is recognized that all creatures vary somewhat. Some will be more likely to reproduce because of their original variations. Other variations will discourage long life and effective breeding. Good variations will become more and more common in later generations, in the same way that border collie owners allowed only the better herders to breed, and neutered or destroyed the poorer herders, resulting in the wonderful herding abilities of today's dogs.

Evolution and Christianity Contradict.

Darwin recognized this idea with finches on the Galapagos Islands. On each island, there is a different, though similar, species of finch that is perfectly adapted to the food and environment of that particular island. It appears that these finches are all descended from a small population of finches that arrived on the islands a few thousand years ago.

This view of creation requires a very old earth and a very old Universe. It matches many accepted scientific facts. However, it ignores the first question - What caused the Big Bang or set up the "brane" of superstring theory? In other words, it may explain most events that have occurred since Creation, but it doesn't explain the Beginning itself.

This position also ignores the very definite statements made by Jesus Christ and the direct evidence for His Resurrection and claim to be God, which is an independent line of evidence that must be examined by everyone who is intellectually honest. The strong evidence for the Resurrection must be accounted for in any comprehensive explanation of the Universe. Naturalist followers typically ignore this evidence.

Naturalism clearly states that miracles are impossible. If you think you saw a miracle -- you must be wrong. Thus, a single proven case of a miracle occurring is complete refutation of this position. The Catholic

Evolution and Christianity Contradict.

Church has been sanctifying Saints for centuries based upon proven, uncontestable miracles. Naturalists argue that the Catholic Church has been wrong 100 percent of the time. Interestingly, a 2005 study by HCD Research and the Louis Finkelstein Institute found that 55% of medical doctors surveyed across a wide range of religious faiths have seen treatment results which they would consider miraculous.[1] These well-educated men and women, who understand biology as well as any group of people, have clearly encountered evidence which has changed their minds about the possibility of miracles.

Naturalism has another problem. It is in direct conflict with my own observation that I am something more than my biology. Now you may say that my thought processes are simply caused by the laws of physics and chemistry as they transfer energy around my body. You say that my thought processes are actually caused by the effect that light beams have on my surroundings combined with certain sensations caused by my chemical digestion of my food -- itself a product of chemistry and physics. So on and so on we go back to atoms and molecules and energy before life itself began. You are saying that I actually don't think -- I simply am a reacting machine made of hydrocarbons and water.

That may be ok for me, but what about YOU, Gentle Reader? Is there anything else to you besides the semi-random collection of atoms and molecules which you have inherited from your food, pulsing in patterns developed by natural selection over millions of years? Are you truly a bio-chemical machine? Or is there something more -- call it Consciousness, Mind, Soul, or Self-awareness -- that makes you more than the sum of your molecules? For you see, if I am a bio-chemical machine, then you must be also. Let's be honest and fair! Think about the logical consequences for a moment. You aren't really thinking. Instead, your body is merely reacting to the physical laws. Your mind has no more significance or capability of independent action or thought than have the gears of a clock.

But does your Soul react with horror to this thought? Got you, didn't I? You KNOW that there is something more to you than biochemistry and physics. You see, it is all very easy to analyze other people as bio-chemical machines with inputs and outputs and DNA programs. But it is different when you analyze your own Self-Awareness in the same way, isn't it?

Naturalism has this fatal flaw -- there must be *Something More*. Perhaps you have just convinced yourself that you can exist as a bio-chemical machine -- but deep down, you rebel at it, don't you? You *KNOW* that it can't be true, for you couldn't know that you are thinking these thoughts if you were merely a bio-chemical computer. Your Mind is something more than just your brain's molecules moving, isn't it? So why don't you apply all of that logic in your Mind to finding a True answer that fits all the facts -- even if it means admitting the existence of a God?

Naturalism has a fatal flaw. In addition, Naturalism does a dis-service to science when it ignores very real facts which call into question certain basic planks of the naturalistic theory, such as the dark energy problem, Big Bang inflation, Neanderthal/Cro-Magnon co-existence, inconsistencies in isotope abundance for isotope dating, the presence of data indicating significant worldwide flooding, the problem of sibling sacrifice, the phenomenon of homosexuality, and the presence of evil in the world. (Also remember the evidence for the Resurrection of Christ!) These facts point out basic flaws in the Naturalistic theory of the Universe. They are ignored as the ravings of mad religious fanatics. Most Naturalists believe that their theory is right and fully proven. If you are a Naturalist, I suggest that you investigate the "why" that underlies these facts.

- *Deism* -- A belief popular 200 years ago, but dying out today, Deists believe that God created the Universe but has kept His hands off the globe for the last couple of thousand years -- some believe since the Creation. Deists believe that God created the rules that the Naturalists are discovering. Deists may or may not believe in the historicity of Christ. A "pure" Deist does not. Thus, this position ignores the very real miracles that were performed by Jesus, including His Resurrection, as well as the presence of the Church. The Deist -- like the Naturalist -- usually deals with the issue of miracles by denying their existence *a priori* rather than discussing them in depth.

Deists do not maintain a Christian position, since a Christian believes that God is still very interested in this world today. Christians believe that God still intervenes in this world today through highly unlikely visible events known as "miracles" and through nearly invisible events that are the actions of individual Christians influenced by the Holy Spirit. Of course, the Naturalists do not accept that God created the Universe, and keep attempting to find a naturalistic explanation for the Big Bang. Thus, Deists find themselves holding a position that is attacked from both sides.

- ***Literal Young Earth Creationism (YEC)*** -- At the other end of the spectrum is pure Young Earth Creationism. This is the dominant view among many Christians, particularly those who claim to be Fundamentalists. These Christians believe that the earth and man were created during seven literal days about 5000 years ago. Many also believe that everything associated with the word "evolution" is a satanic plot. They believe in a truly worldwide Flood that covered the entire earth, including the Himalayas. No mechanism is needed other than God's power. This theory fits the description of the Creation described in the first book of the Bible, Genesis. In fact, the theory simply says that the Genesis account is literally true. If you want to understand this account, read Genesis.

Literal Creationism has a weakness. The theory dismisses the very real evidence that the Naturalists have accumulated as either "made-up", "mis-interpreted", or "placed by God to confuse people", rather than dealing with these facts directly. These facts are ignored as the ravings of mad scientists. YEC proponents believe that their theory is right and fully proven.

Thus, we can see that Naturalists and Deists deny that miracles exist and only scientific evidence is valid. YEC proponents claim that miracles are all that was used for Creation and all scientific evidence to the contrary is invalid. Neither side pays much attention to the detailed claims of the other side, except to set up straw men to be knocked down.

The last two positions are attempts to reconcile both sides of the debate by using evidence from both sides.

- ***Intelligent Design (ID)*** -- The proponents of Intelligent Design argue that the presence of highly complex organs and processes such

Evolution and Christianity Contradict.

as the eye, a self-reproducing cell, and the clotting system point to the presence of an intelligent Designer. They believe that many facts cited by the Naturalists can be re-interpreted to support the presence of God in the direct design of creatures. ID believing Evangelical Christians are beginning to develop a coherent body of knowledge to support their contentions, but still base most of their attacks on the Naturalists by claiming that all scientists are either part of a vast conspiracy or are kept from challenging the Naturalist establishment by fear of the conspiracy. They differ from YEC believers in that they understand that the Naturalist body of evidence is real and needs to be dealt with in a systematic, coherent and scientific manner. ID proponents take the Genesis account as a guide but not as a literal account except in the key phrase "God created..."

ID proponents have also developed strong attacks upon Naturalist orthodoxy. They have pointed out unproven assumptions or "logical leaks" in commonly accepted theories. For example, it has been pointed out that Carbon 14 radioactive dating relies upon the unproven assumption that the proportion of Carbon 14 to Carbon 12 in the atmosphere has been stable for thousands of years. Another unproven assumption of radioactive dating is that the uptake ratio by plants and animals has also remained stable. Still another unproven assumption is that the rate of radioactive decay has remained stable.

ID proponents are split over the age of the earth, with some believing in the Young Earth, and others accepting the scientific/naturalistic view of an old earth that is billions of years old.

In a nutshell, ID proponents believe that the scientific theories of Creation and Evolution are flawed in a *scientific* sense; that key facts and assumptions are being ignored or swept under the rug to support the dominant theories; and that serious research should be done to investigate their objections to the theories. Additionally, in the last decade or two, they have begun to move from simply criticizing Naturalists and begun conducting that research. The ID theory is, ahem, evolving.

- *Theistic Evolution (TE)* -- TE proponents believe that there is nothing inherently contradictory between the Bible and Naturalistic evidence. TE proponents believe that allowing a slight poetic license with Genesis Chapter One (and it *is* a poetic chapter in the original - see Sidebar) allows the seven literal days to become seven epochs. TE proponents point out that the order of Creation described in Genesis agrees exactly with the order propounded by Naturalists. To those who insist upon a literal reading, the TE group says that it would have confused the message if Moses

Evolution and Christianity Contradict.

had been forced to give a detailed scientific account of Creation to a group of people who had no understanding of hydrogen, gravity, the speed of light, the spherical earth, genetics, DNA, or Galapagos finches. What Moses wanted to convey was that Yahweh -- not Ra, Set, Baal, Ishtar, Zeus, Pharaoh, or any other god, or random chance -- had created Man and the world. The details were not important to the Message.

On the subject of evolution, TE proponents point out that a cook who prepares a cake and bakes it can be said to "create" the cake. It is not necessary to say a magic word to "create" something. Without denying miracles, TE proponents point out that God may do *most* of His creative activity through the immensely subtle method of setting up actions thousands or even millions of years in advance and showing His wonderful finesse by letting those slowly developing actions solve the problem rather than solving the problem by a sudden miracle. Which is the better way to create a Grand Canyon, to allow water to work for thousands of years or to take a huge bulldozer and work for a few minutes? What if God prides Himself on His finesse? The slow, gradual method He chose for the establishment of His Kingdom may provide an insight into His preferred method of working.

Evolution and Christianity Contradict.

In a nutshell, TE proponents believe that when the facts are finally in, both evolution and the Bible will have been proven correct.

Thus, you can see that it is not necessary to be a Young Earth Creationist to be an Evangelical Christian.

Discussion Questions

1. Have you ever before heard all five positions?

2. How important has the Creation issue been in your understanding of Christianity?

3. Have you ever been involved in a miracle?

Suggested Scripture Readings

- Genesis Chapter One, of course.

- John 1:1-3 tells specifically of Christ's involvement in Creation.

- Revelation 22:13 reminds of the First Cause.

Evolution and Christianity Contradict.

The Various Questions

As we have seen, there are several positions held by Evangelical Christians. Another point to think about when looking at the Creation issue is that it is actually several different questions.

1. Who/What started the Universe?

    The first question is typically unanswered by Naturalists, although some are beginning to say that it is a natural outcome of Superstring theory. Of course, this is simply putting another step before the Beginning. Who created the Superstring branes that created the Universe? Deists and Christians believe the ultimate answer is God no matter how far back you go.

    The standard Naturalist answer is that there was a Big Bang at which time the Universe came into being. But there is a significant scientific challenge mounting to the Big Bang theory. Because of quantum mechanics, it may be impossible for the Universe to be smaller than a certain size. This, in turn, may lead us back to the oscillating Universe concept, where the Universe alternatively expands and contracts -- or even to the concept that there was a "SuperUniverse" from which our existing Universe came.

Evolution and Christianity Contradict.

2. When?

   Young Earth Creationists believe the answer to the second question is about 5000 years ago. Naturalists, Deists and TE proponents believe about 12.5 billion years ago. ID Proponents are still developing an answer.

   In addition, ID and YEC believers point out that isotope dating assumes that the ratio of isotopes in the air or earth has been consistent over a very long period of time. This may not be a valid assumption -- in fact, recent research seems to indicate that these isotope ratios have clearly fluctuated over time. Another attack is more general -- have fundamental physical constants changed over time? The latest astrophysical research indicates that some may have.

3. How did the Universe and the earth get to today's appearance?

   Naturalists and Deists believe that the physical laws govern the development of the earth. ID and TE proponents agree, but add that God sometimes interferes. YEC believers argue that there hasn't been enough time for much change except due to miracles.

4. Why do we have such a diversity of animals and plants?

   Here is the core of Darwinian evolution versus Creationism controversy. Naturalists,

Deists and TE proponents talk about species which have developed by natural selection (Naturalists) or selection guided by God (TE). YEC and ID proponents talk about "types", which may encompass multiple species, each created by God. Naturalists, Deists and TE proponents believe biological evolution occurs - YEC and ID proponents flat disagree, pointing out several objections. First, evolution has never been directly observed where one species evolves into another. Second, sibling sacrifice and homosexuality don't make sense in an evolutionary context.

Let's take that last item. You see, there is nothing that aids a DNA molecule's desire to reproduce by becoming homosexual. Yet, homosexuality is present in roughly 4 percent of American men. Either it is an acquired trait -- as the moralists of all religions claim -- or it is a genetic trait -- which makes no sense by evolutionary standards. According to natural selection, a homosexuality gene should have been eliminated from the gene pool thousands of years ago, since it is counter-survival.

5. How did mankind come about?

Naturalists and TE proponents claim that man evolved from a common ancestor to the chimpanzee and gorilla. YEC and ID proponents claim that man was suddenly created as *Homo sapiens*. Several objections are pointed out to the evolution theory.

Perhaps the most important is the finding of apparently interbred Neanderthal/Cro-Magnon remains. (Cro-Magnon men are anatomically modern men.) It is interesting that, despite a long history of ape-men, modern man suddenly appears upon the scene. Genesis hints at men who existed before Adam. Was Adam simply the first man selected by God? Or was Adam a new type of Man, created by God after evolution had led to the Neanderthal dead end? (Adam means "mankind" or "first man" in ancient Hebrew.) Although there are a lot of facts regarding the appearance of modern man, these facts are lightly connected -- the prevailing theory is not as strong as it appears at first glance.

6. Was there a Worldwide Flood?

The recent discovery of a village a thousand feet below the current surface of the Black Sea has thrown a new wrinkle into the Flood debate. At the core of the Flood debate are three questions: Was there a Worldwide Flood? If there was not a worldwide Flood, was there a Great Flood that destroyed a large section of the earth? And what difference does this make to the Truth of Christianity?

According to all groups, it appears very likely that a Great Flood happened. Recent discoveries of super tsunami residue indicate that huge cataclysms have occurred which generated giant waves over 1000 feet in height. These waves can be generated by mega-landslides that occur when the flanks of volcanic islands slide into the ocean. Specifically for our studies, islands such as Reunion Island in the Indian Ocean, and Thera in the Mediterranean Sea are known to have had these large landslides. After living through the Christmas Tsunami of 2005, we understand better the tremendous impact such a wave could have had. Many large parts of Mesopotamia could easily have been under water for a couple of months.

In addition, we now know that the Black Sea was once a landlocked sea with a surface well below that of the Aegean Sea. About 7000 to 10,000 years ago, the Bosphorus channel opened up, probably because of an earthquake. The ocean water, which poured into the basin, would have rapidly raised the water level by 1000 feet. Interestingly, the Genesis Flood story talks of the ark coming to rest on Mount Ararat, which borders the Black Sea.

To YEC proponents, the Flood must be worldwide. However, to TE and ID proponents, even a widespread Flood is simply more proof of the inherent validity of the Bible. It is maintained that such a near prediction in what is one of the oldest parts of the Bible should be accepted as proof that the Bible is a reliable document.

Evolution and Christianity Contradict.

Tantalizing pictures exist from Mount Ararat that apparently show a large wooden structure high up the mountain partially buried under snow. In the upcoming years, improved politics in the area should be followed by new expeditions to determine if Noah's Ark still exists.

Exploring Origins

There are many interesting areas to explore in the Origins debate. I personally find the subject fascinating. A careful reading of Genesis brings up a series of other interesting issues:

- Exactly who was Melchizedek? (Chapter 14)
- Where was Eden? (Chapter 3)
- Who were the sons of God? (Chapter 6)
- Why does the Bible give extraordinary long lives to the earliest named men?

Books have been written on each of these subjects. To those who say that these answers will never be known, we should note that the city of Ur (Genesis 11:31) was lost until it was rediscovered in the 1980's by a team of archeologists. Yet it is all beside the point -- an interesting hobby, but it is not the core of Christianity.

Many people love to look at these questions. Many people are also fascinated by the future predicted in the Book of Revelation. The Beginning and the End. These two bookends are always attractive to people. They both tell the same story -- God is in control. He Created us and He controls our destiny.

Evolution and Christianity Contradict.

In the exact middle of the Bible, we have the predictions of Isaiah the Prophet about Jesus Christ. The New Testament is His eternal story.

We love to look at Genesis questions because we know it is important. If God created everything, He created us. If so, then we need to understand Him. We begin that by looking at Jesus Christ today, in the middle of our lives. Only then can we understand what the future holds for us.

Conversely, we often try to make the Genesis debate the core of our objection to Christianity. And it is a silly thing, since many Christians do not believe in a literal seven days of Creation. Yet, the ones that do have deterred many non-believers by insisting that the seven days of Creation is in some way a more important issue than the person and nature of Jesus Christ.

Pizza and Genesis

In some ways, this debate is like three people arguing over whether Domino's makes pizza or not. One man insists Domino's makes the best pizza and further, using all-purpose flour rather than self-rising flour can only make that pizza. The second man says, "Ok, then how can you say that Domino's makes pizza since they use self-rising flour? Clearly they aren't making pizza, then." The third wiser man, not caring a bit about which flour was used, helps himself to a slice of the delicious pizza.

The first man represents the Fundamentalist who insists that Christianity is true, but requires that you

Evolution and Christianity Contradict.

believe additional things about the Origins debate in order to be considered a Christian. The second man represents the atheist who listens to the Fundamentalist and accepts his requirements about what it means to be a Christian. The third man represents the Evangelical Christian who enjoys his Christianity.

Discussion Questions

1. Discuss each of the Origins questions. What new information has come to light recently?

2. Have you ever studied Genesis in detail? Would this be a good topic for a future class in your church?

3. What does it tell us when we find ancient ruins which support a detail found in the Bible?

Suggested Scripture Readings

- The entire book of Genesis.

- The entire book of Revelation.

- Isaiah Chapter 53 predicts the Christ.

Evolution and Christianity Contradict.

The Argument Summarized

At first glance, many people think that believing Christianity requires we disconnect from science. Yet most American scientists are believers in God. Scientists are searching for the Truth - so are Christians. C.S. Lewis, Francis Schaeffer, and myself all became Christians because it was the only philosophy and religion that logically hangs together.

The presence of the ID and TE factions inside Christianity testifies that Christianity is not destroyed by science. On the contrary, there is a large contingent of Christian thinkers who argue that Christianity is the most logical belief system in the world, as proven by the facts. It is completely possible to be a thinker and a Christian at the same time.

> Please note: Whichever position you take on the Creation question, the fact remains that various Christians hold divergent beliefs on this issue. It is not necessary to be a Young Earth Creationist to be a Christian.

The core of Christianity is John 3:16 - not Creation teachings or evolution. In fact, it should be noted that the Bible makes no statements about evolution. It *does* say explicitly that God created everything, including mankind and each of us. But it says nothing about the mechanism. There is no contradiction.

Evolution and Christianity Contradict.

If you are a person who has argued Creation with a Christian before, remember that arguing with a Christian is not the same as arguing about the Truth of Christianity. Individual Christians may be highly skilled in this field -- or they may not be skilled at defending their faith. In the same way that all scientists are not evolutionary biologists or astrophysicists -- a sociologist would be a poor defender of string theory -- remember that all Christians are not trained as defenders of the faith. In addition, the arguments made at the Scopes "Monkey Trial" in Tennessee in seventy years ago do not reflect properly either side of the debate today.

Furthermore, keep in mind that there are more than two sides to this debate. You can't use the Creation/Evolution debates as an excuse anymore to keep from being a Christian -- you've been shown that many Christians accept the Naturalist facts or argue with them from a legitimate scientific basis.

But as interesting as this debate is, it is still secondary to the real question -- what are YOU going to do about the Resurrection of Jesus Christ, which is independently proven and *is* the core of Christianity?

Suggested Scripture Readings

- Hosea 4:4-6 points out the dangers of a lack of knowledge.

Evolution and Christianity Contradict.

- In Mark 1:14-15 Jesus tells us to "repent" (literally "turn about") "and believe in the *gospel*." The emphasis is mine. The gospel is the good news of Christ's ability to save you -- the core of Christian belief.

- In Ephesians 1:7-12 we are reminded of the gospel.

Actions

1. Go on the Internet to read some information from some interesting websites:

    - The Institute for Creation Research
      www.icr.org
    - Answers in Genesis
      www.answersingenesis.org
    - Center for Scientific Creation
      www.creationscience.org

2. Ask a friend of yours who is a doctor, scientist, or engineer whether or not they believe in miracles.

Evolution and Christianity Contradict.

Sidebar - Ancient Poetry Form

Much of ancient poetry is not a rhyming poetry such as we are accustomed to in English. A poetic feel may be constructed in prose instead of in verse. For example, a reading of the first chapter of the Gospel of John indicates a clear attempt to convey a poetic idea.

In addition, much of ancient poetry prefers to use parallelism to convey ideas. Instead of rhyming with a parallelism of sounds, the poetry uses a parallelism of ideas. A series of thoughts is written using similar words. For example, in the Sermon on the Mount, which Jesus originally spoke in Aramaic and then was later written down in Greek, Jesus repeatedly says "Blessed are the..." and then follows later with "Woe to those who..." which is also repeated. This type of construction is a useful memorization aid for speakers, and was commonly used in many cultures to help tell an oral story. We see much the same thing in the Greek classic *The Iliad* and in the old English story of *Beowulf*.

In Genesis Chapter One, we have this parallelism with the Creation account. Each day God creates something and it is good. This phrasing need not indicate a literal six days of Creation -- but then again, it might. Some YEC proponents argue that the original manuscripts are not written in this style at all. If you are interested, YEC proponents and the TE group argue strongly about the ancient words and their exact meaning on many websites. This is one of those intra-mural things that are vehemently

Evolution and Christianity Contradict.

debated by Christians interested in the subject. Feel free to join the debate!

Footnotes

1. Science or Miracle?; Holiday Season Survey Reveals Physicians' Views of Faith, Prayer and Miracles; BUSINESS WIRE; Dec. 20, 2005; home.businesswire.com

Myth #11 - All Groups That Claim to be Christian Are Christian.

> For false christs and false prophets will rise and show great signs and wonders to deceive, if possible, even the elect. Matthew 24:24

As we saw in Chapter 4, standard Christian belief about Jesus is that Christ was both completely God and completely man, and had co-existed with God before the birth of Jesus. Several groups are often seen as Christian or claim to be Christian, yet virtually all the leaders of mainstream, Fundamentalist, and Evangelical denominations would agree that these groups are not Christian.

Our purpose in bringing forth these groups is not to provide an in-depth discussion of their doctrines and the correctness or incorrectness of them. Rather, it is to help you the reader understand that these groups are *not* Christian, despite their claims or public perceptions of their claims. This is especially important if you are a writer, journalist, or otherwise create ideas for the public.

Jehovah's Witnesses

Many people see the Jehovah's Witnesses as Christians. Strictly speaking, this is not true. One of the core beliefs of Jehovah's Witnesses is that Jesus

All Groups that Claim to be Christian are.

is *not* Deity and has not existed from the Beginning of Time.

Jehovah's Witnesses (JW) differ from standard Christianity in their translation and interpretation of John 1:1. JW believers and the New World Translation (the JW standard Bible) poorly translate the Greek to give an interpretation that Jesus is a created creature, rather than the unique Son of God. They argue that the translation should read: "The Word was a god." Their translation argues that since two different Greek words are used for God and the definite article "ho" is missing in the Greek Text, they mean different things. Well, they do. The difference is the same sort of difference in meaning between the words "we" and "us". Your high school English teacher would recognize the difference as one of "case". Koine Greek professors around the world, except for the handful that are Jehovah's Witnesses, would agree that the standard translation is correct: "The Word was God". This is also supported by many other statements throughout John's Gospel and the other parts of the New Testament. Christians believe that Jesus is God.

JW's take this translation mistake and propagate it into many different areas, including the non-celebration of Christmas and other interesting beliefs. Although none can doubt their desire to spread the Word of God, they spread a distorted view of Christ that is at odds with core Christian beliefs accepted for two thousand years by groups as diverse as the Catholic Church, Southern Baptists, Russian Orthodox, and Seventh-Day Adventists.

All Groups that Claim to be Christian are.

Another translation mistake, which JW's make, is to claim that the only proper name for God is "Jehovah". In the Old Testament, there were four Hebrew names used for God: "El", "Elohim", "Eloah" and "YHWH". "Jehovah" is a rough approximation of "YHWH", also pronounced "Yahweh".

Another problem with JW belief is their claim, made before 1930, that "millions now alive will never die", a strong reference to the immediate Second Coming of Christ. Time is rapidly running out on this statement.

Online Information:
http://www.allaboutcults.org/jehovah-witnesses-beliefs-faq.htm

Discussion Questions

1. Have you encountered Jehovah's Witnesses before?

2. What are the dangers of JW belief?

3. How should a Christian deal with a Jehovah's Witness who visits them?

All Groups that Claim to be Christian are.

Suggested Scripture Readings

- John Chapter One tells us of the eternality of Christ.

- Genesis Chapter One talks of God in the plural. The Hebrew word here for "God" is "Elohim", a plural word.

The Church of Jesus Christ and Latter Day Saints (Mormons)

Although the LDS church claims to be Christian, and shares many concepts with Christianity, a critical part of what makes the Mormon a Mormon is the belief that new information was provided to the founders of the LDS church in the early 1800's which is believed by many Christian leaders – Evangelical and otherwise – to be at odds with traditional Christian teachings.

A key part of Mormon belief is the belief in continual revelation of God's will and purposes. Mormons believe that the angel Moroni visited their founder Joseph Smith a hundred and seventy years ago. According to standard Mormon belief, there was a substantial civilization in North America some 1500 years ago, at least as advanced as the Roman civilization and very numerous.

All Groups that Claim to be Christian are.

Unfortunately, archeological evidence does not support this claim.

Mormon theology believes that there is a male Father God and a female Mother Goddess. All people are their spiritual children. Christ was the first-born son -- Adam was next. These spiritual children exist in Heaven before physical birth. Men and women are encouraged to have large families to bring these spiritual children through the cycle on earth. When you die, there are four possibilities.

- Very evil people such as Hitler go to Hell.
- Non-believers and "bad" Mormons go to the lower level of Heaven.
- Very good non-believers and most Mormons go to the middle level of Heaven.
- Very good Mormons go the upper level of Heaven.

A wife's status depends upon the status of her husband. A dead relative may be posthumously consecrated into the faith, which explains the Mormon emphasis upon genealogy.

Mormons who achieve the upper level of Heaven may become the Father God and Mother Goddess of a new Universe or perhaps co-rulers of this Universe. As you can see, this is nowhere near standard Christian belief.

Mormon belief can officially change over the years with progressive revelation given to the leaders of the church. For example, in early days, polygamy was encouraged and widely practiced among Mormons. In the latter years of the nineteenth

All Groups that Claim to be Christian are.

century, a federal law banned polygamy. The church quickly followed by banning the practice, although splinter groups still practice polygamy.

Another older practice in the Mormon church was the prohibition of blacks from the priesthood. This belief also officially changed near the end of the twentieth century.

In the last few years, the LDS church has been moving more and more toward a Christian identity, and has invited Evangelical leaders such as Ravi Zacherias to speak in front of large Mormon crowds. It will be interesting to watch Mormon church beliefs change and the LDS evolve over the next few decades.

Online Information:
http://www.allaboutcults.org/what-do-mormons-believe.htm

Discussion Questions

1. What are the good points of the Mormon religion?

2. What are the dangers of Mormon belief?

3. How is it that a religion can change core beliefs over a period of a century?

All Groups that Claim to be Christian are.

4. What does it say about that religion?

Suggested Scripture Readings

- Revelation 22:18-19 explains the dangers of adding to Scripture. (It is unclear whether or not "this book" which John was referring to was the Book of Revelation or the entire Bible.)

- 2 Corinthians Chapter 11, particularly verses 13-15 helps us understand the dangers of claiming to be an apostle of God.

Christian Science

It has been said that Christian Science is neither Christian nor Science. This group is based upon the works of Mary Baker Eddy, particularly *Science and Health with Key to the Scriptures*, published in 1875. Although Mary Baker Eddy began with the Christian Bible as the basis for her teachings, she ended up simply restating Docetism. This is the heretical view that Jesus was God, but was not human. Docetists believed that Jesus only seemed to be human, but actually was one hundred percent spirit God.

Eddy believed that all that is Spirit is good. Matter is evil. The Mind of God is all that is real. Matter is not real. All cause and effect is mental, not physical. Thus, health is a matter of Mind, not of physical

All Groups that Claim to be Christian are.

condition. Healing can then be accomplished through prayer and the presence of Christ, who is a Spirit and does not have a physical presence.

Standard Christian belief is adamant about the real existence of both Spirit and Matter. God created the Universe -- He is something distinct from the Universe. God is not the Universe. Christ is a physical man who is also God. He is not pure Spirit; He is not pure Man. He is fully both. This is why Christian Science is not Christian.

On the other hand, mature Evangelical Christians will affirm that a tremendous percentage of health issues are caused by breaking God's laws. For example, heart disease is most often caused by smoking (polluting the Temple of the Lord), by excessive drinking (drunkenness), by obesity (gluttony), or by lack of exercise (laziness). Type II Diabetes is generally caused by obesity or lack of exercise. Cancer is more common in those who are obese, have diabetes, or use tobacco. Some types of cancer are actually sexually transmitted diseases, caused by the HPV virus. Overwhelmingly, the cause of sexually transmitted diseases is sex outside of marriage by either the victim or the victim's partner.

Evangelical Christians and scientists will also affirm that prayer appears to cure or aid the cure of many diseases. While scientists will argue that the effect is a psychological one, Christians -- and Christian physicians -- generally believe that there is more to prayer than just a psychological effect.

http://www.allaboutcults.org/christian-scientist.htm

All Groups that Claim to be Christian are.

Discussion Questions

1. Have you ever seen a miraculous healing brought about by prayer?

2. Some people argue that medical doctors can be agents of divine healing. What do you think?

3. Luke was a physician. What does this tell us about medical science?

4. We know that Jesus healed many people. Peter and Paul also healed many people. Can an average Christian do such a thing?

Suggested Scripture Readings

- Luke Chapter Ten tells of seventy disciples being sent to out to (among other things) heal the sick.

- Acts 9:32-43 tells of Peter healing people.

All Groups that Claim to be Christian are.

- Acts 19:11-12 tells of Paul healing people.

- Hebrews Chapter 2 tells of the reality of Christ and the significance of His becoming a man.

Other Groups and Beliefs

There are many groups that trade on the name of Jesus Christ to provide a comfortable feeling about their beliefs, which may or may not be anything like standard Christian beliefs. Still more trade upon the general word "God" to describe their deity or power that they worship. By now, I hope that you understand that Christianity, especially Evangelical Christianity, is a well-defined series of beliefs about a specific Person - Jesus Christ - and a specific God - and the consequences that follow from the message of Christ. It requires more than saying, "I am a Christian" to be a Christian. It requires more than a belief in God. It requires more than simply saying, "I believe that a man named Jesus Christ existed." Otherwise, you are still an Ethnic Christian (see Chapter One).

Becoming an Evangelical Christian

Becoming an Evangelical Christian doesn't require a detailed understanding of Christianity. It only requires a crude understanding that we have personally sinned, that Jesus Christ died for our sins, that he demonstrated He is God by rising from the dead, and that He wants to help you and has the power to help you. Believing this, simply ask Him

All Groups that Claim to be Christian are.

to help you now and He will. You will become a Christian and be given the gift of eternal life.

When you become a Christian, do two things. Tell someone. Go to church. Both are vital steps in making sure that you continue to progress in Christ.

If you have become an Evangelical Christian while reading this book, we want to know. If you still have questions about Evangelical Christianity that we haven't answered, we also want to know. Call us in the USA toll free at 1-888-728-2465 or visit us online at our website: oddparts.com. (Outside the USA, you can reach us through our website.)

Suggested Scripture Readings

- Matthew 22:36-40 has Christ's definition of the Greatest Commandments for the Christian.

- Matthew 28:19-20 includes Christ's instructions for the Christian believer. This is known as the Great Commission.

Discussion Questions

1. How many people are needed for someone to become a Christian?

All Groups that Claim to be Christian are.

2. How do you stop being a Christian?

3. How can you approach people about Christianity?

4. What is the purpose of a Christian?

Actions

1. In your own words, state how to become a Christian.

2. Explain this to a Christian friend, preferably your "Pro".

3. Explain this to a non-Christian friend.

Christians never have fun.

Myth #12 - Christians Are Dull, Unhappy, Weak people Who Never Have Fun.

> But the fruit of the Spirit is love, joy, peace, longsuffering, kindness, goodness, faithfulness, gentleness, self-control. Against such there is no law. Galatians 5:22, 23

Hollywood and the Evening News often portray strong Christians as killjoys. In the 1970's movie *Footloose*, a pastor is portrayed as a controlling father who will not let anyone in the town dance or enjoy music. In most American History courses, the Puritans are portrayed as grim people who dressed in black and worked very hard to eliminate fun from their lives. In the Spielberg classic horror film *Poltergeist*, a preacher shows up to frighten the family with his stern, harsh demeanor. In many TV shows Christian characters are shown as fanatics, holding ridiculous views, and generally are ridiculed.

The truth is that Hollywood is painting a discriminatory view of Christians as badly as they have painted other groups. In the early days, Hollywood painted blacks as stupid, ridiculous, easily frightened servants. Later, Hollywood ridiculed Southerners through *The Beverly*

Christians never have fun.

Hillbillies and rural folk with *Green Acres*. Businessmen, scientists and engineers are usually portrayed as distant, evil, or incomprehensible. Hollywood has a tendency to ridicule that which is not dear to the people that control Hollywood.

Are Evangelical Christians Fringe Elements?

Christians who attend church regularly represent about 25 percent of the American population. Because Evangelicals are found in so many denominations – there are even Evangelical Catholics - over half of these people are considered Evangelical Christians. These people include many people involved in community activities such as food banks, rescue missions, 4-H clubs, Boy Scouts, Girl Scouts, Little League sports, and similar activities. Much of the military is Christian, probably because these men face death more realistically than most people. Christians represent a substantial portion of our elementary and high school teachers, where they help young people in exchange for little pay.

Yes, many Christians become involved in local, state, and national politics. Of our Presidents, Washington, Lincoln, Franklin Roosevelt, Eisenhower, Johnson, Reagan, and George W. Bush were clearly practicing Christians. Reagan and Bush were definitely Evangelicals. Many others claimed to be Christian, including recent Presidents Clinton, George H.W. Bush, Kennedy, and Truman. Winston S. Churchill was very clearly a practicing Evangelical Anglican Christian. In his memoirs of World War II, he talks about the evening that

Christians never have fun.

Churchill and FDR attempted to convert Stalin to Christianity. Clearly, these men were not on the fringe -- and were not weak!

In business, you will find that Sam Walton's business philosophy came from Evangelical Christian teachings. He was raised a Methodist and served as a Presbyterian deacon while growing his first store. While many publicly decry the loss of the local merchant, Walton succeeded because people buy products from his stores in huge amounts. His stores succeed because, in general, Sam Walton worked very hard to treat customers and employees "right". Although starting pay is low, Wal-Mart provides excellent benefits to long-term employees. The company also contributes large amounts of money to community causes. Despite the desires of certain unions and politicians, Wal-Mart is clearly not a fringe element in American society.

Much as Hollywood would like to marginalize Christians, there are a few Christians in key places that have a positive impact. A few years ago, rumors leaked out that Mel Gibson was going to spend over $20 million of his own money making a subtitled Aramaic, Latin, and Greek R-rated movie about the tortures that Christ underwent. It is clear from his passionate desire to make this picture that Gibson fits the definition of an Evangelical Catholic – His picture was a well-crafted attempt to spread his Christian faith.

At first, everyone laughed at Gibson's eccentricity. Then they said he'd never get a distributor for the picture in the USA. Then they began to attack the

Christians never have fun.

picture. But finally, the picture was released and millions of Christians went to see the movie, making "*The Passion of the Christ*" one of the top ten grossing pictures of all time and the top grossing R-rated picture of all time with over $370 million in ticket sales. Not bad for a fringe audience, eh?

In the last few years other pictures with themes dear to Evangelicals have come to the big screen. The *Lord of the Rings* trilogy is a fantasy about the interplay of good and evil and the difference a handful of committed "good guys" can make. J.R.R.Tolkien, who wrote the original books, was a committed Christian. Likewise C.S.Lewis, whose book *The Lion, the Witch, and the Wardrobe* was written to intentionally show how Christ might enter a fantasy world with talking animals. It also became a major motion picture with tremendous sales.

More directly, the *End of the Spear* is a movie about the first contact made by Christian missionaries with a new tribe. It shows Evangelicals from Wheaton College demonstrating the Evangelical concept of Christianity. Another movie, *The Gospel*, tells of the ways a black Evangelical church works in Atlanta. Also, the *Love's Long Journey* series of movies provides a look at Evangelical Christianity in action in the 1870's. Walden Media and Fox Faith are just two of the many new ventures into Christian movie making which are targeting the growing Evangelical Christian market.

Christians never have fun.

The True Impact of the Holy Spirit

Why does Evangelical Christianity continue to spread?

Truth

First, Evangelical Christianity happens to be true. Truth cannot be kept hidden forever. Gradually, gradually, people have found out the entire story of what happened two thousand years ago. Those who investigate Christianity find out that it is true. And that is what ultimately matters: Is Christianity True? C.S. Lewis said that the entire value of Christianity depends upon its Truth. If it is not true, than it is of no worth whatsoever. But if it is true, then it is the most important piece of knowledge you can ever know.

There are many barriers to understanding Christianity.

- Some people are arrogant. "If Christianity is the most popular religion, then there must be something wrong with it -- as an intelligent, well-educated person, I am capable of seeing that there is something deeper and more profound." Yet these people rarely investigate Christianity in depth, preferring to believe what a non-Christian told them rather than take some time to find a Christian "pro" to explain the faith to them. They begin by assuming it must be false, since ordinary people have understood it. Their failure to understand Christianity is not a failure of understanding, but a failure

Christians never have fun.

- of knowledge -- they haven't taken the time to investigate the faith with one who understands the faith. Have you taken the time to investigate Christianity? Have you spent a few hours with a Christian pro asking about the points that are confusing to you? Or have you dismissed them out-of-hand?
- Other people are depressed. "Christianity cannot be true because all religions are false." These people have been burnt by false religions so much that they will not spend the time to learn about the True Religion. It reminds me of the time I was marketing manager for a major industrial electronics product line. Our product was extraordinarily easy to use. A senior design engineer spent a couple of months investigating our competitor's top products. His conclusion? "I understand now why no one will try our products. [The competitor's] products are so difficult to learn how to use that no one would ever want to try to learn another one!"

  Are you so disgusted with false religions that you will not spend the time to learn about the one True Religion? Have you ever considered that there might be -- as Evangelical Christians believe -- an evil power that wants you to miss the Truth?

- Still other people have been misled. "I used to go to church as a child. It was boring and useless -- and my parents hated the people there." These people have not seen true

Christians never have fun.

> Christianity -- only a poor imitation of it. I have visited many churches. The difference between a good church's Christianity and a poor church's Christianity is like the difference between a five-star restaurant and a fly-ridden roadside hot dog stand. Keep looking until you find a good church and taste real Christianity!
>
> - Another group of people are captured by their sins. "I enjoy a promiscuous lifestyle - Christianity would make me quit that." These people are quite correct in their analysis of their situation -- as far as it goes. If they became believing Christians, they would immediately need to change their lifestyle. They would find themselves accountable to someone - God - for once in their lives. However, the part that they miss in their analysis is this: They would re-evaluate their activities and see them for the self-destructive behavior that they are. Then they would *enjoy* giving up their vices and have a more satisfying life.
>
> Are you one of these people? If so, look carefully at what you are holding onto. Which is better -- your vice or eternal life in peace?

Whatever your barrier, you owe it to yourself to investigate Evangelical Christianity and determine whether or not it is true. Because if it is true, it is of immense importance. And if it is not true, then it is of no importance whatsoever and you can make a fortune with a book explaining why it is not true.

Christians never have fun.

The Holy Spirit

The second reason Evangelical Christianity continues to spread is because of the Holy Spirit. Christianity is more than a true idea. It is actively being promoted by an immensely wise Being who wants everyone to hear about Him. The Holy Spirit works within believers to spread the Word and improve each believer. We truly "become better people", and that arrogant-sounding statement is why we attract more and more people to Christ. Christians change for the better. Other people notice and wonder why the change occurred. In his letter to the Romans, Paul says "Let each of us please his neighbor for his good, leading to edification." (15:2) "Edification" means "to build up". Evangelical Christians are constantly at work to understand the mind of God and to help each other understand, for as we understand more we become more fully attuned to God, in the same way that each violin in the orchestra is gradually tuned to the sound of the oboe by twisting the tuning knobs. Only as we come into tune can we play properly in God's orchestra -- otherwise we still will sound like the fourth grade orchestra trying to play Mozart.

If this is your first detailed study through Christianity, you should find yourself much closer to understanding Our Lord than you did at the beginning. But there are two final things to keep in mind:

- First, although we can develop many different spiritual habits, such as reading the Bible daily, praying several times a day, and talking about Christ with everyone we meet,

Christians never have fun.

none of these habits is necessary for eternal life. Furthermore, even if we do all of these things, it can never be *sufficient* to get us eternal life. Christ gives us that gift solely because we *chose* to follow Him and acknowledge Him for Who He is. Everything else we do is simply done to allow us to follow Christ more completely, allowing Him into the rest of our lives.

We start by allowing Him into our mind intellectually on Sunday mornings. Then we acknowledge His provision for us by saying Grace at meals. We begin spending time with Him praying. One day we realize that He can help us with our children, our job, our business, and our relationships.

Gradually, gradually, it really sinks home that He is truly walking beside us 24 hours a day and is ready to talk with us at all times and to help us out. Like Jimmy Stewart in the movie "*Harvey*", we have an invisible friend who no one else sees, but who is very, very real. And then, we move onto the next level of understanding. And the next. And the next. Even Paul said that He was continually learning more about Christ as he approached Him.

This is normal, for we know ever so much more about our spouse today than we did when we were first married. Christ is ever so much more complex than any spouse! How wonderful it is when my wife and I spend time together with Him! We both get to

Christians never have fun.

> experience a wonderful guest in our home, who will stay as long as we want.

- The second point is the essential simplicity of the Gospel. Christ died on the cross so that we would have a ticket into the mansion of God. We now have eternal life with God -- start living your life that way! All is forgiven -- nothing needs to be patched up. Don't make it complicated -- the Party has begun. Just have fun with your Host!

Suggested Scripture Readings

- Romans 12:9-21 explains how Christians should live.

- Romans 15:7 explains how to treat the other guests in the mansion.

- Revelation 19:6-10 Talks about the wedding feast of Christ.

Discussion Questions

1. How has your relationship with Christ grown over time?

Christians never have fun.

2. How do you treat other people when your parents are watching?

3. How can an awareness of Christ's constant presence help you love your neighbors?

4. Have you ever thought about Christianity as an invitation to a Party?

Actions

1. Rent the 1950 movie "*Harvey*", Jimmie Stewart starred in this comedy. Consider how Harvey is like Christ.

2. Throw a dinner party for your friends. Invite your Pro to mingle with the guests. Let the Spirit and your Pro lead the conversation.

3. Take your spouse and the Lord out for a walk or a dinner.

Christians never have fun.

Appendix - How Do Mormons Fit into Evangelical Christianity?

The Mormon Church, officially known as The Church of Jesus Christ and Latter Day Saints, is often associated with Evangelical Christianity. It is by far the dominant religion in the state of Utah, and is very strong in nearby states such as Arizona, Nevada, and California. But it has an odd relationship to Evangelical Christianity that needs to be understood, particularly with the appearance on the national scene of leaders who are Mormon. Mormons prefer the use of "LDS" to describe their church, considering "Mormon" to be an inaccurate description of their faith.

History of the Church

The LDS church was founded in the 1830's by Joseph Smith, who claimed to have been visited by the Angel Moroni and who was given twelve golden tablets which further explained the travels of the ancient nation of Israel, and gave additional revelations about God, Jesus Christ, and their relationship to men. Smith began in Western New

Christians never have fun.

York State, and quickly moved to Missouri, where he established his religious movement. The LDS became seen as a cult in Missouri. Violence soon erupted, resulting in the death of Smith in Carthage, Illinois in 1844. Under their new leader, Brigham Young, the group had a mass migration to the area of the Great Salt Lake in what is now Utah, arriving in 1847, where a near theocracy was established.

Differences between LDS and Christianity

The LDS believe that their church is a restoration of the original Christian church. They believe in the inspiration of three volumes in addition to the Bible, the *Book of Mormon*, *Doctrines and Covenants*, and *The Pearl of Great Price*. These books contain the basis for the departure of the LDS from standard Christian teaching.

In the early years of the LDS church, plural marriage was practiced. A church council officially discontinued this practice in 1890. Thus, officially, the "Utah Mormons" who practice polygamy are not part of the LDS church and are rebuked by the LDS leadership.

More to the point, most evangelical Christians see the LDS as non-Christian because the LDS have a different concept of the natures of Christ and of God than traditional Christianity. The LDS believe in a female mother goddess as well as the traditional male God. This heavenly couple has spiritual

Christians never have fun.

children – the first was Christ, Adam was the second. Ordinary men and women must bring spiritual children down to earth. (This is why LDS members have an extraordinary number of children.) The LDS believes that, even though you have forgotten it, you lived as a spirit with God before your earthly birth.

The LDS claims that Joseph Smith received a vision in which God and Jesus Christ were present, telling him not to join any of the existing churches. Later, Smith claimed to have received repeated visits from an angel who directed him to the location of some golden tablets, inscribed in "Egyptian, Chaldaic, Assyriac, and Arabic" characters. Smith translated some of the Egyptian characters with aid of supernatural stones found with the tablets, and it was supposedly confirmed that this was an accurate translation.

Eventually, these tablets were published as the Book of Mormon, which describes a pre-Columbian civilization in America. Unfortunately, unlike standard Christian belief, no archeological evidence has been found for this civilization. And the angel has taken the tablets back...

Other LDS concepts

LDS members have an intensive interest in the family and in genealogical research. This is theologically driven.

The interest in the family is directly related to the concept that there are children in Heaven who are

Christians never have fun.

awaiting earthly birth. Thus, good LDS members strive to have as many children as possible.

The interest in genealogical research is because the LDS practices ancestor baptism. LDS members believe that their ancestors are unsaved and doomed to an eternal life apart from God unless they are baptized. If certain information can found, these ancestors can be baptized into the church, centuries after their deaths.

Another concept of the LDS is the concept of eternal marriage. While most Christians argue that something fundamentally changes in marriages at earthly death, the LDS believes that a very good LDS couple will go onto an eternal life together, as the spiritual father and spiritual mother of a new universe, giving spiritual birth to billions of new souls. (However, the marriage must be performed in a LDS temple.) In the LDS theology, there is not only a heavenly father, but there is also a heavenly mother.

Perhaps the most interesting LDS concept is the concept of continual revelation, which is shared by the charismatic and Pentecostal movements. Most evangelical Christians and, indeed, all other major Christian groups believe that the Bible is the final revelation of God to man before the events shown in the Book of Revelation. However, the LDS believes that God is continually adjusting the position and beliefs of the church.

Most Christian denominations regard their policy books and policy statements as the interpretation by men of God's will. If the denomination realizes that

Christians never have fun.

it holds a position that may be wrong, the denomination admits this and makes the necessary changes. An example is when the Southern Baptist Convention apologized for supporting slavery at the time of the American Civil War.

However, the LDS goes much further. The documents written by the founders of the LDS are seen as revealed scripture. Thus, when the LDS needs to change a position, it is necessary to receive a revelation from God.

This was seen in the late 1800's when the LDS publicly disavowed their former belief in polygamous marriages. In the late twentieth century, the LDS moved away from banning blacks from the priesthood. In both cases, the move was presented as a formal revelation from God to the ruling body of the LDS. It will be interesting to see if further doctrinal issues are changed over the next few years.

Attitudes towards the LDS by Evangelical Christians

The LDS appears to be attempting to move toward being seen as a Christian denomination. Towards that view, evangelical Christian leaders have been invited to speak to large LDS gatherings in Salt Lake City and elsewhere. Most evangelicals have responded positively. We like the general God-fearing, family friendly attitude of the LDS, but we are cautious about their less public beliefs.

Christians never have fun.

LDS politicians have found that they are viewed with suspicion in the evangelical community, and are not fully embraced. There is a strong suspicion in the evangelical community that Joseph Smith fabricated most of his story upon which the LDS has been built. Or, worse, that the "angel" that revealed the tablets to Smith was an agent of Satan.

The LDS has not helped with this suspicion by keeping the temple and many ceremonies closed to the public. LDS websites, advertisements, and videos appear to be constructed to intentionally emphasize the similarities with standard Christianity and to obscure the differences. Perhaps they will be more open in the future.

Christians never have fun.

Index

addiction, 165, 172, 309, 310
agnostics, 36
alcohol, 48, 163, 164
Alexander, 149
Amish, 48, 216
angel, 41, 183, 184, 185, 187, 189, 197, 367
Anglican, 23, 163, 201, 215, 240
Anthropological, 270, 274
Arianism, 115, 118
atheist, 12, 84, 85, 270
atheistic. See atheist
Attendee, 55
Attending Christians, 33
baptism, 118, 211, 212, 213, 214, 215, 216, 217, 218, 222, 288
Baptist, 19, 23, 36, 164, 211, 226, 247, 248, 294
baptized, 37, 214, 216, 217, 218. See baptism
Believer, 298
Bible, 21, 36, 39, 45, 52, 53, 54, 55, 97, 98, 107, 108, 111, 119, 120, 121, 150, 157, 158, 160, 163, 166, 167, 168, 180, 184, 186, 188, 200, 203, 204, 208, 213, 215, 217, 231, 232, 236, 237, 240, 247, 252, 276, 280, 283, 290, 291, 292, 293, 294, 295, 299, 300, 302, 303, 312, 313, 314, 317, 328, 329, 330, 331, 332, 334, 335, 336, 337, 338, 339, 346, 348, 350, 355, 356, 357, 358, 359, 365, 370, 383
Billy Graham, 54, 161

Index

BSF, 52, 55
Buddhists, 90, 93
C. S. Lewis, 51, 108
C.S. Lewis, 10, 97, 122, 380
Calvinist, 251
Catholic, 9, 19, 21, 23, 36, 115, 116, 177, 201, 215, 240, 241, 243, 244, 246, 333, 341, 365
Charismatic, 206, 208
Christ, 20, 22, 23, 34, 71, 74, 75, 78, 83, 110, 111, 114, 115, 116, 117, 118, 119, 120, 123, 126, 128, 135, 140, 141, 142, 147, 154, 157, 158, 159, 160, 162, 163, 168, 169, 182, 185, 190, 193, 194, 196, 197, 204, 209, 214, 215, 216, 222, 237, 238, 240, 242, 243, 252, 256, 275, 279, 289, 298, 304, 305, 306, 308, 311, 313, 316, 339, 341, 344, 345, 350, 357, 358, 360, 361, 364, 365, 366, 367, 368, 371, 373, 374, 378, 383, 384, 385, 386
Christian Science, 370, 371
Christianity, 1, 6, 9, 10, 11, 12, 13, 19, 20, 21, 22, 23, 32, 36, 37, 38, 39, 41, 42, 43, 46, 47, 49, 50, 51, 52, 53, 54, 55, 56, 74, 84, 106, 109, 110, 115, 119, 147, 163, 165, 180, 199, 213, 218, 237, 264, 266, 275, 277, 280, 286, 290, 291, 293, 302, 304, 305, 307, 313, 314, 328, 329, 350, 354, 356, 359, 360, 365, 373, 374, 375, 378, 380, 381, 382, 383, 386
Commandments.
Communion, 163, 199, 200, 219, 220, 221, 222, 223, 242, 294
congregation, 166, 200, 202, 203, 205, 206, 209, 210, 220, 221, 225, 226, 227, 228, 231, 232, 239, 310
Consistency, 270, 275
Coptic, 23
Cosmological, 270, 273
crabby, 69, 70, 73

Index

Creation, 107, 336, 338, 339, 340, 341, 344, 346, 348, 350, 351, 359, 360, 361, 362
Creationism, 345, 346, 352
Creator, 20, 76, 79, 80, 107, 108, 109, 157, 290
creatures, 76, 151, 187, 274, 338, 339, 340, 347
crucifixion, 20, 128, 129, 130, 131
Deists, 345, 346, 351, 352, 353
denominations, 21, 116, 199, 221, 224, 364
Disciples of Christ, 23
Divorce, 224
Ethnic Christian, 35, 373
Eutychianism, 115, 117
Evangelical, 1, 6, 19, 21, 23, 246, 247, 248
evolution, 9, 247, 274, 345, 349, 350, 352, 353, 359
Evolution, 91, 328, 339, 348, 360
Existence, 85, 264, 269, 270, 277
forgive, 80, 82, 154
Fundamentalism, 247, 248
Gnosticism, 115, 119
God, 8, 9, 19, 20, 34, 37, 42, 43, 45, 48, 50, 53, 63, 65, 66, 67, 69, 70, 72, 73, 74, 76, 77, 78, 79, 80, 82, 84, 86, 90, 93, 94, 95, 96, 97, 102, 103, 104, 105, 106, 107, 108, 109, 110, 111, 114, 115, 116, 117, 118, 119, 120, 121, 122, 123, 125, 126, 139, 140, 147, 148, 149, 150, 151, 152, 153, 154, 157, 158, 159, 162, 166, 167, 169, 170, 171, 172, 173, 176, 178, 180, 184, 186, 187, 188, 190, 191, 192, 202, 203, 208, 226, 232, 238, 240, 241, 242, 251, 252, 256, 264, 266, 269, 270, 272, 273, 274, 275, 276, 277, 278, 279, 280, 281, 282, 283, 284, 285, 288, 289, 290, 291, 294, 296, 297, 298, 299, 300, 301, 302, 304, 305, 306, 307, 308, 309, 310, 311, 312, 313, 314, 316, 317, 331, 336, 339, 340, 341, 344, 345, 346, 347, 349, 351, 352, 353, 354, 356, 357, 359, 362, 364, 365, 366, 367, 368, 370, 371, 373, 383, 385

Index

Gospel, 20, 109, 111, 116, 127, 139, 170, 174, 203, 205, 206, 209, 211, 244, 249, 295, 313, 365, 385
gray" reasoning, 44, 45, 46
Greatest Commandment, 73
Heaven, 8, 20, 69, 80, 118, 154, 160, 183, 188, 190, 193, 195, 214, 215, 236, 289, 294, 305, 306, 307, 308, 311, 368
Hell, 8, 9, 70, 74, 188, 190, 192, 195, 196, 198, 305, 368
heterosexual, 166, 167, 168
Hindus, 90, 93, 95
Hitler, 118, 152, 161, 162, 191, 368
Hollywood, 11, 12, 13, 41, 183, 187, 189, 190, 195, 208, 376, 378
Holy, 8, 34, 50, 154, 157, 160, 165, 166, 203, 207, 214, 228, 240, 256, 291, 294, 316, 331, 345, 380, 383
homosexual, 9, 147, 166, 167, 168, 169, 353
hypocrites, 9, 37, 179, 305, 311
Intelligent Design, 346
Islam. See Moslem.
Jehovah's Witness, 19, 366
Jehovah's Witnesses, 364, 365, 366
Jesus. See Christ.
Jewish. See Jews.
Jews, 21, 35, 36, 47, 49, 65, 93, 95, 105, 109, 128, 136, 148, 185, 297
Legalism. See Legalistic.
legalistic, 22, 47, 48, 49, 289, 304, 310
liberal, 22, 252, 330
logical, 11, 12, 89, 92, 94, 101, 266, 343, 347, 359
Lutherans, 21, 116, 213, 246
Mankind, 77, 186
Marriage, 193, 242
Martin Luther, 10, 21, 51, 254
Mary, 9, 50, 121, 133, 185, 186, 241, 242, 253, 370

Index

Mature Christian, 13, 35, 38, 39, 55, 56
Methodist, 23, 36, 201, 378
Monarchianism, 115
Mormon. See Mormons.
Mormons, 19, 367, 368
Moses, 65, 78, 121, 148, 294, 295, 348
Moslems. See Mohammed.
Myths, 1, 10, 84
Narnia, 97
Naturalism, 341, 342, 343, 344
New Age, 42
New Testament, 21, 53, 127, 185, 198, 289, 295, 297, 332, 333, 337, 357, 365
nice, 38, 43, 69, 70, 73, 96, 182, 232, 302, 312
Old Testament, 21, 65, 96, 118, 148, 198, 273, 295, 366
Ontological, 270, 274
Orthodox, 21, 23, 115, 116, 163, 201, 215, 365
Pentecostal. See Charismatic.
Perfect Policeman, 72
philosophy, 13, 49, 86, 87, 88, 89, 92, 99
Pope. See Catholic.
prayer, 66, 80, 82, 153, 204, 207, 209, 235, 300, 301, 302, 312, 371, 372
preachers, 10, 55, 166
Presbyterian, 23, 201, 215, 378
Protestant, 21, 23
Purpose, 78, 90, 92, 188, 214, 220, 223, 296, 298
reality, 37, 74, 86, 87, 88, 89, 190, 199, 202, 251, 265, 373
Reformation, 21, 23, 216, 254
religion, 12, 21, 22, 32, 34, 35, 36, 37, 40, 41, 42, 43, 45, 47, 50, 51, 87, 88, 89, 90, 97, 105, 112, 115, 169, 291, 333, 369, 370, 380
Resurrection, 117, 134, 135, 136, 139, 140, 141, 142, 339, 341, 344, 345, 360

Index

Sabbath, 66, 131
sacrifice, 78, 79, 81, 83, 344, 353
salvation, 21, 214, 243, 311
Scientologists, 93
Seventh Day Adventists, 243
Sin, 77, 78, 147, 149, 176, 182, 297
Social Justice, 252, 253
Solipsists, 85, 86, 87, 88
Son of God. See Christ. Teleological, 270, 273
Temple, 78, 118, 166, 173, 296, 297, 371
Ten Commandments, 65, 66, 148
Theistic Evolutionists, 348
Theists, 95, 97, 98, 103, 106, 108, 109
Theology, 200, 240, 246, 247, 251, 252
Tiger Woods, 40, 51
Tolerance, 98, 101, 103, 104, 105, 106, 237
Trinity, 9, 50, 154, 155, 157, 159
Truth, 12, 42, 98, 99, 101, 105, 106, 109, 116, 119, 125, 266, 267, 270, 277, 329, 354, 359, 360, 380, 381
Ugliness, 78
Universe, 20, 42, 63, 74, 85, 86, 87, 88, 90, 91, 92, 94, 96, 99, 105, 107, 108, 109, 240, 266, 273, 290, 314, 338, 340, 341, 344, 345, 351, 352, 368, 371
wisdom, 34, 179

Contact Information

For Additional Copies of this Book or to arrange a Speaking Engagement or Workshop, Contact us via our Website:

oddparts.com

www.ingramcontent.com/pod-product-compliance
Lightning Source LLC
Chambersburg PA
CBHW020941230426
43666CB00005B/105